CW01510268

LAST RITES

Also by Ozzy Osbourne

I Am Ozzy
Trust Me, I'm Dr Ozzy

OZZY OSBOURNE

WITH **CHRIS AYRES**

LAST RITES

SPHERE

SPHERE

First published in Great Britain in 2025 by Sphere

3 5 7 9 10 8 6 4 2

Copyright © Ozzy Osbourne 2025

The right of Ozzy Osbourne to be identified as author of this
Work has been asserted by him in accordance with the
Copyright, Designs and Patents Act 1988.

Lyrics: page 160 'Ordinary Man' by Duff Rose McKagan,
Ozzy Osbourne, Chad Gaylord Smith, Andrew Wotman and Billy Walsh.
Copyright © EMI April Music Inc., Pimp Music, Avanails Publishing,
Andrew Watt Music, Nyankingmusic, Wmmw Publishing.
Page 199 'Mama, I'm Coming Home' by Zakk Wylde and
John Osbourne. Copyright © Monowise Ltd.

All rights reserved.
No part of this publication may be reproduced, stored in a
retrieval system, or transmitted, in any form or by any means, without
the prior permission in writing of the publisher, nor be otherwise circulated in
any form of binding or cover other than that in which it is published
and without a similar condition including this condition being
imposed on the subsequent purchaser.

A CIP catalogue record for this book
is available from the British Library.

Hardback ISBN 978-1-4087-2405-7
Trade paperback ISBN 978-1-4087-2406-4

Typeset in Bembo by M Rules
Printed and bound in Great Britain by
Clays Ltd, Elcograf S.p.A.

Papers used by Sphere are from well-managed forests
and other responsible sources.

Sphere
An imprint of
Little, Brown Book Group
Carmelite House
50 Victoria Embankment
London EC4Y 0DZ

The authorised representative
in the EEA is
Hachette Ireland
8 Castlecourt Centre
Dublin 15, D15 XTP3, Ireland
(email: info@hbgi.ie)

An Hachette UK Company
www.hachette.co.uk

www.littlebrown.co.uk

People say to me, if you could do it all again, knowing what you know now, would you change anything? I'm like, f★★★ no. If I'd been clean and sober, I wouldn't be Ozzy. If I'd done normal, sensible things, I wouldn't be Ozzy.

I mean, yeah, it's f★★★ed up, what happened.

But when you get to your seventies, you don't just get a cold or a sprained ankle, do you? You get major s★★★. And if you've lived the kind of life I have, you're gonna get major s★★★ squared.

Look, if it ends tomorrow, I can't complain. I've been all around the world. Seen a lot of things. Met some phenomenal people – King Charles, Queen Elizabeth, presidents, actors, celebrities, some truly great fans. I've done good. Done bad.

But right now, I ain't ready to go anywhere. I've lost a lot of things, but I've still got my marbles … or whatever marbles I ever had. It's good being alive. I like it. I want to be here with my family. And more than anything else in the world, I'm just happy I made it back to where it all started – Aston, Birmingham.

In 2003, when I was more famous for being on the telly than I was for being a singer, I crashed my quad bike in the fields behind my house in Buckinghamshire, England.

The bike flipped over, then landed on top of me − breaking my neck, fracturing eight of my ribs, puncturing a lung and severing the arteries to my left arm.

I was in a coma for eight days.

It was the good old NHS that put me back together again − turning me from the bloke who sang 'Iron Man' into an actual iron man, my shoulder and spine held together with metal plates, rods and screws.

For the next sixteen years, whenever I set off an airport metal detector, I couldn't help but smile . . . thinking of how I'd cheated Death once again.

But you never cheat Death, not really.

He's always keeping score.

And sooner or later, he's gonna call in his final debt.

This book tells the story of how he called in mine.

Spoiler alert: I told him to f★★★ off.

I'm busy.

Contents

1

The Demon Awakes

Just before I turned seventy, a thought suddenly occurred to me.

I wonder when it is you start feeling old?

I mean, there I was, six years older than my own father when he left this world, and as far as I was concerned, I was still basically a young man.

Okay, so my hands and legs were a bit shaky thanks to my Parkinson's. I was going deaf. My short-term memory had been on the blink since about 1992. But I could run around the stage at Donington Park for two hours, shooting a foam gun at the crowd. I could belt out 'War Pigs' and 'Crazy Train' without dropping a note. And although a part of me missed the wild times of waking up in the middle of a twelve-lane freeway or surfing on the roof of a Swiss cable car, I was happy just to chill out in my hotel room with my four-legged friends Wesley, Pickles, Elvis and Rocky (God rest his soul) after a show.

In many ways, I'd never been so physically fit. I'd catch a glimpse myself in a mirror and think, fucking hell, I look better *now* than I did in the video for 'Bark at the Moon' . . . and that was forty years ago! Not that it's hard to look better than a bloke who was knocking back four bottles of cognac a day.

The point being, getting old had turned out to be absolutely nothing like I'd expected.

When I was growing up in Aston, you were lucky if you made it to retirement age. More often than not, you'd just drop dead on the factory floor. When my dad passed away in his early sixties, none of us Osbourne kids batted an eyelid. As far as we were concerned, he was *ancient*. In those days, almost no one made it to seventy. The few who did were so craggy they made Gandalf from *Lord of the Rings* look like Timothée Chalamet. Bits would be falling off 'em as they shuffled off down the pub.

But that wasn't even close to the case with me.

At the age of sixty-nine, I was still touring the world. Still making TV shows. Still lording it up with big houses in LA and Buckinghamshire. And every night, I'd stage-dive into bed like I'd done since I was a little kid living at 14 Lodge Road.

Whheeeeeeee . . .

THWUMP.

'OZZY!!!' my wife Sharon would scream. 'Why can't you *step* into bed like a normal person?'

'You wouldn't like me if I was normal.'

'You'll break the bloody thing, you idiot!'

Heh-heh-heh.

Ah, yeah . . . them were the days.

When death still seemed like something that only happened to other people.

Now, I obviously ain't the best person to ask about dates or whatever. There are holes in my memory so big most of the eighties and nearly all of the nineties slipped through. But the chain of events in this book began at the end of 2018 – around October time, I believe – when I was halfway through what was supposed to be my farewell tour.

It was called *No More Tours II*, I should probably mention. The original *No More Tours* had been in the nineties, before I realised there's only so much time you can spend in your back garden wearing wellies before you lose your mind. But this time, with my seventieth birthday approaching, I was serious about slowing down. Sharon was even talking about me taking up one of them golden-oldie residencies in Las Vegas when I got back. Not that I fancied the idea of becoming the next Barry Manilow.

Looking back now, of course, I should have known the schedule was on the ambitious side. I mean, sixty gigs on four continents is no joke for any singer, no matter what their age. But the way I looked at it, it was my last goodbye to fans in places I knew I wouldn't be playing again.

To be honest with you, before the tour started I was worried if anyone would even turn up to the shows. It had been a few years since I'd last been on the road. For all I knew, I couldn't fill a broom cupboard, never mind sixty major arenas. But in the end, *No More Tours*

It turned out to be an absolute blinder. From Mexico City to Moscow, Toronto and São Paulo, every show was sold out. And the whole vibe of the thing, from the stage design to the mood of the crowds, was absolutely phenomenal.

Every night, before I made my entrance, images of my life flashed across this huge screen above the stage. An old black-and-white photograph of me as a kid, still in short trousers, scared of my own shadow. A colour picture of me in Black Sabbath, wearing a tasselled suede shirt with a necklace that was actually a tiny coke spoon. On stage with the great Randy Rhoads – God bless you Randy, wherever you are – to promote *Blizzard of Ozz*. All mixed in with flame effects and clips from the video for 'No More Tears', set to a choir chanting Carl Orff's *Carmina Burana*.

DUH, DUH, *DUH-DUH!!*

DUH, DUH, *DUH-DUH!!*

DUH-DUH-DUDH DUUUUUUH DUUUUUH, DUH DUH!!!

Then out I'd run from the wings in a long purple cloak while Zakk Wylde ripped into the opening riff of 'Bark at the Moon', his hair down, legs astride, looking like a Viking about to set fire to a village. Believe me, there's no drug on earth that comes close to that kind of high. I should know, I've taken 'em all.

Even the *reviews* were good, which freaked me out a bit. The critics had hated everything I'd ever done, so if they'd changed their minds now, maybe I was doing something wrong. But I didn't care, I was having too much fun.

What made it even more special was the lack of any

tension behind the scenes. I mean, Zakk ain't just one of the best guitarists out there, he's also one of the loveliest, most salt-of-the-earth guys you'll ever meet. A lot of people in this business only want to know you when you're riding high. Not Zakk. He's always been there for me, no matter what, no questions asked. Up on the drum riser, meanwhile, was Tommy Clufetos, a guy whose idea of a good time is a trip to the gym and an early night. He's been keeping me out of trouble for years, has Tommy. On bass was Rob 'Blasko' Nicholson, who's been by my side as long as Tommy. And on keyboards, Adam Wakeman, whose dad Rick I've known since he played on Black Sabbath's 'Sabbra Cadabra' – for a fee of two pints of Directors bitter. I don't think I'd be giving away any national secrets if I said Rick was a bit of a pisshead back then. It's why we got on so well.

What I'm trying to say is that *No More Tours II* was like being with family. And the fans seemed to be having as much fun as we were. Every night, I'd hear tens of thousands of 'em singing back the lyrics to everything from 'Fairies Wear Boots' to 'Crazy Train'. Absolutely fucking magic, man.

But as always with me, the devil was only a few steps behind.

I'd been sober about five years at this point. I ain't pulling that number out of my arse, I've got an app on my phone that tells me exactly how long it's been. The chains had been broken, as far as I was concerned. But that's what all addicts tell themselves. Then the voice of your addiction starts talking to you, and it sounds just like you, and you can't tell the difference. It's weird, having a disease that keeps telling you you don't have a disease. Next thing you know, it's talked you into having a little sip of this, or a little toot of that. Then you're in prison, or broke, or dead, or your wife's left you . . . or all of those things at the same time.

Being an addict's like carrying around an unexploded bomb that you can never put down. Look at the *Friends* guy, Matthew Perry. He used to come to our house for AA meetings, or so my wife tells me. The funniest, most talented bloke. And he was trying so hard to stay on the right path. Then one day he listened to his addiction telling him it was okay to get loaded, and that was it – game over. I felt so sad when they said he'd been found in his hot tub, unresponsive, with ketamine in his system. He'd given everything he had to stay clean. But it wasn't enough.

For me, it was around the time of the Black Sabbath album *13* – 2012, I suppose – when I last fell off the wagon. Why it happened, I can't tell you, other than I was riding high and my ego was running the show. Buying myself a Ferrari 458 Italia with a wrap that made it look like a stealth bomber was the first sign of trouble. Then I got another one, but this time one of them drop-top California models in gunmetal grey. Fabulous cars, both of 'em. The only problem being I didn't have a licence and had never learned to drive. But with the help of my assistant at the time, I soon started to get the hang of it . . . although I think I gave him a bit of PTSD along the way.

I don't know exactly *when* it happened, but at some point I decided I could handle a drink. Probably a pint of Guinness. I dream about Guinness almost every night. I fucking love the stuff, it's like drinking a glass of pudding. The problem is, one's too many, and ten's not enough. And the first thing I want after a Guinness is to go looking for some coke. Cocaine's the alcoholic's best friend, 'cos you can drink around the clock with it. Otherwise the booze would drop you to your knees. But of course when the coke wears off, you get the comedown, and the only way to handle the comedown is with some pills. Well . . . either that or more coke. But there's only so long you can do that 'til you're taking a very long nap.

Next thing I knew, we'd moved back to Buckinghamshire and I'd bought another rocket on wheels, this time an Audi R8. By then I could legally drive, 'cos I'd managed to pass my test in LA, which is a piece of piss compared with the test in England. All you've gotta do is drive around the block at this place in Hollywood and not crash into anything. They don't even make you park, never mind do a hill start. It's an absolute joke. They wouldn't even know what a hill start *is* in LA, the cars don't have clutch pedals.

So there I was, back in England with my California driving licence, blasting around in the R8, while Sharon was in LA doing her TV thing. And of course I lost control, started womanising . . . the whole thing. It got really ugly, really fast.

Eventually Sharon gets suspicious, calls my dear friend Billy Morrison – he's the guitarist in Billy Idol's band, and my AA sponsor – and he takes the overnight flight from LA to Heathrow, drives up to Buckinghamshire and finds a note from a drug dealer in High Wycombe in the R8.

To this day, I have absolutely no memory of ever going to High Wycombe – although it's a fitting name for a place to go and buy coke. That's the thing about being an addict, you live in two worlds. The drunk world and the sober world. And what happens in one is like a half-remembered dream in the other.

I break into a cold sweat and shudder when I think of what I did in the drunk world. It's like someone walking over my grave. Flat out around a blind corner on a country lane in a Jaguar XJ12, with just enough room for a car and a half to pass. Trying to strangle Sharon, the woman I love, thinking she was the devil. Setting myself on fire more times than I can remember. Popping Klonopin pills like they were sweeties. Hitting a bloke in the face with a pint glass. He went to hospital, apparently, but was okay in the end. It's so fucking easy to kill somebody in the drunk world. You push someone, hit someone, you've no idea what medical shit they've got going on, how they're gonna fall, what they'll hit on the way down. You're temporarily insane. And when you're behind the wheel, all it takes for a tragedy is a tractor, a cyclist, someone walking their dog.

I've fallen through roofs. Fallen *off* roofs. Woken up in my Range Rover in my driveway, icicles on my nose, jeans soaked through with piss. I'd been at my local, the Hand & Cleaver, which was only a hundred yards from my house at the time, Bullrush Cottage in Ranton Green, near Stafford. One time someone had to come out and put a sleeping bag over me, 'cos they couldn't drag me out of the car and my lips were turning blue.

If a cat has nine lives, I must have thirty-three.

I had some great times in the drunk world, of course.

And my drunk world friends were the funniest group of guys you could ever meet. Dave Tangye, the welder turned roadie turned personal assistant. Charlie Clapham the fruit and veg guy. Dennis McCarten, Barry Dunnery, Don McKye, Bobby Thomson, Chris Sedgwick – all in the music game, in one way or another. You knew you were part of the gang when you'd woken up after a night of heavy drinking to find one of your eyebrows missing. That moment when you looked in the mirror and realised you looked like absolute shit, but you couldn't for the life of you understand *why* ... it was just absolutely priceless, man. It's thanks to those guys I know exactly how long it takes to grow one eyebrow back after it's been shaved off. Three weeks. Which is longer than it sounds, believe me. The funniest of all those guys was my old friend Pete Mertons. He had the driest, sharpest wit of anyone I've ever met.

He's dead now, God rest his soul. They all are. Throat cancer. Liver failure. Heart attacks. You name it.

Why I'm still here, I don't know.

I really thought I'd beaten that shit. After Sharon busted me and sold all my cars – that one bender cost me north of half a million quid – I did the 'ninety meetings in ninety days' thing at the AA log cabin in West Hollywood. That's literally what it is, a log cabin that's been there since 1930-something. It used to be home of the Boy Scouts of America, or so I'm told. Baden-Powell would turn in his grave if he knew I'd been in there.

Sometimes you have some fun at those AA meetings. Sometimes you hear some fucked-up shit. Other times it's just really sad. Addiction is cunning, powerful and baffling, they tell you. It helped me, all that AA stuff. Got me started on the way back to being sober. If you're on your own, the voice in your head is too persuasive. But I don't want anyone to think I'm the patron saint of recovering alcoholics. If you want to drink, and you think you can handle it, good for you. But I had to be honest with *me*. I couldn't handle it.

It terrifies me now, alcohol, because I turn into somebody else. One drink, and the demon awakes. I used to be a fun drunk, or so I thought. But now I just argue. All the little niggles I have with people, I bring them up.

The moment I thought I'd finally managed to break free from my addictive personality was when Sharon had some ketamine treatment. Not the off-the-books stuff Matthew Perry was supposedly doing, but a controlled medical thing, with a shrink involved. It's very effective for depression, I'm told. Every time she went for a session, she'd come home with her eyes all swollen from crying. And I was like, 'Sharon, what the fuck are they *doing* to you in that place?' She said they were helping her face the demons in her past, and that maybe I should try it too, 'cos maybe the reason I couldn't ever stay sober was some buried shit.

So I went down there and gave it a try. It seemed like a better idea than going on psych meds or whatever they were talking about giving me at the time.

They started me on this tiny dose. A microdose, they call it. But the second I felt it kick in – a very small but unmistakable altering of the mind – I was like, *oh yeah, I could have some serious fun with this.* It's totally different from the way Sharon reacts to drugs. She can take 'em as needed. I just want to keep doing it until I'm blacked out and dribbling in the corner. But this time, I recognised it immediately for what it was, and I was like, you can fuck right off with that, no, absolutely not.

For the first time in years, I was able to be really honest with myself.

They say it's physical and spiritual, addiction. The physical part is the craving from the brain. And that robs you of your spirit. And by getting sober, you're earning your spirit back. When I walked out of that ketamine clinic, I told myself I'd never let addiction steal my spirit from me again.

For a long time after getting sober, I found harmless things to get addicted to. Yorkshire tea. Wordsearch books. English sweeties. Doodling. Exercise machines. Texting funny shit with Billy Morrison and other friends.

But nothing is really harmless when the word 'moderation' ain't in your dictionary.

I remember the time I decided to give up cigarettes and have the occasional cigar instead. It was after a tour, and I was starting to get freaked out by the damage I was doing to my vocal cords. The idea was that quitting cigarettes would let my voice recover, while the cigars would allow me to enjoy the taste of tobacco once in a while without inhaling the smoke.

Next thing I knew, I was smoking thirty Montecristos a day, inhaling every single one of 'em, and I'd converted half my house into a walk-in humidor. When the time came to start singing again, my voice was so rough my arsehole hurt. So I thought, fuck it, and went back to the cigarettes. But by then I was used to inhaling cigar smoke, so even a pack of full-strength Marlboros felt like having half a wank. It took me *years* to wean myself off those things. Nicotine is the most addictive substance I've ever put into my body, without any shadow of doubt. People whose lives are wrecked with emphysema and lung cancer, they still carry on smoking. That tells you something about the nature of that drug.

Of all the supposedly harmless things I've been addicted to, though, the most dangerous have been doctors' prescriptions. Whether it's Vicodin or cough medicine, it's always been the slipperiest of slopes for me. So when I got sober, I forced myself to stay away from the medical profession as much as I could.

But during *No More Tours II* I started to come down with a bad case of vocal strain. I mean, try screaming your lungs out on stage for an hour and a half every other night for months on end, with the humidity and temperature changing at every venue . . . at the age of sixty-nine.

Don't get me wrong, for some singers it's no problem at all. Take Elton John. I was talking to him one day and he said he'd just come back from a tour. I asked him how many shows. 'Forty-eight,' he said. And I was like, 'That's a lot of shows, Elton . . . How long was the tour?' He just shrugged and said, 'Forty-eight days.' I couldn't believe it. The guy's unstoppable. He'd do his residency in Las Vegas during the week, then fly halfway around the world to do a couple more shows over the weekend. He works every day of the year, that bloke. The work ethic is insane. I can't keep up with that. There comes a point when my body just says, fuck off, no.

For as long as I can remember, the answer's been a drug called Decadron, or dexamethasone. It's a type of steroid, basically, used to treat inflammation. It gives you a bit of a shove, y'know? One shot and you can sing higher than the moon. Now, I ain't gonna lie, I've pushed my luck with Decadron in the past. I've bullshitted doctors to get more than I needed – whether it was in pill form, liquid drops or injections into my throat. But until *No More Tours II* it had never given me any serious problems. A lot of singers, they go too far with it. They scream so hard they end up with nodules on their vocal cords that have to be removed with surgery. Not me.

So as soon as I felt my voice giving out I went straight to my gig doctor – not sneaking around this time, but with Sharon's knowledge – and got myself a couple of bottles of liquid Decadron.

At first, it was like a magic elixir. I could get through a whole show, no problem at all. My range and stamina were so good I could have added a couple of Bee Gees numbers to the setlist. But as with most drugs, it was 'play now, pay later' . . . and before long, the cure became worse than the disease.

To be fair, of course, the doc had told me to take just two drops of the stuff every night with dinner. But those couple of drops soon became five or six, dinner or no dinner. Then a few more before bed. Then a top-up the next morning. Then it was back to the old, 'Hi Doc, it's Ozzy – *can I please have some more?*'

'Ozzy, your voice is fine, you don't *need* steroids,' Sharon kept telling me.

'But what if it stops being fine when I'm halfway through a show?'

'That's why you do warm-ups. So you can tell how you're feeling.'

'But the doctor says—'

'You've got that doctor wrapped around your bloody finger. STOP. TAKING. THEM.'

But Sharon was busy doing her talk-show stuff back in LA, and I was hopping between cities on the other side of the world, so there wasn't much she could do other than give me a bollocking whenever she called.

Which was all well and good until the old 'roid rage kicked in.

Next thing I knew, I'd somehow given myself a black eye that even a couple of layers of stage make-up couldn't hide. Sharon got heavy with me after that. She hired this military guy with a neck wider than the Watford Gap to come and watch over me. Where she found this bloke, I've no idea. He just appeared by my side one day, like an angry mountain in human form, and never left. Sharon kept telling me I was hallucinating at night, either just as I was about to fall asleep or when I was waking up. She said that's how I'd head-butted a coffee table, giving myself the shiner. I had no recollection of that. To her, that proved her point. To me, it felt like everyone was getting on my case for no good reason.

Sharon kept wanting me to see a neurologist. My son Jack was worried I might have the same thing that took down Sharon's dear friend Robin Williams – Lewy body dementia. I mean, it wasn't like I was seeing Martians floating over the bed or anything. But it was bad enough that I was talking to people who weren't there. I would think the kids were throwing parties in my room, or I'd get angry and pieces of furniture would end up broken – and I'd wake up with no idea how it had happened.

My Parkinson's was part of the problem. When most people think of Parkinson's, they think of what the actor Michael J. Fox has got. My case is nowhere near as severe. In fact, my doctors have told me it's pretty mild. Having said that, the disease has stiffened my muscles, which affects the way I walk and talk, and the pills I take to keep it in check have side effects. This one drug I was taking back then, Sinemet, is known to cause confusion in some people – along with agitation, nightmares, nervousness and all kinds of other shit. And when I added a bottle a day of steroids to the mix, I became more wired than the National Grid.

On top of that, I'd been getting this really bad stage fright, partly 'cos I was so paranoid about my voice giving out. That had given me terrible insomnia, which had thrown me off even more. Sharon was so worried she got the kids to take it in turns flying out to each gig to keep an eye on me.

Jack came one weekend, Kelly the next, Aimee after that. I even got to hang out with some of the grandkids. I've got *ten* of 'em now, if you can believe it. There's Jack's daughter Pearl, who was six at the time. Andy, who must have been three. And Minnie, who was just a baby then. (His daughter Maple hadn't been born yet.) Since then, Kelly's had her little Sid, who's a proper tearaway. I get knackered just watching him. My other grandkids are from my first marriage. Maia and Elijah from my son Louis, and Harry, Isabelle and Kitty from my daughter Jessica.

Anyway, it did the trick, all the extra support. By the time *No More Tours II* reached North America, just before my birthday, I was feeling a lot better. Which was just as well, 'cos we still had thirty arenas left to play.

Everything seemed fine again.

But I wasn't fine. I was heading straight for a brick wall.

Because the Decadron was doing damage no one could see.

2

Clever Accident

When we opened *No More Tours II* in Jacksonville, Florida, it had been fifty years since I started out as a singer. Where the fuck had all that time gone? Nobody warns you that one day you'll wake up and half a century's gone by.

It was a totally different world when I first got into the music game. Telly was still black and white. Steam trains were still running from Birmingham Snow Hill to London Paddington. And the future king of England was still a teenager, like I was – although that was the only thing we had in common. He certainly hadn't just done six weeks for burglary.

The question I constantly got asked when I was doing press for *No More Tours II* was, how did you do it? How did you get from there to here – becoming this well-known name, keeping your career going over five decades?

I didn't have an answer. I still don't. None of it was

planned. When you're on the inside looking out, you're just doing your thing, riding the rollercoaster. There's no good reason why I'm still here, still working – or trying to, anyway – and others aren't. Maybe I just got lucky. Or maybe it's just my trip, and everything's meant to be.

I first became a performer at school, I suppose, in the days when I was still John, not Ozzy. I couldn't read properly 'cos of my dyslexia, and I couldn't concentrate 'cos of my ADHD. Whenever I had to read something out loud in class, everyone would piss themselves laughing. But if I hammed it up, did crazy things to distract them, I didn't feel so ashamed.

The first time I sang in front of anyone was at one of my sisters' talent shows at 14 Lodge Road. I did a Cliff Richard number – 'Living Doll' – of all things. It can't have been that bad, 'cos no one booed, and none of the windows shattered. But never in a million years did I think singing could be a career. In my mind, I had a better chance of becoming the next prime minister of fucking Sweden.

The first proper band I joined was the Polka Tulk Blues Band. I was nineteen at the time, and straight out of prison. The name came from the brand of talcum powder my mum used. It was me on vocals, Tony Iommi on guitar, Geezer Butler on bass, Bill Ward on drums. We also had a slide guitarist and a saxophone player, but they only lasted about two gigs. Mainly 'cos they couldn't play the slide guitar or the saxophone.

After a few weeks of gigging, we changed our name to Earth. The only problem with that was, when you said it in a Brummie accent, it sounded like you were throwing up. *UURRRGGHHHFFF.* So we changed our name again, to Black Sabbath, after an old horror film. We were all into that black magic shit, especially Geezer, who was always carrying around a pile of Dennis Wheatley books with titles like *The Satanist* and *The Devil Rides Out.*

In the beginning, it was all Tony Iommi. He'd been in the year above me at Birchfield Road Secondary Modern, which they knocked down not long after we left. Everyone knew Tony, 'cos he had a bright red electric guitar that his parents had given to him one Christmas. He was also tall and good looking, and unbeatable in a fight. Then he lost the tips of his fingers in an accident at the sheet metal place where he worked. I only heard about what happened later, but I'm told this huge machine press came down on his right hand, and when he pulled it out, he could see his finger bones sticking out. Fucking horrible, man. That should have been the end of his guitar playing. But Tony's an inventor. So he just invented himself a set of new fingertips using an old Fairy Liquid bottle, then he re-taught himself how to play. To this day, I don't understand how he even knows his fingers are hitting the strings.

After the accident, Tony started using lighter strings – like the ones you'd get on a banjo – 'cos he was in so much pain. He also loosened his strings for the same reason, which lowered the tuning. Not that I knew much about any of that stuff at the time. But his plastic fingertips and de-tuned guitar gave him this really dark, distinctive sound. He was so good Jethro Tull made him a job offer just as Earth was starting to take off. We were devastated when he broke the news. But lucky for us, Tony didn't like being an employee in someone else's band.

He was back after two gigs.

At some point over the years, Black Sabbath got credited with inventing heavy metal. People even call me the 'Godfather of heavy metal', whatever the fuck that means. But I'm not totally sure that's right.

For me, the first proper 'heavy' song was 'You Really Got Me' by The Kinks, which came out the summer I left school. When I first heard that riff – DUH-N-N-N-*NUH*! DUH-N-N-N-*NUH*! – it *did* something to me. It was like a drug. Listening to it was like having a fucking orgasm. I had to buy the single five times, 'cos I kept wearing out the grooves. It might have been the first thing I ever got addicted to. It drove my poor old man halfway round the bend. 'IF I HEAR THAT ONE MORE TIME, I SWEAR I'LL ...'

I did eventually stop playing it, but only 'cos I blew out the speaker of his record player. It was one of them polished wood things with a built-in radio that took up about half the living room. And of course there was no way I was ever gonna own up to doing that kind of damage. There was just this sudden, very suspicious silence ... until eventually he put on one of his Al Jolson records and all that came out was this dribbly, farty noise. *PPFFTTHHHHHH.*

You could hear the scream from a mile away.

Years later, I was lucky enough to meet Ray Davies from The Kinks. We were at the Rock & Roll Hall of Fame's twenty-fifth anniversary show at Madison Square Garden in New York. I was playing with Metallica, jumping around on stage like a jackrabbit. I told him I thought 'You Really Got Me' was basically the perfect song. He couldn't have been nicer about it. He even returned the compliment, saying he liked 'Paranoid'. You couldn't wipe the grin off my face. I wanted to phone my dad and tell him what he'd said, but of course he wasn't around any more by then.

Whatever the history books decide when it comes to heavy metal, it's certainly true we wanted the first Sabbath album to be heavier than anything that had come before. Not just the music, but also the lyrics. Back then, no one was singing about Satan, demons and corpses. I mean, okay, Fleetwood Mac had done 'Black Magic Woman', which Santana then covered. But you didn't see girls running out of Fleetwood Mac gigs screaming 'cos they were terrified. You did at *our* gigs. You've gotta remember, a lot more people went to church back then. They thought the Devil was real. So when they heard that spooky three-note riff with me howling about a figure in black with eyes of fire coming to take me away, they thought he'd be coming for them next.

At the same time, the image that first album created was so strong, for a long time people thought Devil stuff was all we did. That's why people started calling me the Prince of Darkness, supposedly after a line in *Paradise Lost*, the John Milton poem . . . not that I knew who the fuck John Milton was.

The truth is, although Sabbath always had a dark vibe, the song 'Black Sabbath' was basically the only full-on 'scary music' thing we ever did. I mean, go and listen to 'Changes', a soulful piano ballad about a marriage falling apart, or 'Supernaut', with that awesome funk-rock rhythm break, or the trippy 'Planet Caravan', which I'm told they played in the SpaceX Crew Dragon before it docked with the International Space Station.

Still ... we did all right in the end. So it ain't like you're gonna hear any of us complaining.

It's a miracle I had any kind of career after Sabbath.

After I got fired – for being too fucked up, according to them, but that's a story for later – I ended up living in a little apartment with its own kitchen and living room at a temporary housing place called Le Parc in West Hollywood.

I had no clue what I was gonna do next. The stress was killing me. I just kept ordering in booze from Gil Turner's on the Sunset Strip, keeping the blinds drawn all day, running the AC full blast – with the gas fire on at the same time, 'cos it reminded me of home – while drinking and smoking myself into oblivion. Meanwhile, my wife at the time was back in England with the kids, waiting for me to land a new gig so we wouldn't go broke.

The problem was, I'd just turned thirty-one, which was dangerously close to over the hill for a rock star. In my mind, there was a good chance I'd end up draining whatever was left of our savings, leaving me with no choice but to go and find a job on a building site somewhere.

It was Sharon who saved me.

The crazy thing is, I barely knew her at the time. She was working for her father, Don Arden, who was then Sabbath's manager. He called himself Mr Big and looked and acted like an East End gangster. He'd supposedly once hung the Bee Gees' manager Robert Stigwood out of a window for trying to poach the Small Faces, Don's biggest band. There were other stories of him stubbing cigars out on people's foreheads, or bribing DJs to get radio play. I had no idea how much of it was true. I just stayed the fuck out of his way.

I'd bumped into Sharon once or twice during the early days of Sabbath, thanks to our dealings with Don. But it was only on recollection I realised it was her. She was his receptionist initially. She says she remembers me once coming into Don's office on Berkeley Square in London, not long after *Paranoid* came out, with no shoes on and a hot water tap around my neck. She couldn't have been older than eighteen at the time. It was all just a haze to me. I was stoned out of my mind. She also went to one of our gigs at the Marquee Club in Soho. She was used to seeing the American pop stars her dad represented and couldn't believe the difference. The volume. The sweat dripping down the walls. Me on stage, reaching out and touching the fans in the front row. We were a people's band, Sabbath. When we did a gig, it was like we were a part of our own audience.

The first time I saw Sharon and *knew* it was Sharon was when she came walking out of a hotel in Copenhagen. Don had sent her there to collect the door money from an ELO gig or something. *Wow*, I thought, *what a good-looking chick*. Then she smiled at me. And I was like, *you've got no chance with her, don't even think about it*. I mean, Sharon was this educated, high-class woman. She'd wear diamonds and all the latest fashions. Her dad was a famous multimillionaire. Besides, I was still married to my ex-wife then ... not that I was exactly Husband of the Year material.

After I got kicked out of Sabbath, I was convinced Don would keep managing 'em and I'd get dropped. I mean, Sabbath had the name recognition. Who the fuck had heard of Ozzy?

Then came the knock on the door.

It was the moment I'd been dreading. But it wasn't the apartment manager or one of Don's heavies coming to throw me out. It was Sharon, dressed to kill, standing there looking at me in my underwear, unshaven, drunk, beer cans all over the floor. It takes a lot to shock Sharon – when you've grown up the daughter of Don Arden, you've seen everything – but the smell alone was enough to make her take a step back.

'If you get your shit together,' she said eventually, 'we'd like to manage you.'

I was so surprised, all I could say was . . . '*Me?*'

'No, the other Ozzy Osbourne, the one standing behind you,' she said. 'OF COURSE YOU.'

I'd be dead without Sharon – of that, I'm absolutely, 100 per cent fucking sure. But when it came to my first two solo albums – *Blizzard of Ozz* and *Diary of a Madman* – they couldn't have happened without Randy Rhoads. He was a gift from God – there's no other way of putting it. I was incredibly fortunate that I ever crossed paths with him.

After Sharon came over to Le Parc, she told me I needed to start holding auditions. It was a wake-up call, that was. I mean, Sabbath only had to find one man to replace me. I had to find a whole band, starting with the guitarist.

Then the clouds parted, a choir sang and out of no-where, Randy appeared.

I had no clue who he was at the time – there were so many guitarists out there, and we'd auditioned so many of 'em – but I later learned he was in a band called Quiet Riot. They'd been going through a tough time, or so I was told, and the only deal they'd got was in Japan. That's why Randy was putting out feelers for a new gig.

All I remember of his studio audition was him plugging in and warming up. That was enough, as far as I was concerned. It's not that Randy was in another league to everyone else ... he was playing a different game. He was also just the *epitome* of a rock star. He couldn't have been more than ninety-five pounds wet, and he stood at just five-two – the same size as Sharon. And he had these beautiful features, long blond hair, and he wore the leather trousers and low-cut T-shirt. When I first set eyes on him, I couldn't tell if he was a bloke or a chick. I'd never met anyone who was so careful about their appearance. If it was too windy, or raining, he didn't want to go outside in case it messed up his hair. Mind you, he was meticulous like that about everything, including his guitar. It was part of what made him such an incredible player.

The thing I really couldn't get over was how skinny he was. I could lift him up with one arm. That's probably why he didn't drink much or do a lot of drugs. When he *did* drink, he'd have one of those milky White Russian things. A girl's drink, or at least it was in those days. Two or three maximum. Then he'd get all giggly and go to sleep. And yet he had this really deep voice, with an almost Southern twang.

What I came to realise was, Randy didn't *eat* food. He just picked at it. The one thing he liked was chicken skin. Just the skin, not the meat.

'Why d'you eat *that*?' I asked him once, as he was pulling apart this chicken leg.

'I like the taste,' he shrugged.

But even though he was skinny, he had the body of an athlete. He'd wear these high-heeled boots in a woman's size – the only ones that would fit – and he could run around a stage in 'em for hours.

I told him he'd got the job before his warm-up was even over. He looked surprised.

'But I haven't started yet,' he said.

If my career after Sabbath came down to any one moment, it was the release of *Blizzard of Ozz* in America.

When you think of all the singers from huge British bands whose solo albums went down like wet turds in the States, it's unbelievable. And I was no one compared with most of 'em. There was no reason to think I'd do any better.

The release date was around March time, 1981. The album had already been out for a few months in Britain on Don's Jet Records label, and had done okay – more than okay – getting to number seven in the charts. To support it, we'd played smaller shows, but we'd packed 'em to capacity, creating a lot of buzz. At the same time, though, the single of 'Crazy Train' had barely scraped into the top fifty. I mean, that wasn't a huge surprise. The UK charts at the time were full of novelty acts like Shakin' Stevens and Bucks Fizz, with the occasional new wave hit by Soft Cell or The Human League. And metal was about *albums*, not singles. It was a reminder of the uphill battle we had ahead of us, especially in America.

By the time we arrived in LA for the US launch the

pressure was off the scale. And the only way I knew how to handle pressure was to drink all night, then keep drinking the next morning. So that's what I did on the day of our big meeting with the marketing department of our American label, Epic, which was owned by CBS Records. It was something all new signings had to do at the start of each quarter, or something.

When Sharon drove me to the CBS building in Century City from her dad's house up in Benedict Canyon, I was already out of my tree. All the way there she was bending my ear about how important the meeting was, how Epic didn't have a clue what to do with a metal album 'cos their other acts were The Jacksons and a bunch of new-wave and synth-pop groups. 'Why the fuck did they sign me then?' I asked her.

'Because CBS already has a huge distribution deal with my father,' she said.

The plan was, I'd make an impression by taking two white doves out of my pocket – someone at Jet Records had gone out and bought 'em from a pet shop the night before – open up a window, say 'peace' or 'rock 'n' roll' or something, then let 'em fly away.

I wasn't keen on the idea, to be honest with you. Especially since the birds kept shitting in my jacket pocket.

But Sharon insisted I had to do it. 'This is your *one* chance to make an impression,' she said. 'You need to give them a show.'

The thing is, I'd been in the music game long enough to know exactly what the deal would be. If the record company was having a marketing meeting, it wouldn't just be *me* going. There'd be a rapper in front of me, a folk singer behind . . . a fucking didgeridoo player in between. And the marketing people with their suits and Rolexes wouldn't give a flying fuck about any of us. They wouldn't be *fans*. It would just be another day at the office for them.

It was only when I saw the cameras in the room that I made up my mind what to do. *They want a show,* I thought, *I'll give 'em a show.* I knew exactly the shot I wanted: horror – just absolute horror on everyone's faces. As for Sharon, she had absolutely no idea what was coming. She'd have confiscated those doves in a heartbeat if she'd thought they were in any danger.

So we walk into this board room. There must have been at least twenty-five executives there – and they'd all just been listening to 'Crazy Train' and other tracks off *Blizzard of Ozz.* For some reason I sit myself down on the knee of this young woman near the front. Then after a couple of minutes of listening to all their fake bullshit, I pull out one of the doves – just like we agreed – and say 'peace' or 'rock 'n' roll' or whatever.

Aww, goes the room.

Then I took a deep breath, smiled for the camera, and bit the dove's head off.

The place went absolutely fucking nuts. People scream-ing. Crying. Throwing up. Calling for security. Calling for the cops. At this point, I'd thrown the dove's body down on the conference table, but I still had its head in my mouth, so then I popped it out and grinned again for the camera. I had blood and bird shit and feathers all over me, it was absolutely horrendous. To this day, I've no idea what I was thinking – I mean, I wasn't thinking, I was thirty-six hours into a seventy-two-hour bender. Then these big blokes with earpieces and guns come running in, grab me and Sharon, drag us away, and throw us out on the street, where Sharon *literally* pisses herself, she's laughing so much – out of shock, I think, more than anything. Meanwhile, I'd let the other dove go, so we knew it was still fluttering around up there somewhere, with about half a dozen massive security guys running around in circles after it.

Later that day, we got a call from CBS's lawyers saying if I pulled any more stunts like that, they'd bury the record and not let me out of my contract. But the early pressings of 'Crazy Train' had already gone out, and by the end of the day, it was being played back to back on every metal station in the country. That was the moment the US label realised, okay, this guy's fucking nuts, but maybe he'll sell some records. I mean, that was their whole game, man – selling more records.

Funnily enough, it was my game too.

The first thing I should say about it all is that the poor dove didn't deserve it. Now that I'm older and living full time in the sober world, I can't stand any kind of cruelty to animals. What happened to that bird, I'll take to my grave. But I can't change what I did. And the truth is, as bad as my behaviour was, it changed everything for *Blizzard of Ozz*.

By the time the US tour got started a few weeks later, people thought I was an absolute fucking lunatic. So we had some fun with it, chucking buckets of pigs' guts and whatever into the crowd. What no one expected, though, was that the fans would play along, chucking stuff at *me* on the stage. Meanwhile, the authorities were losing their minds over the atrocities they thought we were committing, even though it was nothing worse than throwing around some slop from the nearest butcher's shop.

Every night, things got crazier and crazier, until finally, early in January – by now it was 1982 – the tour reached the Veterans Memorial Auditorium in Des Moines, Iowa. That was the night someone threw what I thought was a joke-shop bat at the stage. And I caught it. And I don't need to tell you what happened next. Other than to say, when I bit down on its neck I realised very quickly it wasn't made of rubber.

From that day on, my reputation would precede me whenever I went into a new town. And of course, human nature being what it is, the story about the bat got exaggerated every time it was passed on. It was like a game of Chinese whispers. When it starts, Johnny's cut his finger. But by the time you've gone around the circle, Johnny's cut his head off.

But I was lucky, y'know? Once you get on the horse, you've gotta go wherever the horse takes you. You've got to be prepared for the good and the bad. You can't go back and redo it. The saddest part for me, the part I still think about all the time, is what happened on that tour to Randy and our hair and wardrobe lady, Rachel Youngblood. If anyone deserved to die, it was me. But when tragedy struck, it was so fucking random. I still don't understand how it happened. But for now, all I'll say is that not a day goes by when I don't ask myself, why am *I* still here, not them?

What I'm trying to say is, there was no clever plan that got me from the Polka Tulk Blues Band to *No More Tours II*. If anything, it was all just a clever accident.

It was the same story with the one thing in my life that had nothing to do with music – *The Osbournes* TV show.

For the longest time, the TV people in LA had wanted to make a sitcom based on my life, a kind of a rock 'n' roll *Addams Family*, but with a retired rock star as the dad. But they didn't think a straight-up documentary-type show would have enough of a plot. Then we did that *Cribs* special on MTV at the end of 2000 – kind of like the old ITV show *Through the Keyhole*, but for rock stars and rappers or whatever – and the thing just blew up. It became the highest-rated episode in the history of the channel or something.

After that, the TV people were like, fuck it, let's just stick some cameras in their house and see what happens.

We started a whole new thing with that show. As the actor Jack Black joked at my Rock & Roll Hall of Fame induction ceremony, it might have been the most evil thing I ever did. Before us, there were no reality shows about famous families that didn't have pre-written plots. Now everyone and their fucking hamster has one.

We had some good times making *The Osbournes*, looking back. Well, for a while, anyway. But that kind of fame is impossible to hold on to. I mean, I'd been sort-of famous for most of my adult life. But being a TV star was something totally different. It was what I imagined it would be like to be Tom Cruise or Meryl Streep.

I got addicted to the fame for a while, if I'm being honest with you.

At one point, Sharon threw a party at our house and it was just a who's who of fucking everybody. George Lucas was there. Elizabeth Taylor. Robin Williams. Sylvester Stallone. Rod Stewart. Then I walk out into the back garden and Elton John's playing the piano by the swimming pool. Every day, something crazy happened. Donny and Marie Osmond filmed an advert with me. I went to the White House Correspondents' Dinner, where President Bush joked that his mum was a huge Sabbath fan. I probably shouldn't have drunk three bottles of wine and stood on the table at that thing . . . but whatever, you live and learn.

At the end of the day, though, I'm a singer, not a TV personality. I mean, I liked being in *The Osbournes*, but I hated working in TV. It's a vipers' nest, TV, it really is. It's not like being in music. You've got no friends in TV. The rivalry's off the charts. Everyone just wants what you've got, it's so phoney all the time.

By the time we got into the fourth season of *The Osbournes* I knew it had to end, like everything does. I'm fucked if I know how the Kardashians have lasted this long with their shows. They must be on season sixty by now.

For us, by the end of our run, we all were desperate to get our lives back. Jack was on drugs. Kelly was on drugs. I was sneaking up to my room to smoke weed at every opportunity. Then Sharon got cancer. The toll was bad, man. My poor wife was so sick, it took her the longest time to get over that. It took all of us a long time to come down from the high of the show, the stress of it . . . to go from reality TV to actual reality again.

When the final camera guy left, it was such a relief, man.

To take a shit without a boom mic over your head.

To get your leg over with the missus without three producers taking notes.

And best of all . . . to get out of the house and go back on the road again.

3

Hand of Doom

The last gig of *No More Tours II* before the Decadron caught up with me was West Valley City, Utah.

We were almost done with the North American leg of the tour by then. We only had Mountain View, San Diego and Las Vegas to go, plus a big night at the Hollywood Bowl. It should have been a breeze. The gigs were so close to my house in LA I could sleep in my own bed at night.

But life's never that easy, is it? Even the calmest, bluest ocean has a turd bobbing around in it somewhere. And there was a massive one headed right for me.

The first sign of trouble was my fingernails, of all things. I'd been biting 'em like crazy, 'cos the Decadron made me so tense. Then one day I noticed the cuticle on my right thumb was all red and swollen. But instead of doing what I was supposed to do – dab some antibiotic cream on it and leave it the fuck alone – I'd started to pick at it. I was so agitated all the time, it was like a nervous tic. Then somehow I banged it against a door, making it bleed. Meanwhile, the cuticle on my middle finger was starting to go the same way. I wouldn't have cared, but the pain was really bad – a kind of constant low-level throbbing that made it hard to focus on anything else.

What I didn't realise was that I had bacterial infections in both fingernails. And although those kinds of infections can heal on their own, the way Decadron works is it suppresses your immune system – that's how it reduces swelling, which is what makes your voice feel so much better. But if you do enough Decadron, your immune system goes from suppressed to totally shut down. And that was what had happened, which might not have been a problem if I hadn't been exposing myself to all kinds of new viruses and bacteria at the events we were holding every day.

'Meet-and-greets', they were called.

Now, the way a meet-and-greet works is, if a fan pays more dough, they get the best seats in the house, some signed gear and a few minutes to chat and take a selfie before the show. In the old days, they'd just hang around the back of the venue, hoping to get your autograph on your way out. Not any more. Like everything else in the music game today, that side of touring's become a kind of mini-industry in its own right.

I ain't gonna lie – part of me finds the whole meeting people for money thing creepy. Also, tickets are expensive enough as it is. The bean counters have pulled so many fees out of their arses over the years, it's a wonder they don't charge people to *leave* when a gig's over. That said, if meet-and-greets were a free-for-all,

only the pushiest fans would ever get to the front of the
queue . . . and they'd probably just turn around and flog
whatever you signed for 'em on eBay. Besides, the older
I get, the more I enjoy meeting the fans and having a
bit of fun with 'em, especially when whole families of
metalheads turn up, from the little kids to the grandparents. Not that grandma or grandpa can ever remember
much about the old days – they were as off their tits as
I was.

Honestly, the only worry I had about meet-and-greets
during *No More Tours II* was that someone crazy would
get through. I mean, it's hard to forget what happened to
Dimebag Darrell, one of the greats of metal guitar. Out
of nowhere, a guy jumped on stage and shot him dead,
along with three others. It must have been twenty years
ago now, but it still shakes me up whenever I think about
it. Spookily, it all went down on 8 December, the same
date John Lennon was killed. Probably no coincidence,
but we'll never know, 'cos the shooter was taken down
by a cop before anyone could ask him why the fuck he
did what he did.

I've certainly had no shortage of lunatics following me
around over the years. There was a bloke who kept showing up at my gigs with a five-million-year-old mammoth
tusk. Why, I've no fucking idea. Another guy painted my
name on every single thing in his house – the walls, the
sofa, everything – then sent me a home video to prove
it. A lot of the crazies came out of the woodwork after
the bat thing happened. But it was when the evangeli-
cals said I was putting Satanic messages in my songs that
it really got out of control. I mean, when you get that
kind of fame in America, there's always someone out

there who'll say, *I'll stop this little game you've got going on, bang-bang, you're dead.*

But the thing is, crazy people are *everywhere.* If you thought about it too much, you'd never leave the house. So I was like, fuck it, the whole point of this tour is to say goodbye to the fans, so why not meet as many of 'em as I can? That's why, every afternoon before a show, I was at the venue, my cuticles all fucked up, infections raging, shaking hand after hand . . . before going back to my hotel to do more Decadron.

All while I was getting sicker and sicker.

Whheeeeeeee . . .

THWUMP.

'Gaagh! *Fuck!*'

'Whatever you just broke,' said Sharon from under the covers, 'it serves you bloody right.'

I'd just stage-dived into bed again, like I did every night. 'I think something's wrong with me,' I moaned, staring at the dodgy finger I'd just landed on.

'It's taken you this long to realise that?'

'I'm serious, Sharon . . . something weird's happening to my hand.'

She sighed, and I heard a *BZZZZZZZZZZ* noise as her side of the bed started to lift. That's one of the best things about being a rock star – having all the latest toys. Our bed's got a bigger brain than ChatGPT. Me and Sharon each have a little remote control, and with the press of a button we can set our side of the bed to whatever height we want, all without affecting the other person. Meanwhile, all the motors, wires and gear wheels and whatever are hidden under the mattress in this metal platform thing.

'This had better be worth it,' said Sharon once she was fully upright.

'Look,' I showed her my thumb. 'It's fucking *killing* me. And my middle finger, too.'

She took a closer look. 'You've got swollen cuticles,' she said. 'Just put some cream on. And stop *biting* them all the time, it's disgusting.'

'But—'

BZZZZZZZZZZ.

Back down she went.

I must have put a couple of tubes of antibiotic stuff on my fingers that night. But when I woke the next morning my thumb was throbbing so hard it felt like it was hooked up to a diesel generator. And when I lifted it up to take a look, I just about shit the fucking bed. Overnight, it had ballooned at least ten times its normal size. It looked like it belonged to one of those giant foam hands you see at baseball games. My middle finger was massive as well. I could barely move any part of my hand, the swelling was so bad. And the pain – the pain was on another level.

'Sharon . . .' My voice was shaking. 'I think I need to go to hospital.'

'Oh, for God's sake, Ozzy. Stop being such a bloody drama— OH MY GOD!!! YOUR HAND!!!'

She couldn't believe it. My thumb was the size of a hundred-watt light bulb and glowing almost as brightly. Neither of us could stop staring at it. It was like something from the circus. We could have sold tickets.

We had no choice but to get it looked at – even though the next gig of the tour was that night in Mountain View, a one-hour flight from Van Nuys airport in the Valley.

So Sharon phoned the tour manager and he came over – not looking very happy at all – then off we all went to the Cedars-Sinai Urgent Care place down on Wilshire Boulevard in Beverly Hills. It's a separate building to the main Cedars ER, 'cos it's for non-life-threatening things. You wouldn't walk in there with an axe in your head, put it that way. But for a swollen thumb, it was just the job.

All I really wanted was something for the pain. As bad as my hand looked, I still thought it would just get better on its own. I mean, my sister Jean had swollen cuticles all the time when we were kids, and she just got on with it. If she'd asked for a day off school, she'd have got a clip around the ear.

But when the doctor took a look at my hand, the blood drained from his face.

'How did this happen?' he asked, giving me this very stern look.

'Beats me. I just woke up with it like that.'

'Did you shake anyone's hand recently?'

'Are you taking the piss?' I said. 'I must shake a thousand hands a night.'

'I see,' said the doc. 'And have you been feeling run down lately, for any reason – say, from a cold?'

I shook my head and gave him my best 'It wasn't me, officer' look.

Sharon kicked me. 'Just bloody tell him, Ozzy,' she hissed.

'Okay,' I coughed, 'I might have been taking … the odd drop of Decadron.'

'Steroids?'

'Yeah. For my voice.'

'I see. And just the occasional drop?'

'Yeah. Ow!' Sharon had kicked me again, but harder. 'Okay . . . a few drops.'

'You mean a few drops a week?'

'More of a . . . daily thing.'

He went very quiet for a moment. 'Mr Osbourne, *how many drops a day exactly*?'

'How many do you get in one of them little bottles?'

The doctor rubbed his temples and muttered something that sounded a lot like 'Jesus fucking Christ'. I was expecting a proper bollocking. But when you get to a certain age, docs stop lecturing you. They think you're a lost cause. Which to be fair, wasn't all that far from the truth with me. He also seemed to have more important things on his mind. 'Mr Osbourne,' he said, 'you appear to have an advanced staph infection in your thumb – and another one in your finger. And they're spreading fast, because your immune system has been completely wrecked by all the steroids you've been taking . . . or rather, abusing.'

'So . . . you can give me some pills for that?'

'No, no. Pills won't be enough. We need to get you to an emergency room.'

'What?!! But I've got a—'

'They'll put you on an intravenous drip of antibiotics to try and get the infection under control. Then they'll need to operate. The clock's ticking.'

I almost fell off my chair.

'It's just a sore fucking thumb!'

'Mr Osbourne,' said the doc, looking straight at me, 'this is very serious.'

*

If there's one thing I've learned over the years, it's that the absolute worst thing you can do after being told you've got some heavy-duty medical shit is look it up on the internet. I mean, half the stuff on there is made up – and the other half is usually wrong. So all you're gonna do is freak yourself out.

That's why I had Sharon look it up instead when we were on our way to the ER.

'Okay, here we go – staph infection,' she said as she scrolled through the search results on her phone. 'There's a whole Wikipedia page on ... oh ...'

'What?'

'Nothing.'

'Sharon, just fucking—'

'Oooh look, the sun's coming out. Maybe it's not going to rain this afternoon after all—'

I grabbed the phone and squinted at the screen.

The Wikipedia page, it turned out, was a list of very famous people who'd been totally fucking fine until they got a staph infection. Then they became very dead. One of 'em was President Reagan's Secretary of State Alexander Haig. Another was the big-time movie star Roy Scheider from *Jaws* and *The French Connection*. Even a president of the World Bank had popped his clogs after coming down with the same thing.

Let's just say, at this point I was starting to get a little bit concerned.

Next thing I knew, I was being squeezed into one of those paper hospital gowns that your arse hangs out of. Then off I waddled to the operating room.

It was obvious by now the Mountain View gig wasn't happening. Sharon and the tour manager were already on their phones, trying to move hell and earth to re-schedule, which is always the last thing you ever want to do. *No More Tours II* was employing thousands of people, from the band to the crew and all the workers at every venue. When you cancel a gig, every single one of 'em loses out. When I was younger and fucked up all the time, I didn't think so much about that side of things. But now it felt like this huge responsibility weighing down on me.

Worse than that was the feeling of letting down the twenty thousand or so fans who'd bought tickets. They would have hired babysitters or taken time off work or whatever so they could come to the show. If we'd been cancelling with more notice, that would have been one thing. But this was last minute, which felt like a below-the-belt move. But we didn't have a choice. Like the doc had said, the clock was ticking.

The shock of it all was just starting to hit me when they put the antibiotic drip into my arm. Then a nurse came in and started numbing my thumb.

The strange thing is, whatever was in the numbing stuff, it suddenly made me very emotional. I've no idea why. One minute I was watching her work, the next I was sobbing. I just totally broke down. It was crazy. Looking back now, I suppose it was the suddenness of it all. When an infection takes a bad turn, it happens so quickly. And it was all because of such a mundane, stupid fucking thing – an infected fingernail.

Okay, *two* infected fingernails.

At the back of my mind, there was also the worry that the bacteria would turn into one of those mutant flesh-eating things that antibiotics can't control.

What if it got into my bones?

My lungs?

My heart?

By the time the surgeon came in with his scalpel, I was thinking, Maybe this is it, maybe this is how it all ends . . . maybe tomorrow they'll be printing my—

'GAAAAGGGGHHH! I thought you fucking *numbed* it!!'

'Seriously? You can feel that?' The surgeon looked very surprised. He'd just sliced my thumb open.

'You didn't even warn me! What happened to the old "This might sting a bit"?'

'Mr Osbourne, your hand has been *completely* numbed. Only a person with a truly *incredible* tolerance to . . .' At that point he seemed to remember who he was talking to. 'Oh . . . er . . . I see,' he said. 'Sorry about that.'

'Well, get on with it then!'

The funny thing is, watching him work actually calmed me down. I love a bit of gore, me.

With my thumb now wide open, he started cleaning all this shit out of the wound. It was like pus, but . . . worse than that. He said he was trying to stop the bacteria from getting into my bloodstream. Then he *really* got to work, cutting out the dead tissue, whittling down the bone underneath, getting under my fingernail and scraping out more infected bits of whatever. After that, he moved on to my middle finger, doing the same thing again. It was the most riveting thing I'd watched since the camera feed of my first colonoscopy. Then all of a sudden it was done – my thumb and finger all bandaged up like I was a boxer getting ready for a prize fight. He hadn't even messed up my black nail polish.

I was so relieved, I almost burst into tears again. Then someone brought me an ice cream in one of those chocolate-dipped waffle cone things, and I just about inhaled it, I was so ravenous. But of course that just made me want another ice cream, 'cos if something's good, I don't know how to stop until I've made myself sick. I had a full-on addiction to ice cream for a while, actually. Always Häagen-Dazs or Ben & Jerry's. Vanilla or coffee. Okay, *sometimes* strawberry – but only if the other two flavours weren't available. It got to the point I was eating so much of the stuff, I decided to save money by hiring a chef who made her own. Big mistake, that was. The ice cream she made was un-fucking-believable. I didn't even need a cone, I would have eaten it off the floor. But after a few weeks of going to town on that, I became pre-diabetic and had to stop.

One more thing to add to the list of fun things I ain't allowed to do any more.

Anyway . . . after finishing the ice cream, things were all a bit of a blur. Kelly and Jack stopped by at some point. And of course we had to put something on Instagram, since we'd cancelled the show. If you're famous and so much as scratch your bollocks these days, you've gotta put it on social media. I mean, if you don't do it, someone else will. Before smartphones, you had to be in *really* deep shit before the paparazzi showed up. On a few occasions, I've had 'em jumping out of the bushes and parachuting onto my back lawn to get the best shot. I think it's a liberty, I really do. But now *everyone's* a pap. You can't walk down the street without someone sticking a phone in your face. But I don't complain about it any more. I'm like, fuck it, if you can't beat 'em, join 'em. So now my every last burp and fart gets beamed to my six million followers.

'I can't wait to get out of here tomorrow,' I wrote in the post, under a picture of me with my bandaged hand. I also made sure to thank the doctors and nurses.

Meanwhile, Sharon had worked a miracle with the venues. They'd agreed to delay the shows by a few days, so the North American leg could be wrapped up by the end of the year – just like we'd planned. I'd finish 2018 by headlining a blow-out New Year's Eve Ozzfest in LA.

I could hardly believe what a close call it had been. For a few moments there, I'd been convinced I was about to have a very short conversation with St Peter in front of the final velvet rope. 'Osbourne,' he'd say, not even looking at his golden clipboard. 'You're not on the fucking list.'

CLANK. Whaaaaaaaaaaaaaaaa . . .

But it all seemed so silly now. I even started to laugh. Or at least I did until the surgeon came marching back in with a bad-news look on his face.

'Your test results are back,' he said. 'The infections are more stubborn than we'd feared. We'll need to keep you on the drip for at least another five days.'

It was like the air had just been sucked out of the room. I couldn't get any words out.

That wasn't even the worst part. 'And we're going to need to operate on your hand again because the scan showed there's still dead tissue in there,' he went on. 'If we don't get it all out, it could be life-threatening.'

I looked over at Sharon, thinking there was still a chance we could do the shows. She had her head in her hands. Five days in the hospital were five days too many. It would totally fuck up the rescheduled dates. The juggling act she'd just pulled off had been for nothing. It was game over – for 2018, at least. We'd have to pick up the pieces in the new year.

Assuming the infections didn't get me first.

4

Countdown

They kept me in hospital for the rest of the week. I would have tried to sneak out sooner, but that's easier said than done when you've got an IV drip hooked up to your arm and doctors and nurses popping in and out of your room the whole time. And it ain't like I'm the most inconspicuous-looking person, what with my name tattooed across my knuckles and smiley faces on both knees. Besides, the doc said I'd had *three* staph infections in total – not two, like they originally thought – so it was probably a good idea to let the medicine run its course.

Even after I got home, it seemed like the swelling would never go down. For a while I was worried I'd be stuck with a giant thumb for forever ... although to be fair, it would have made hitchhiking a lot easier.

But by 3 December – my birthday – everything was back to its normal size. I was almost starting to feel like my old self again.

Since I was turning seventy – a number I just could *not* get my head around – Sharon wanted to throw a party at our place in LA. It's one of those grand old Spanish mansions down on the flats near Paramount Studios, built in the twenties for some mogul or other. We bought it when I was feeling flush after the last Sabbath tour. My favourite thing about it is the sign on the gate – 'Never Mind the Dog, Beware the Owner'.

The problem was, after all the cancelled shows, I wasn't in the mood to celebrate. 'I don't want a party,' I said to Sharon. 'I just wanna get back on the road.'

'Oh, don't be such a misery guts,' she told me. 'Seventy's a big number – we've got to mark the occasion somehow. After all, it's amazing you're still here.'

'Trust me,' I said, 'no one's more surprised than me.'

The truth was, of course, there was another reason I didn't want a big song and dance for my seventieth. Because I'm an addict, a party just ain't a party for me. If I'm not getting fucked up, I don't want to be there. You end up just sitting there at the end of the table, twiddling your thumbs, while you feel the mood of the room start to rise. And you're thinking, Is it my imagination, or is everyone getting a bit friendly with each other? Then you remember it's 'cos they're getting happy and you're not.

Sometimes even Sharon forgets I can't have so much as a sniff of shandy on a special occasion.

'Oooh, try this,' she'll go when someone gives her some new whizz-bang cocktail that tastes like chocolate or strawberries or whatever. And I'll be like, *are you serious?* One sip of that, and you'll go home to your bed tonight and I'll still be here in the morning! Next thing you know, you'll be throwing pots and pans at my dealers, and I'll be back in rehab, throwing up into a bucket. All my life, the same shit, over and over.

What I don't understand is *why*. Why are some people good company when they drink? But when I do it, I'll have a grand old time but no one else will? Nothing clears a room faster than, oh shit, Ozzy's back on the sauce.

The way I look at it, when you're an addict, your basic problem is that you can't handle reality. Your marriage is in trouble: you get shitfaced. You're going broke: you get shitfaced. You've been fucked over or betrayed by someone: you get shitfaced. That's the thing with drugs, they give you an escape from whatever's bugging you in the sober world. Or they boost your confidence when you need it. Or they help you bury some dark shit in your past.

It's all of the above in my case.

Because of my dyslexia, I spent my whole childhood living in fear. It sounds stupid now, but having to get up and read in class when I couldn't make sense of the words felt like a fate worse than death. It gave me this sense of impending doom that followed me wherever I went. I'd walk around with this black cloud over my head, waiting for the world to end. Then once I'd stammered and mixed up my words and everyone had laughed, the fear was replaced by this overwhelming shame.

On top of that was the shame of us not having the money to do what other families did. I mean, my parents tried their hardest in their own way, but we were always less than. Growing up, there'd been six of us Osbourne kids – me, my older sisters Jean, Iris and Gillian, and my

younger brothers Paul and Tony – all crammed into a
tiny terraced house with no indoor toilet. We never had
a car. Never went on holiday. You'd see other kids going
off on their summer holidays with their mums and dads,
and you wished you were doing the same. And when the
ice cream van showed up, you were the only kid whose
mum and dad didn't have a spare penny to buy him a
cone. That probably only happened a couple of times, but
it felt so crap, man. Everything seemed to be an anticli-
max, even Christmas. You'd get all excited about it for
weeks, then suddenly it was over and you realised your
parents could barely afford to feed and clothe six kids,
never mind stuff your stocking with presents. Even after
I made money, that feeling of financial insecurity – the
fear of not being able to pay the rent, of waiting for the
bailiff's knock – never went away.

The way I avoided reality as a kid was by living in a
fantasy world. If I found a stick on the street, I could disappear inside my head for the rest of the day. The moment
I picked it up, it wasn't a stick, it was gun, a spear, whatever the fuck I wanted it to be. I feel bad for kids who
can't do that today. An iPad's an amazing thing, but it's
got nothing on a kid's imagination.

As far as I know, addiction wasn't something that ran
in my family. Not that working-class people knew how
to talk about that kind of thing in them days.

My father would drink, but nothing out of the ordinary. He liked Mackeson Stout. It was a milk stout,
sweeter than the usual bitter. Every so often he'd reach
for the top shelf, have a whisky, get a bit merry, play some
snooker. But I only saw him properly out of his shitter a
handful of times.

When I started to drink myself, the first thing I realised was that it made all the bad feelings go away. Same
with coke or pills. But no one warned me of the dangers.
There was no sit-down talk with my mum and dad: Here's
what to do, here's what not to do. Even if they'd tried,
I wouldn't have listened. So I learned from the street,
which is a dirty way of learning. I worry about that with
marijuana. Now it's legal in a lot of places, it seems like a
disaster waiting to happen, 'cos once you get started on it,
you want something stronger. It's a gateway drug. Or at
least it is for people like me. Although I suppose *anything's*
a gateway drug for me.

What I don't understand is, once I became successful, and my shame and worries went away, why did my
drinking and using just keep getting worse?

If I don't know the answer by now, I suppose I probably
never will.

In the end, I spent most of my birthday party in the
kitchen, popping my head round the door every so
often to say hello to the guests. Some of the guys from
Metallica and Faith No More stopped by. So did my old
friends Billy Idol, Slash and Marilyn Manson – and of
course Billy Morrison, the guy who got me sober, for
which I'll always be grateful. I appreciated 'em being
there, even if I wished we were still out there raising hell.

The funny thing is, I got to know most of those guys
at the same place, the Sunset Marquis hotel in West
Hollywood. It was weird seeing 'em together in my house
so many years later. The Marquis was the centre of the
rock 'n' roll universe for a while. According to Sharon,

we were staying there once when Kelly was little, and Kelly snuck away, and when we found her she was in the hot tub with Cyndi Lauper. All of the kids came to absolutely adore Cyndi and, many years on, she's become a great friend of Sharon's.

That kind of shit happened all the time at the Marquis. You'd see Keith Richards propping up the bar. Bruce Springsteen eating his breakfast. And every so often someone out of their fucking skull on coke would cannonball off the roof into the pool. Not that *I* ever did that. Flea from the Chili Peppers did it once, I'm told. But I wasn't there to see it.

The first time I ever met Slash was at the Marquis.

Sharon had arranged an afternoon birthday party for Aimee – she was turning five, I believe – and I remember Zakk Wylde was there. This would have been right after Zakk started playing with me, during the *No Rest for the Wicked Tour*. It was that moment in time when you couldn't go anywhere without hearing 'Sweet Child o' Mine' or 'Paradise City' blasting from somewhere.

Now, I can't speak for Zakk, but I must have started drinking early in the day – or even the night before, I dunno – and just kept going. And at some point I heard Slash was also staying at the hotel, and I got it into my head that we should go and find him.

So off we went to find Slash's room, and ended up barging in on him in bed with his chick. He was all groggy and said he needed to sleep a bit more, but promised he'd come and find us later for a drink. I didn't understand. I thought everyone else was like me, and spent every waking hour getting drunk or high, or both.

Slash did eventually come and try to find us. But by

then I'd passed out and been dragged away by security . . . or at least that's what I'm told. When I asked Slash what time I was thrown out – thinking it must have been really late – he said it was like three o'clock in the afternoon. I'd had so much fun getting ready for the party, I missed the fucking party. But that's how it worked in those days. I'd go to a bar and come back two or three days later. It drove Sharon crazy.

After that, our paths kept crossing, and slowly but surely Slash turned into a great friend, one of the kindest people I've ever known. What's weird is that until very recently I'd never met Axl Rose, although I'd admired him from a distance. I mean, when Axl sings, you could never mistake him for anyone else.

I hung out with Metallica a lot at the Marquis, too. I'd met them during *The Ultimate Sin Tour*, when Sharon booked them as our support act. It must have been right after *Master of Puppets* came out. It was obvious even then they were something very special. The army of followers they brought every night was unbelievable. They just absolutely blew the roof off every venue we played. At the same time, they were so nice and down to earth – huge Sabbath fans, too, which meant a lot to me. The only problem was they were such a hard act to follow. Well, that and the fact James Hetfield kept falling off his skateboard and breaking something every other fucking night. Not that it stopped him playing. He'd just get up there in a cast and push through.

With Marilyn Manson, on the other hand, I never saw him at the Marquis, probably 'cos he was a bit younger and I'd moved back to England when he really took off. But I must have seen him at hundreds of functions over the years.

The first time we met was when he joined the Ozzfest tour at the end of the nineties. The whole thing was an absolute stage-five shitshow. We had bomb threats. People praying outside venues to save the souls of everyone inside. We even had to take the New Jersey Sports and Exposition Authority to court so one of the shows could go ahead. People were terrified of Marilyn back then. They thought he was gonna turn their kids into serial killers. What he was *really* doing was giving them an escape, a way to let off steam. That's healthy. That's what rock 'n' roll is *for*. But no one wanted to hear that. They just wanted someone to blame for everything they thought was going wrong with the world.

Marilyn had a big ego thing going on at the time, which didn't help. But he soon got over it. We've all been there. Everyone who performs has an ego – you have to, or you couldn't get up on stage. But in this game, you quickly realise your shit *does* stink, even though your millions of adoring fans might be telling you the opposite.

I've no idea what landed Marilyn on the undesirables list in recent years, 'cos I don't read any of that tabloid shit. But he took the whole shock-rock thing a lot further than I ever did. Things started to get hot for him after the Columbine high school shooting, which was very unfair. Then it was 9/11, which made shock rock seem much less shocking than before, then the MeToo thing blew up. The mood of the planet just changed. People turned on him. I feel bad for him, 'cos he's not a bad guy. I've also come to learn he's a very talented painter. Jack owns a few of his pieces. He could make a living out of that if he wasn't a musician.

The thing is, we both walked a fine line, and when you become known for doing crazy things it's the easiest thing in the world to take a step too far. Or just get your timing wrong when society changes. Every generation has someone who plays that role.

The fact me and Marilyn are still here to tell the tale is nothing short of staggering.

To be fair to Sharon, she went all out on the entertainment for my birthday party, hiring a bunch of circus acts, a little guy dressed as Donald Trump who handed out drinks and a Britney Spears impersonator called Derrick.

There were a couple of moments when I wondered if I could sneak a couple of cocktails from Tiny Trump's tray. But after the health scare with my immune system and the three staph infections, there was no way I could risk falling off the wagon right before the tour was due to start up again. So I stayed absolutely stone cold fucking sober that night.

The party ended with a choir singing 'Mama, I'm Coming Home' while someone wheeled in a cake of me sitting in an armchair with fireworks coming out of my arse. All in all, given how much I'd been dreading the whole thing, it was an okay night. But even as the party was going on, I was itching to get back on the road and finish what I'd started, before anything else could go tits up.

Sharon and the tour manager had been pulling all kinds of levers behind the scenes.

The next gig of *No More Tours II* would be in Dublin at the end of January, followed by half a dozen more dates up and down the UK, including a big night at the O2 in London. Then we'd do nine more shows in Europe, two in Australia, two in New Zealand, and one at the Download Festival in Japan.

After that, I'd finish the North American leg – twenty-seven shows in total, including Madison Square Garden – and wrap it up with the four gigs we'd cancelled.

Just thinking about it all – the flights, the hotel rooms, the meet-and-greets, the stage fright, the exhaustion – was enough to make me want to go to bed for a year. But at the same time, it was what I'd been put on this earth to do, y'know? So the truth is, as much as I probably complained about it, and worried I couldn't handle it, I wouldn't have had it any other way.

Due to all my health issues, we only managed to save one gig before the end of 2018: the Ozzfest on New Year's Eve. Since Ozzfest was a separate thing to *No More Tours II*, I looked at it as kind of a trial run, a way to make sure we could still kick arse before the *real* show got back on the road again. There'd also been so much guilt for letting people down with the cancelled shows, it was just incredibly exciting to finally be playing live again.

A lot of people don't like to work over the Christmas and New Year period. It's the opposite for me. When you're an alcoholic, the holidays, as they call 'em in America, are hands down the hardest weeks of the year. I mean, if you're an alcoholic who's still drinking, they're amazing, 'cos it's an excuse to get extra loaded, no ques-tions asked. In the old days, I wouldn't even wait 'til December before ordering in the barrels of beer. These days, I've gotta ride out a whole month while everyone else is knocking back hot toddies and getting merry under the mistletoe, all while being tortured by 'Jingle Bells' on endless repeat.

It was the twenty-second year of Ozzfest, amazingly enough – and all 'cos Lollapalooza refused to put me or any other metal bands on the bill in the nineties, which pissed off Sharon so much she decided to do her own thing. Since then we've done Ozzfests everywhere from Japan to Texas. This time, the venue was closer to home, thank God – the Forum, down by LAX.

It was just after lunchtime when they started letting the fans in. The way it usually goes, people spend the afternoon outside at the smaller stages, get some burgers and beer and whatever from the food trucks, then head inside for the bigger acts. Sharon said there were close to fifteen thousand people there, making it another sell-out crowd.

What always strikes me when we do an Ozzfest is what a broad spectrum 'metal' is. I mean, some of the stuff you hear on those outdoor stages sounds like people being *tortured*. It's way above even *my* head. I almost want to apologise to the kids in the crowd. But to each their own, y'know? If you like listening to a noise like someone having their eyeballs removed with a pneumatic drill, go ahead, knock yourself out.

It's the same with the fashions. Especially tattoos. I just don't get it any more. The big thing in the eighties was to get your whole arm done, so it looked like you were wearing a sleeve. Back then, it made you seem a bit dangerous, a bit nuts. And if you were even *crazier*, like me, you'd also get some ink on your chest, or on your legs, or across your knuckles.

These days, that barely raises an eyebrow. People are

tattooing their *entire faces* – and then having surgery to remove their lips and ears, so they look like aliens. Whenever I see those guys, I'm like ... what the fuck are you thinking? How are you gonna get a job on any day that's not Halloween? And how's your kid gonna feel when you're reading him *Thomas the Tank Engine* with a full-face skull tattoo and no nose?

It makes you wonder what'll happen when genetic engineering takes off. People are gonna be walking around with two heads and three dicks. Looking like a freak will be so normal, it'll be the normal ones who stand out.

Personally speaking, I can't wait.

To say I was nervous before the New Year's Eve gig would be an understatement to say the least. It didn't help that I was getting emotional again.

Then, finally, just before midnight, it was my turn to go on.

Now, after fifty years of touring and probably a thousand gigs or more I've had plenty of time to think about what makes the difference between a good and a bad show.

The first rule I've learned is don't ever go on stage when you're loaded. Even when I was a massive pisshead, I was pretty strict about that. The day of a show was the one day I absolutely *had* to stay sober. The rest of the time was my own, and when I was on tour I always made sure to build in a day of recovery after each gig. The few times I did go on stage when I was drunk or high, I got really down on myself. That was the one thing that could shock me into going cold turkey for a while.

One of the saddest things I ever saw was Amy Winehouse

on stage when she was fucked up. It was heartbreaking. She was so talented, so beautiful, and she was up there slurring and stumbling around. Kelly was friends with her. She told me she was into smack. Those boyfriends of hers that were giving it to her needed a kick in the head. What an absolute tragedy.

The only other time I saw someone throw away a gig like that was when Van Halen played the US Festival. It was a three-day thing in San Bernardino, out in the desert near LA, organised by the Apple bloke Steve Wozniak and the promoter Bill Graham, who died a few years later in a helicopter crash. It must have been 1983. What I heard was, Van Halen's management had negotiated a clause in their contract that no one could get more money than them. So when David Bowie was paid a half million dollars to headline the whole thing, they got the same.

They were like kids who'd robbed a fucking sweet shop. The whole thing was just one big celebration. They had trailers, dancers, dealers, you name it – a little party city backstage. And it went on for *days*. By the time it was their turn to go on, they were totally fucked up. Dave Lee Roth was off his face. That's taking the piss, in my opinion. Nothing against Van Halen, they were a great band, and they put Black Sabbath to shame when we toured Europe with them right before I got fired. But you're letting down the fans if you can barely stand up straight.

Some people can pull it off, mind you.

I'll never forget seeing Steve Marriott in action at the Akron Rubber Bowl. Don't ask me the year, but we're talking a long time ago. He was in Humble Pie at the

time, not the Small Faces. And he was doing coke backstage with the guys in his band like it was going out of
style. I was just standing there, looking at him, thinking,
okay, there's no fucking way this bloke's singing a note
after putting that much shit up his nose. I mean, for me,
one bump of coke and my vocal cords are shot for the rest
of the day. I wouldn't be able to get through the first verse,
never mind a whole set.

So I'm watching Steve from the wings as he walks out
onto the stage, picks up his guitar, adjusts the mic . . . then
starts to sing like he's had nothing more than a sip of hot
lemon tea. The guy was pitch perfect . . . for the whole
gig! I couldn't believe it. Then he comes off stage before
the encore, walks over to where some roadie's set up a
little table with a Quaalude and another pile of coke on
it, he snorts the blow, pops the Quaalude, then goes back
out and does not one but *three* encores.

You could have knocked me down with a feather. To
this day, I've never seen anything like it. The guy must
have had some kind of cocaine superpower.

At the other end of the spectrum, you get bands that
want to treat a gig like a science experiment. I've known
American bands that come off stage, go to the back of the
tour bus and put a tape on of the show they've just done.
Then they listen to the whole thing again, analysing every
note. No fucking way I'd ever do that. When the show's
over, it's over. What's the point of sitting around arguing
about who fucked up and when? To me, it all comes down
to one question: *did you have fun?* Because chances are, if
you were having a good time out there, so were the fans.
Mind you, sometimes I think I'm doing a great gig and
I'm told afterwards it was shit . . . and sometimes I think

it's shit, and everyone says it was great. So it's not *always* the case. But it's generally true.

The best gig I ever did – in my opinion, anyway – was the Monsters of Rock festival at Castle Donington, 1984. I wasn't even headlining. I was third on the bill behind Van Halen and AC/DC.

The night before at the hotel, I'd been absolutely off-the-charts shitfaced. We're talking peak human wrecking ball days. And this German guy came up to me – it could have been Wolf Hoffmann from Accept, or someone else in his band – and he goes, 'Ozzy, vy you get so crazy before show? You have responsibility! Don't you vant to prepare?!'

I was like, 'What do you think I'm doing?'

He just shook his head and walked away.

But the thing is, playing with a hangover after you've had a great night out is a lot different to going on stage wasted. The next day, I rolled out of bed in the afternoon, got shot up with Decadron, went on stage and absolutely killed it. It's sod's law. You over-prepare, and it's shit. You wing it – going out there with a steaming hangover – and it's amazing.

Speaking of hangover gigs, another great one was Rock in Rio a year later. I'd just got out of the Betty Ford clinic in Palm Springs, and I thought the flight to Rio would be just a couple of hours. But after three hours had gone by, I realised it would be more like nine or ten. And in my mind, getting through it without a drink was impossible. By the time we came in to land, I was blacked out in the aisle and Sharon was so pissed off with me she was stabbing me with a fork.

You can see for yourself what the gig was like, 'cos

someone's put it on YouTube. For me, it was almost up there with Donington. The only thing that took away from the fun was the smell of the place. The organisers had provided almost no toilet facilities, so people just pissed and shat where they stood in the ninety-degree heat. And they'd been there for almost a *week*. At some point, someone threw a raw chicken at me – as everyone did in those days, for some reason – and when I bent over to pick it up the stench almost knocked me out. Normally, I'd have fucked around a bit with the thing and taken a bite out of it or whatever, but even my booze-sozzled brain was like, fuck no, not a good idea. A live bat was one thing. A shit-smeared raw chicken was something else.

Queen played after us, and they must have had pretty bad hangovers, too.

Not that I partied with Freddie Mercury or anything. But he was staying in the suite directly above ours, and every time we went up to our room, day or night, the lift was jam-packed full of these kids going up to his penthouse. The ruckus at night, it was unbelievable. I mean, the night we arrived, I was black-out drunk from all the miniatures I'd downed on the plane and it *still* woke me up. I was like, what's he *doing* up there? Beating people with sticks? The whole building was shaking.

But I've got to hand it to Freddie and the guys, they were on fire that night. Then a few months later, they stole the show at Live Aid. There's nothing like it when that happens. The Gods were with 'em. They absolutely killed it as the whole world watched. They hadn't over-prepared. They weren't fucked up. They just went out there and had the time of their lives.

*

For whatever reason, the stage fright I got before the New Year's Eve Ozzfest was up there with the worst of my life. But it all came back like second nature in the end.

My life flashed before my eyes on the giant video screen above the stage.

Carmina Burana kicked in.

DUH, DUH, *DUH-DUH!!*

DUH, DUH, *DUH-DUH!!*

DUH-DUH-DUDH DUUUUUUH DUUUUUH, DUH DUH!!!

Then off I went, legging it up and down the stage as I belted out 'Bark at the Moon' like the whole staph infection thing had never happened. Better yet, my old foam cannon had been upgraded to a *snow* cannon. Meaning the cold wet stuff, not the white powdery stuff that made Geezer write a lyric about climbing mountains on the moon.

I had so much fun shooting that thing at the crowd. And of course I got snow all over myself as I was doing it. Then it melted under the lights, so my T-shirt got soaked through with all this freezing-cold water.

But I barely noticed. I was having an absolute ball.

There did come a point, though, during Tommy's drum solo, when I thought, fucking hell ... what kind of deal must I have done with the devil to still be up here doing this? I mean, I was the last man standing in many ways. David Bowie was gone. George Michael was gone. Prince was gone. Tom Petty was gone. Michael Jackson was gone. All these icons, these huge names from the seventies and eighties, and *I* was the one still on tour. It made no sense to me. I was the one who'd been to prison. Whose tour bus had been hit by a fucking plane. *While I was still in it.* Whose guitarist had been killed tragically. Who'd been charged with attempted murder. Who'd broken his neck and spent eight days in a chemical coma, technically dead, after falling off a quad bike. Who'd been a hopeless drug addict and world-class alcoholic for more than half a century.

The biggest shock for me was when David Bowie died. I thought he'd outlive me by decades, he seemed so young and healthy. I was devastated when I heard the news. I kept thinking back to the time he'd shouted out to me from across the street in West Hollywood, 'OZZZZYY!!' – but I was so starstruck I could barely even wave back. I was walking into Hugo's, this breakfast place on Santa Monica Boulevard. Then he came in after us and sat a few tables away. But by that point it was weird, 'cos we hadn't talked or anything. He just read his newspaper.

For years, I thought I'd blown my one and only shot at ever shaking his hand and telling him how much he meant to me. But we did end up crossing paths again at the AA log cabin many years later. He even called my house in LA a few times to talk about recovery stuff. I've no idea what the last thing I said to him was. That's the thing when you're younger, it never occurs to you that you might never get to see or talk to someone again.

You just carry on like we're all gonna live for ever.

Halfway through the set, we stopped playing to watch the clock on the video screen count down to midnight.

TEN . . . NINE . . .

As I shouted out the numbers with the crowd, I thought I was counting down to a new start.

. . . EIGHT . . . SEVEN . . .

To the rest of my farewell tour.

. . . SIX . . . FIVE . . .

To that cushy residency in Las Vegas that Sharon kept talking about.

. . . FOUR . . . THREE . . .

But the rock 'n' roll gods, they had other plans.

. . . TWO . . . ONE.

What I was *really* counting down to . . .

HAPPY NEW YEAR!!!!

Was the end of it all.

5

Lights Out

The flu.

Of course I got the fucking flu.

And bronchitis for good measure. With a bit of pneumonia on the side.

The doc at Urgent Care didn't seem all that happy to see me again. 'Mr Osbourne, you really *must* remember you're in your seventies now,' he said. 'Have you been making sure to wrap up warm now that it's cold outside?'

'Of course I have, doc,' I croaked. 'I can't afford to be ill. I'm back on tour in a couple of weeks.'

'So you're telling me you've had no prolonged exposure to cold temperatures whatsoever?' he asked with this sceptical look on his face.

'Not that I can think of.'

The doc sighed and scratched his head. 'Well, it's a mystery how your flu became this bad.'

'Oh, wait.'

The doc gave me a look like he wanted to punch a hole in the wall. 'Yes?' he said.

'I did get wet from the snow cannon.'

Mystery solved, apparently. Turns out running around a stage in a T-shirt on New Year's Eve while soaked in freezing-cold water ain't a good idea, whether you're seventy or seventeen. But the doc said if I rested and drank plenty of fluids I should be better again in a week to ten days, just in time for the tour. So off I went back home, made myself a few gallons of hot lemony shit to drink, threw a pile of logs on the fire and sat down to watch every Vietnam War and serial-killer documentary on Netflix until the virus fucked off.

I was so pissed off, man. It always seemed to be something. And 2019 had started off so well. After Ozzfest – which had been an absolute blinder of a gig – me and Sharon had a few days of seeing old friends and sharing memories.

But the most mind-blowing thing I did before the flu kicked me in the bollocks was go over to DreamWorks in Glendale to record the voice of King Thrash for *Trolls World Tour*. I mean, okay, it didn't exactly take Daniel Day-Lewis to read the couple of lines they gave me. But the fact a Hollywood studio wanted to cast *me* in this blockbuster family movie was hard to wrap my head around. It still feels like yesterday to me that the same people thought I was either Satan or the enemy of Western civilisation, or both.

But bring it on, that's what I say.

If Disney ever need a new Snow White, they know where to find me.

No matter how much rest I got, or how many fluids I drank, the flu wasn't going anywhere. Meanwhile, I was on antibiotics to try and take out the bronchitis and pneumonia. I even ended up in hospital one night to get checked out.

I was losing my mind.

Every day I spent shivering on the sofa was another day closer to when *No More Tours II* was supposed to start up again in Dublin. I hadn't played Ireland since *The End Tour* with Black Sabbath in 2017, and I couldn't wait to get back there. If I closed my eyes, I could almost *taste* the Guinness. I was also excited to hang out with my old friends in Judas Priest, who'd be opening for me. Between 'Diary of a Madman' and 'You've Got Another Thing Comin'', it was gonna feel like 1982 all over again. We were gonna have an absolute blast.

But as the days counted down – and the virus just wouldn't take the hint and fuck off – the reality of the situation became impossible to ignore. Not only would we have to call off the Dublin gig, but also all the UK ones that followed.

Normally, I'd have at least tried to put a brave face on it all for the fans. But between the fatigue and brain fog from the flu, the cost of the cancellations, the disappointment and the guilt of letting everyone down – *again* – I couldn't do it. 'It seems that since October, everything I touch has turned to shit,' I wrote in a statement that we put out on social media.

I felt so fucking down, man. When I was younger and burned out from touring, I'd try and get *out* of gigs. I'd shave my hair off. Disappear on a ten-day bender. Check myself into a psych ward somewhere. But as corny as it sounds, now that I was seventy, I realised that every gig was a gift.

The worst part was the feeling that the universe was trying to tell me something.

Maybe I just wasn't up for this any more.

Maybe I wouldn't get to experience anything like the New Year's Eve show again.

Maybe my days of touring were over, and I just didn't know it yet.

Sharon did her best to talk me down from the ledge. *Anyone* can get the flu, she said. *Anyone* can get an infection. I just got unlucky – twice in a row. Besides, she said, hundreds of thousands of fans had already bought tickets. I needed to finish what I'd started. Then I could decide what's next.

After a few more days of frantic phone calls, there was a plan. We'd start the tour again in March, giving me plenty of time to get back on my feet again. Instead of trying to reschedule the shows we'd missed, we'd jump straight ahead to the Australia, New Zealand and Japan gigs, followed by the remaining twenty-seven or so dates of the North American leg – most of which would be in summer, making it less likely that I'd come down with something. Meanwhile, Sharon would find a way to get the Dublin and UK shows back on the books.

It should have been a relief.

But something still didn't feel right.

I told myself it was just that horrible heavy feeling you get when you're all stuffed up.

To say that I didn't have high hopes for February would be an understatement. At this point, I'd learned to just expect the worst. Which was a good job, 'cos that's exactly what February was about to give me.

I mean . . . where do I even start?

Okay.

This is what I remember.

It was a Saturday night, I'm pretty sure. The first weekend of the month.

I've no clue exactly what I was doing that day, but it wouldn't have been much, 'cos I was still feeling about as fresh as a gorilla's arsehole. I probably had a bit of soup for lunch, if I ate anything at all. Took some flu medicine. Started watching a war documentary. Took a bit more flu medicine. Finished the war documentary. Finished the flu medicine. Then at around midnight I would have switched off the telly, gathered up my little pack of four-legged friends, got into my private elevator – that's not a joke, my house really *does* have a private elevator – and toddled off to bed.

Sharon was already under the covers, tossing and turning, trying to get to sleep, her face lit up by her phone every so often when she checked her texts.

Now, it's a rule of being a seventy-year-old bloke that you never go to bed and stay there. Every other minute, your brain gets an urgent message from your bladder saying if you don't get up and piss *right now* you're gonna explode. But it's a pain in the arse to get up, so you end up leaving it longer than you should, until suddenly you have to do an Usain Bolt to the bog.

That's exactly what went down that night. I needed to piss, but it was pitch dark in the room and my head felt like it was floating in an ocean of snot. So I waited . . . and waited . . . *and waited* . . . until finally – *oh, for fuck's sake!* – I flopped out of bed and staggered off to shake the ol' snake.

Ahhhhhhhhh . . .

That was better.

Then back I came, banging into walls, feeling my way around in the dark.

I could have switched on the lights, I suppose. But I didn't want to wake up Sharon, who was by now fast asleep. And unless I went and got my reading glasses – a major operation, since I can never remember where the fuck I put them – there was no way I was gonna find the flashlight on my phone.

But whatever.

I found my way, mumbling and cursing as I went.

Then, once I was a few steps away from the bed, I did what I always did.

Whheeeeeeee . . .

BLA-*BANG!*

'Ozzy?'

'Ozzy?? *Ozzy!!?* What the fuck just happened?'

I could only gurgle.

The first thing I felt was this incredibly sharp pain in my eyes.

It was Sharon, switching on all the lights.

She was confused, her brain still booting up. She couldn't see me anywhere.

'Ozzy?! Ozzy, where are you? What on earth—'

She saw me.

'*Oh my God.*'

I was on the floor. Absolutely nowhere near anything resembling a bed. To this day, I don't understand how the fuck I could have missed it. The thing's massive. It's like having a Sherman tank parked in the middle of the room.

There was so much I wanted to say.

Like how I couldn't feel anything.

Like how I couldn't stand up.

Like how I couldn't remember what had happened just a couple of seconds ago.

Like how the pain was worse than anything I'd ever felt before.

But once I was done with all the gurgling, all I could manage was three words.

'*My fucking neck!*'

The second I hit the floor, my mind was back in the nineties, just after the original *No More Tours* tour.

At the grand old age of forty-five, I'd just bought myself a 'retirement' present: a Yamaha Banshee 350 quad bike. It had red fenders and gold rims.

I loved that thing, man. It was like a bullet on wheels. I could spend days racing it around the three hundred acres behind Welders House, the old Second World War officers' convalescent home we'd just bought in Buckinghamshire. I had many, *many* years of enjoying that bike, to the point where I'd pretty much forgotten just how powerful it was.

Then on 8 December 2003, I took it out while we were filming for *The Osbournes*. The crew were complaining about something or other, so I sped off ahead of them, skidding down this muddy embankment, and at the bottom of it my front wheels hit a pothole. I later found out it was one of the craters left by Luftwaffe pilots who didn't fancy getting shot down in flames over London. They'd just empty their bomb bays over the fields, turn around and fuck off home.

Anyway, the crater wasn't a problem. The Banshee was built for that kind of thing. But the bike had this really stupid throttle design. It wasn't a twisty thing on the handlebars. It was a lever you could accidentally push with your hand if you slipped. Which is exactly what happened.

The engine went WAAAAAAAHHH, the bike shot out from under me and flipped over in the air, meanwhile I was thrown backwards and fell flat on my arse in the mud.

Other than feeling a bit silly, I was fine.

Then the bike landed on top of me.

I wasn't fine any more.

To cut a long story short, by the time I woke up, after an eight-day coma, I had more nuts and bolts inside me than a B&Q superstore. The docs at Wexham Park Hospital in Berkshire – where I'd been airlifted – had done an incredible job. They'd somehow repaired my punctured lung. They'd saved one of my arms from being amputated after the main artery was severed. And they'd rebuilt my collarbone with rods, plates and screws.

Then off I went back to America.

A few months later, one of my docs in Beverly Hills took a look at the work and whistled through his teeth. 'How much did all that cost you, then?'

'Bugger all.'

'Haha. But seriously, how much?'

'Well, we did have pay 50p for the car park,' I said. 'Which was a bit fucking steep.'

He couldn't believe it when I explained to him that when you get work done on the NHS – even the most complicated surgery, using the very latest technologies – Her Majesty's government (as it was back then) picks up the tab.

'You Brits are lucky,' he told me. 'Over here, you'd be getting bills 'til the day you died.'

Sharon says I still had my hands by my side when she saw me all crumpled up on the floor. From the moment I'd started the dive onto what I thought was the bed, to the moment I hit the floor, I hadn't broken form. That's how sure I was there was a pillow-top mattress underneath me. What was I thinking? Why were my hands *by my side*? Did I think I was Batman or something? Sharon thinks I must have slipped on the edge of the rug when I jumped, hitting my head on either the frame of the bed or the side table, ending up in the middle of the floor. I have no idea.

None of it made any sense. It still doesn't.

As soon as Sharon touched me, I found my voice again. 'Don't move me!' I screamed. 'Call an ambulance! It's my neck, *I've broken my fucking neck!*'

Sharon didn't want to believe it. But she knew my medical history better than anyone. I was held together with screws. Or at least I had been until the fall. I didn't need a doctor so much as I needed a mechanic.

The fire brigade were at the house within a few minutes. Big blokes, all of 'em. Maybe a dozen in total. They put one of those massive braces on me, the kind that make it look like you're wearing Dracula's collar. Then they gathered around me, counted down from three, lifted me up and carried me down the stairs to an EMT van with its lights flashing.

They don't fuck around, the LA fire brigade. They don't go in for any of that celebrity bullshit, either. If they knew who I was – or cared – they didn't let on. Not that I was in any state to be signing copies of *Paranoid*.

Then off I went in the van – siren wailing, the driver gunning it through all the red lights on Beverly Boulevard – back to Cedars-Sinai, the same place I'd gone for the operation on my staph-infected hand.

What I hadn't fully appreciated was just how busy it would be on a Saturday night. It made sense, I suppose. It's by far the biggest hospital in LA, and LA is one of the biggest cities in the world. And Saturday night is when the shit hits the fucking fan. Every motorway pile-up. Every gang shooting. Every bar fight. Every domestic accident. If you've still got a pulse, you're gonna end up at the ER – the American equivalent of accident and emergency. The place was part butcher's shop, part zoo.

Now, in my imagination, I pictured all these white-coated doctors running out to meet my ambulance the moment it pulled up to the hospital. Checking my vitals. Asking questions. Hooking me up to a morphine drip.

Not to disappoint anyone, but that ain't how it works in real life.

If you ain't bleeding from the eyeballs and seconds away from death, you ain't a priority. All they did was wheel my stretcher into a corridor and leave me there. Then some bloke told Sharon to go to the reception area, get a ticket with a number on it, then settle in for a long wait. Meanwhile, all these guys kept staggering in with gunshot wounds and limbs missing, which made a broken neck seem like a minor inconvenience.

Don't get me wrong, I ain't complaining. I've done some hard jobs in my time, from working on a car horn assembly line to killing cows with a bolt gun, but if you ain't a doctor or a nurse, you can't have any idea what it's like to put in a twelve-hour shift in an ER, where every decision is life and death. I have the greatest respect for anyone who can handle that kind of pressure.

I could tell by the look on Sharon's face that even *she* realised she couldn't pull any favours in the Cedars ER. Not that it stopped her trying. I could hear her going off in the reception area. 'DO YOU KNOW WHO MY HUSBAND IS?'

'No, ma'am,' came the weary reply.

'He's Ozzy *bloody* Osbourne!'

'He could be Father Christmas, ma'am. He still needs to wait his turn.'

'He's broken his fucking neck!'

'Ma'am, this is a level-one trauma centre. Everyone in here's broken something.'

The funny thing is, a weird calm came over me as I waited there in the corridor. I'm fascinated by hospitals, these gateways to the other side that we drive by every day without thinking. When I was younger, I used to visit hospitals a lot when we were touring, usually to meet wounded troops.

I'll never forget going to the Walter Reed National Military Medical Center in Maryland, the place they did John F. Kennedy's autopsy. It was full of these very young men with glittery eyes and bits missing, bouncing off the walls. It was nuts, man. If you ever want to see what war really does to people, don't watch a Hollywood movie, check that place out.

I remember opening the door to one room and it was pitch black, but I could make out the silhouette of a guy on the bed. They told me, 'Sir, maybe don't go in there.' Which of course made me want to go in even more.

I regretted it as soon as I got my first proper look at the guy. Half his head was gone, like it had been hollowed out and the hole sewn back up. He was totally brain dead. The worst thing was, he couldn't have been more than a year or two out of high school. When you're a father yourself, it hits you hard. It was so fucking sad, man. The injuries some people get while serving their country are truly a fate worse than death.

In England, meanwhile, when I went to visit soldiers in hospital they weren't usually in a special building, they were just mixed in with the regular patients. One time, I remember talking to this squaddie with horrendous injuries from a roadside bomb. Then I moved on to the next bed, and the guy was in even worse shape. Both his arms were broken. His leg was up on one of those wire-and-pulley things. His face was fucked up like you wouldn't believe. I was worried he'd have PTSD, but I couldn't help but ask what kind of mission he'd been on when it happened.

He looked confused. 'Mission?' he said.

'Yeah,' I said. 'I mean . . . it's okay if you don't wanna talk about it. Or if it's classified or whatever. I was just wondering what happened.'

'Oh,' he said, sounding woozy from all the painkillers. 'Well . . . I fell off the ladder.'

'The ladder?' I said. 'What the fuck were you doing on a ladder in a war zone?'

At that point, one of the doctors pulled me aside. 'Mr Osbourne, that patient's not a soldier,' he whispered. 'He fell off a ladder while painting his shed.'

Sharon tried a few more times doing her 'do you know who my husband is?' thing. But she packed it in eventually. By now it must have been two or three in the morning. We were both knackered. As far as the hospital staff were concerned, I was just some seventy-year-old bloke with long grey hair, still in his pyjamas, who'd had a bad fall but was in a stable condition.

At some point Kelly and Aimee came. Neither of 'em could understand how a trip to the bog in the middle of the night had landed me in hospital . . . and I wasn't doing a good job of explaining it, 'cos I didn't have a fucking clue myself.

Finally, at God knows what time, they found me a room. But the doc had no idea what to do with me. The medical file showing all the previous surgery on my neck was back at Wexham Park, so he had nothing to work with. Mind you, a full set of blown-out schematics with bolt sizes and assembly instructions wouldn't have made any difference. When he ran me through the X-ray machine, all he could see was this huge mass of swelling. Whatever damage I'd done was hidden behind it.

By the end of the whole ordeal, we were told the main issue was bruising and that everything was fine. Then they sent me home with two paracetamol and the number of a neck surgeon to call first thing on Monday morning.

I'd gone in there at midnight on a stretcher. I came out at dawn in a wheelchair . . . although I managed to get to my feet and hobble the last few steps to the car.

My Count Dracula neck brace was still on. Bruises were starting to show on my face. And I had a hospital blanket around my shoulders to keep me warm, 'cos the temperature had dropped overnight and there was a wind blowing.

I must have been a very, *very* sorry sight.

Still, I told myself, at least I could stop wondering when I'd start feeling old.

Round about now was the answer.

6

No Choice

The nurses must have wondered what the fuck was going on when they walked past my room. 'Electric Avenue' by Eddy Grant was blasting out of the speaker of Jack's laptop. Sharon was dancing around like a crazy person, singing the chorus at the top of her voice. Jack was in stitches, holding up his phone, getting the whole thing on video. And I was propped up on a stretcher bed, wearing my neck brace on my head like it was a hat, rocking backwards and forwards to the beat ... which, believe me, is easier said than done with a broken neck.

This was six days after the accident. Friday 8 February, or so I'm told.

When I'd got home from the Cedars ER I was so knackered I almost didn't notice how bad a state I was in. My right arm was going numb. My legs felt weird. I couldn't stand fully upright. When I walked, I was all hunched over and less steady than usual. Meanwhile, I'd

been ordered not to take off my neck brace until a specialist had taken a proper look.

Sharon sent someone out to buy a Zimmer frame – or
a walker, as they call 'em in America – so I could move
around the house safely, but I was having none of it. I told
her I'd walk on my own two feet if it fucking killed me.
She couldn't watch. She was terrified I was gonna go arse
over tit and end up paralysed from the neck down like
Christopher Reeve.

I didn't wanna believe it was that serious. I couldn't
handle the reality.

One of the few people outside the family we told about
the accident was Zakk. I mean, he's basically family
anyway. He kept saying, you should call this bloke, Dr
Fix-It or something. And in my mind, I was like, Zakk's
one of my closest, dearest friends, and the first person I'd
ever go to with a question about guitars. But what the
fuck could he *possibly* know about neck surgery? Besides,
Dr Fix-It sounded like one of them dodgy blokes who
put adverts on the back of LA buses. 'INJURED? CALL
DR FIX-IT!'

'Look, I appreciate the tip,' I told him, 'but I'm gonna
call the guy the ER doc recommended.'

'Just promise me one thing,' said Zakk, 'whatever they
tell you, get a second opinion.'

The trouble was, I was so freaked out by the whole
thing, I wasn't really listening. I didn't want to believe
surgery would even be necessary, to be honest with you.
In my mind, I was still going back on tour in a few weeks.

When Monday morning came around, Sharon called
the number we'd been given by Cedars. I dunno who
she spoke to, but they said they needed to check me out

straight away. I'd be seeing two docs, apparently. The first was a surgeon who specialised in neck problems. The other was an expert on Parkinson's disease. At this point, I should probably mention I didn't think I had *full-blown* Parkinson's disease. All I knew was that I had this hereditary thing called Parkinsonian syndrome, which gave me muscle tremors and stiffness. I'd been taking pills to manage those symptoms for years. I mean, deep down I suppose I knew it was a form of Parkinson's. But it was so mild I didn't like to call it that.

Anyway . . . off we went, driving to this massive medical place. It was like a mini city of hospital buildings connected by sky bridges, arranged around a quad with a lawn, with all these pathways for visitors to walk around.

It was drizzling when we got there – and freezing cold by LA standards – and I was starting to get that horrible feeling you get when you go somewhere unfamiliar to get heavy-duty medical shit done. Suddenly it doesn't matter who you are, who you know, how much money you've got in the bank. You just feel like a number on a wristband.

As we went up in the lift, I found myself thinking back to when I was a kid, going to Dr Rosenfield's surgery in Aston. It was on the corner of Fentham Road, opposite a tripe and cow heel shop, right by the Villa football ground. I hated that place, man. It was bleak and dark, and Dr Rosenfield smelled of old leather. You only went there when you were really fucked up. The last thing your parents wanted to do was take you to the doctor's. They'd try everything else first – usually Vicks VapoRub or that 'black salve' drawing ointment shit that's probably illegal now.

He also did house calls, Dr Rosenfield. But if that happened, you were basically dead. The only time he came to 14 Lodge Road was when I got whooping cough. I must have been six at the time. There wasn't a vaccine then, so whenever a kid started coughing up a lung, it was always touch and go. I came down with it the same week the Halfords headquarters caught fire, which was a major disaster 'cos it was full of chemicals. It burned for a whole week. Every firefighter in the Midlands was called up. My dad said it was the worst fire he'd seen since the end of the Birmingham Blitz.

My cough was so bad, I had to be sent away to a special quarantine hospital. The only thing I remember about it is that it was next to a golf course. When I peered over the window sill, I could see all these white balls flying by. I must have been pretty ill, 'cos I don't remember crying 'cos I missed my mum and dad. What I do remember is when my dad came to pick me up, and the smell of him, the relief, it was fucking great. Then we took the bus together back home, and it was the best bus ride of my life. I was my dad's first boy, so we had that special bond, y'know? He must have also been pretty relieved. I mean, he came from the age when you just *expected* to lose a kid or two. It's one of the reasons my parents had six of us. Well, that and the fact my mum was Catholic, not that she ever went to church or made us study for confirmation or anything.

My dad's attitude to doctors was that he wanted nothing to do with 'em. No matter what was wrong with him, he'd just grin and bear it. Or at least he did until his cancer spread so much my mum had to call for an ambulance. He felt the same way about priests. He'd cross the street if he saw one coming. In his mind, if you found yourself in the company of a priest or a doctor, you were as good as six feet in your grave.

And in the end, for him, that turned out to be true.

They were a strange pair, the docs I saw. The neck surgeon looked like a Range Rover salesman with a shiny suit, tasselled loafers, a pocket handkerchief and manicured hands. 'Dr No Socks', Sharon called him, 'cos he didn't wear any. Meanwhile, the Parkinson's guy looked like he'd just walked off a Margaritaville cruise. I suppose 'cos I grew up in England, I was expecting tweed suits and posh accents. But in LA, it's anything goes. The guy who's about to drill a hole in your skull can walk in wearing flip-fops and a tie-dye Jimmy Buffett shirt, and no one bats a fucking eyelid.

Still, they obviously knew what they were talking about.

I told 'em about the quad bike accident in 2003, how I was half man, half rivet. I told 'em how I'd stage-dived for the bed with the lights off and missed. I told 'em about my all-nighter at the Cedars ER.

After a lot of umming and ahhing, each one asked if they could take a look. So off came my neck brace, and they had a good old feel around my neck and shoulder area to see if they could tell what kind of damage had been done. It hurt like fuck in a few places when they poked and prodded, but otherwise it wasn't too bad . . . although my addiction was already whispering in my ear, telling me this would be a great time to score some yummy pills.

'Well,' said Dr No Socks, 'it seems you've dislodged some of the metal bolts that were put in your collarbone fifteen years ago. We can take care of those right away. It's an outpatient procedure. Very straightforward. But there's still far too much swelling to know what's going on with your neck. And we need to be *extremely* cautious with an injury like this.'

Sharon shot me one of her 'I told you so' looks.

'What d'you mean?' I said.

'Well, for a start, we need to get you into intensive care *right now*,' he said. 'With an injury of this nature, by far the biggest risk is making it worse. Once you're in the ICU, we can safely monitor the swelling until it's gone down enough to give you an MRI scan. After that, we can regroup, see what's going on and assess what kind of spinal surgery you'll need.'

'*Spinal surgery?!*' I spluttered. 'Who said anything about *spinal surgery?*'

'Well, as I'm sure you already know, Mr Osbourne, your neck is made up of the top seven vertebrae of your spinal column – we call them C1 to C7,' he explained. 'And it's highly likely you've damaged more than one.'

I didn't want to hear it. I mean, I knew the fall had been serious. But I'd managed to kid myself it wasn't that bad. Certainly not bad enough for spinal surgery. 'Can't I just go home? See how I feel in a few days?' I asked.

There was this awkward silence as the doc made a face and looked at the floor. Sharon wasn't helping me out. Fuck me, I thought, there's no getting out of this. I'm gonna be spending the next God-knows-how-long in bed with a tube up my arse, eating hospital food, until they tell me I'm ready for the scan.

And after that?

Honestly, I didn't even wanna know.

*

Other than being bored out of my mind, I don't remember much about the rest of the week. The surgery on my collarbone was done the same day I went in. Then a day or two later the kids came to visit, which was a good distraction. Zakk also stopped by with his lovely wife Barbaranne. He told me again to make sure I got a second opinion, and I just thought, *second opinion on what?* The docs hadn't told me anything other than to stay in bed.

By Friday, I was feeling much better. The bruises on my shoulders were turning from black to green. My right arm felt a bit less numb, although I still had very limited movement. I was desperate to get out of bed and start walking around again. But the docs said they needed to get the MRI scan done first. The good news was that I was finally ready for it.

Now, they're weird things, MRIs. You lie on this tanning bed thing, which gets rolled into a glowing tube with a huge magnet around it. A lot of people freak out from the claustrophobia, so they give you a little panic button to press in case it gets too much. But if you press it, it messes everything up, meaning they have to start again. So you're better off just letting 'em get on with it. For me, the biggest worry was all the metal in my shoulder. If any of it was made of steel, the magnet would rip it out of me. I'd be going in there in one piece and coming out in a bucket. But the MRI guy said implants are made out of titanium, which is non-magnetic for that very reason. Even ones put in fifteen years ago by the NHS.

Still, I held my breath – and everything else – when he pressed the big red ON button.

I was in the tube for so long I was starting to think they must have gone off on their lunch break. But then someone came and rolled me out and took me back to my room to wait for Dr No Socks to tell me what the deal was.

Since I was feeling so much better, I was half expecting him to go, actually, your neck is healing up nicely, Mr Osbourne, all you need is a bit of physical therapy, then you can go back on tour. Oh, and here's a bottle of Vicodin . . .

But no. I wasn't having that kind of day.

Or week.

Or year.

'I wish we had better news,' said the doc, with this heavy-duty look on his face.

Oh God, I thought. *Here we go* . . .

'This is what I'm most concerned about,' he said, handing me this black-and-white image of what must have been the back of my head. It just looked like a bunch of blobs to me. Then he pointed to an area and told me it showed I had no spinal fluid between five of my vertebrae just below my skull. The fluid was supposed to be flowing freely between 'em, he said. But the impact of the fall had compressed my spine or fucked it up in some way – I've no idea what the exact technical term for it is – which had blocked it. Without the fluid, he said, my spinal cord and brain had no protection. Which was very bad news, according to him.

'So what's the plan?' asked Sharon. 'How do we get the fluid moving again?'

'Well, uh . . . there are a few options,' said the doc, which to my ears sounded suspiciously like 'fucked if I know'. Then he said the only way to know *exactly* what he needed to do to 'get in there and take a look'.

'Get in there ... *how*?' asked Sharon. I could tell she was starting to get pissed off.

'Well, we make an incision in the throat—'

'THROAT?! He's a fucking *singer*! What if you nicked one of his vocal cords? He'd never sing ag—'

'Mrs Osbourne,' said the doc in this firm voice, 'no surgery is without risk. But with no spinal fluid between those five vertebrae in your husband's neck, he's just one slip of the foot away from being paralysed from the neck down.'

It all happened so quickly.

The worst part of the meeting with the doc was looking over at Sharon and seeing the fear on her face. She doesn't get that look easily. She's a warrior, my Sharon. I mean, we both knew how dangerous a neck injury could be. But no one had mentioned anything about never walking again, or the surgery affecting my voice. It was too much to take in. The moment the bloke said that, I felt like I was in one of those movie scenes when the sound cuts out and all you hear is this high-pitched whine.

By the time I snapped out of it, the doc was explaining there was *another* way to do the surgery, but that came with all kinds of other possible complications. Instead of making the incision in my throat, he said, they could go in through the back of my neck. As for the complications, I didn't catch any of 'em, 'cos my mind was racing so fast. All I remember is Sharon asking him when he'd want to do the operation, and him looking at his watch. 'We can have the OR ready in an hour,' he said.

I don't even remember if we talked it over after he left the room. I mean, what was there to say? It wasn't like I was gonna check myself out and go walking around with no spinal fluid in my neck. It would be like driving a car with wooden wheels, with my brain on the fucking passenger seat. If I tripped or slipped, I'd be eating my dinners through a straw and shitting into a bag for the rest of my life. Compared with that, the risk of spinal surgery seemed like nothing. Especially since they could go in through the back of my neck instead of cutting a hole in my throat.

Although the doc said he didn't know *exactly* what he'd need to do after opening me up, he had a general idea. The main thing was to widen the area around my spinal cord, he said – apparently there was a special tool for this – which would allow the spinal fluid to start flowing again. The operation would take about two hours, with a week in hospital to recover.

Look, it ain't rocket science, I told myself. *Besides, he probably does this this all the time.*

At the back of my mind, I suppose, I was also thinking the surgery could hardly be any worse than what had happened after my quad bike accident. I mean, I was technically dead – or in a chemical coma – for eight days. I had eight fractured ribs. A punctured lung. My collarbone was broken so badly it had severed the main artery in my arm, cutting off the blood supply to the point where I almost lost the thing.

But the NHS had patched me up, no problem at all. And when I woke up from the coma, they gave me some jolly juice to help with the pain and I was on my way. I even checked out early, although they'd wanted me to stay.

I mean, okay, I was sore for a while. And I had to be

careful for a few months not to re-break anything. But the recovery was just a temporary thing. So in my mind, I could easily handle a bit of spinal surgery, even if I was in my seventies now. In fact, I was feeling so confident I almost called Dr No Socks back in and told him to hurry up and get on with it.

While the nurses got the operating room ready, Jack drove down to the hospital to try and keep our spirits up. He's a great guy, Jack. We've had a lot of fun together over the years, including travelling the world for three seasons of our TV show, *Ozzy & Jack's World Detour.* While Kelly is very much her father's daughter, Jack takes after his mother. After getting into some trouble with drugs when he was seventeen, he's been sober ever since. I greatly admire him for that. I wish I could be that strong. He's good at business, too. Most of all, though, he's just great company, and can always make me laugh. Which was exactly what he started to do, loading up a music app on his laptop and getting a dance party going.

The looks we got through the open door were priceless, man.

It's funny, people think 'cos I'm the Prince of Darkness, I must only listen to organ music while hanging upside down from the ceiling or something. But I love all kinds of music, me. When I was growing up, I was crazy about The Beatles. When I discovered their music, it was like I'd gone to bed in black and white and woken up in colour. Nothing was ever the same again. I used to carry around my copy of *Please Please Me* wherever I went. I even fantasised that one of my sisters would marry Paul McCartney. When it comes to melodies, no one has ever come *close* to The Beatles. That includes McCartney's bass lines. They're so playful and clever, they're like a second melody hidden inside every song.

Later on, right after we finished the first Sabbath album, it was Elton John I was obsessed with. I'd come home from singing about Satan and witches, and get all teary-eyed to 'Your Song'. I loved that whole record, man.

In the eighties, the album I just could not stop playing was *So* by Peter Gabriel. There's not a bad track on there. 'In Your Eyes'. 'Red Rain'. 'Mercy Street'. They sound as fresh today as they did then. For a whole year after it came out, I blasted it everywhere I went. It became a problem, actually, 'cos it was around the time I was fighting all those lawsuits about subliminal messages, and I had a security guard by my side every second of the day. He really didn't like Peter Gabriel at all. It just wasn't his thing, y'know? But he couldn't escape it. When my cassette wore out, the poor bloke even had to come with me to buy the CD. I'd play it all day on the tour bus. I'd play it all night at whatever hotel we were staying in. I'd crank it up on my boombox if I was by a swimming pool. And at all other times – other than when I was on stage – I'd be singing one of the songs from it at the top of my voice. It got to the point where the guy couldn't take it any more. It broke him, that record. He had to take time off, just so he could go a day without hearing 'Sledgehammer'.

And as it so happened, on his first day back – after however long it took him to do a Peter Gabriel detox and get the album out of his head – I was staying at this hotel in Midtown Manhattan. So, that morning, he meets me at my suite, gets into the lift with me and I hit the button for the ground floor. And as it starts to go down, I can see him breathing this huge sigh of relief, 'cos I'm not singing or playing anything off *So* any more. He's like, thank God, the spell's been broken.

Then the lift stops at the mezzanine level. The doors open. And this bloke gets in.

And it's Peter fucking Gabriel.

I couldn't believe my luck. I was like, 'Oh, I've gotta tell you, Peter, I love your album so much, it really is an absolute masterpiece, just seeing you here in person makes me want to listen to it another thousand times.'

He couldn't have been nicer, actually. Before he got out, I asked him how it long had taken to make, and he said, 'Oh, a long time ... at least three months.' And I was, 'Fuck me, if I tried to make that record like that, it would take me thirty years.' Then we said our goodbyes and he was gone. When I looked around, the security guard was in the corner, shaking and sweating. I don't think the bloke lasted the rest of the day.

I loved Phil Collins, too, of course. Still do. Every time I hear 'In the Air Tonight', it sends a shiver down my spine. That drum fill ... fucking hell, man. It's gotta be one of the best moments of any song, ever. I also got to meet Phil, but not in a lift. He was the drummer in the house band for the Party at the Palace to celebrate the Queen's Golden Jubilee. I was nervous as fuck, 'cos I thought my voice was gonna give out – and Her Majesty wouldn't have been amused if I'd croaked my way through 'Paranoid'. But Phil put me in touch with his vocal guy, and he sorted me out. I was so grateful to Phil, I sent him a big thank you. Then when I ran into him later in Las Vegas for a VH1 thing, one of the red-carpet guys asked for a picture of the two of us. I said, 'Ask Phil.' When Phil saw it was me, he was like, go on then, and gave me a big hug. I love that picture.

It's funny – when I look back at all the records I've been hooked on over the years, so many of 'em are pop or electronic. I loved all of Kraftwerk's albums. 'Rock Me Amadeus' by Falco – amazing. Prince's '1999' is another great one. And of course Eddy Grant killed it with 'Electric Avenue'.

The only kind of music that leaves me cold, or mostly cold, is hip-hop. I mean, is it music . . . or is it poetry? I can never tell. Once you've heard one song, you've heard the lot, as far as I'm concerned. But I did *try* to get into it. In fact, back in 2001, I got a call from Busta Rhymes saying he wanted to do a cover of 'Iron Man', and asking if I'd sing on it. I was happy to give it a shot. If it meant introducing more people to Black Sabbath, that was all good with me – and rap and metal have always gone together in a weird way. So he gives me this address in Manhattan, tells me to go there on such and such a day, and says we'll put down the vocals together.

When I got there, I couldn't get in the door. It was barricaded from inside or something. So I call Sharon, and she says, 'Yes, Busta says you've got to knock *really* hard.' So I'm there on this New York sidewalk pounding on this door until eventually one of them little peep-hole things pops open, and a voice on the other side goes, 'Who's there?' And I'm like, 'It's Ozzy.'

'Ozzy who?'

'Ozzy fucking Osbourne, who the fuck do you think?'

'Oh. Okay.' The door opens, and this guy's standing there packing heat. Meanwhile, there are two blokes behind him, and they're also packing heat. And I'm like, fucking hell, I should have been a bit more polite. Anyway ... it was one of them 'walk-up' buildings with no lift, and the studio was on the top floor. By the time I got up there, I felt like I'd run ten marathons.

It was just me, Busta and this engineer guy at first. They were very nice, very respectful. But before we got the tape rolling for the first take, they give me a printout of the lyrics. I'm like, guys, I've been singing 'Iron Man' since before either of you were born, I think I know the words.

'Oh, I've rewritten them,' says Busta.

'Okay,' I said, a bit confused. No one had told me about this. 'So what's it about now?'

'Loyalty ... and vengeance.'

'But won't people think a song called "Iron Man" is about a bloke made of iron?'

'Yeah. That's why I'm changing the title too.'

'*What?*'

'I'm calling it "This Means War".'

'So what the fuck do you need me for?'

'To sing the chorus. Same tune, different words. Trust me, man, it's gonna be cool.'

It didn't take long to get it done. After the final take, I remember looking out of the control room window, and I couldn't believe my eyes. The studio had been empty when I walked in. Now there were like three hundred people in there, all with these massive reefers. I would have hung out and smoked a bit myself, but there were enough guns in the room to start World War III, and it was making nervous. So I fucked off back down the five hundred flights of stairs and went back to my hotel room.

As for the song, it ended up being called 'Iron Man: This Means War (feat. Ozzy Osbourne)'.

It's one of the few hip-hop tracks I like, actually.

But it's got nothing on the original.

Our dance party ended soon enough with Sharon and Jack getting kicked out of the room. Then it was time for another kind of party to get started: the nurses hooking me up to a drip of propofol to knock me out for the surgery.

I'd be lying if I told you I hadn't been secretly looking forward to that part.

It's incredible stuff, propofol. At the height of my alcoholic days, I had it once for surgery on my toe. It's like being fucking dead. One minute you're thinking, I wonder when they're gonna give me the . . . then ZONK, you're out.

But I've gotta say, propofol is one of the few drugs I'd *never* take for fun. There are some things you don't just fuck around with. The fact Michael Jackson used to take it every night to get to sleep is absolutely insane to me. He called it his 'milk', apparently. They said he'd been doing it every night for ten years before it finally killed him. The doc who gave it to him got off very lightly, in my opinion. I mean, okay, he was a cardiologist or something, but he wasn't an anaesthesiologist. He was totally out of his realm. It would be like if you or I had given it to him. Except if I'd killed the King of Pop, I'd have been locked away for ever.

Anyway . . . as I was waiting for it to kick in, they unlocked the wheels of my hospital bed and started rolling me out of the room, towards the OR.

Sharon and Jack were waiting for me outside. Jack was filming on his phone.

'See you in a couple of hours,' I said, giving him a thumbs-up and a big smile for the camera.

'Zakk called,' said Sharon, kissing me on the forehead. 'I said you'd call him back after.'

'We're ready,' said a voice from somewhere.

A thought popped into my head about Zakk. Didn't he say I should get a—

ZONK.

Two hours later . . .

Two days later . . .

Two weeks later . . .

Another week later . . .

7

Keeping my Head Up

I woke up desperate for a piss.

I had no idea what time of day it was. How long I'd been under. Whether they'd managed to fix my neck or not. I couldn't see Sharon or Jack anywhere, but I was guessing they were still waiting for me outside in the corridor.

All I remember is trying to get the attention of this nurse at the other end of the room. She was leaning over a little sink with the water running. But I was having trouble speaking. My mouth was dry. The muscles in my throat weren't working right. My brain was all foggy. Must have been the Jackson juice, I thought. Meanwhile, my right arm was so numb I almost couldn't feel it at all. I couldn't sit up straight either, no matter how hard I tried. And the new Count Dracula collar they'd put on me was so tight I felt like my neck was encased in a block of concrete.

I would have panicked, but I didn't have the energy.

I'd never felt so wiped out in my life.

Finally, I managed to croak loud enough for the nurse to turn around.

'Oh, Mr Osbourne, you're awake,' she said, before coming over, wetting my lips and giving me a glass of water. 'How are we feeling today?'

'Where's the bog?' I asked.

'Bog?'

I forgot I was in America. 'The toilet,' I said. 'Bathroom.'

'You can feel the urge to go?' she said. 'Oh, that's *great*. Would you like me to bring you a urinal bottle, or would you prefer the catheter? It's getting cleaned right now but I can get a new one fitted right away.'

'I just wanna piss!' I told her. I didn't know why that was so hard to understand.

'I'll get you a bottle.'

I was so frustrated at that point, I tried to get out of bed. Which was a problem . . . 'cos my legs wouldn't work. They were almost as numb as my arm.

That was when the panic kicked in. I remember just lying there, paralysed, my heart suddenly racing, thinking, *what the fuck has happened to me??*

I didn't know it at the time, but I'd been in critical condition for a few weeks by this point. After leaving the operating room, they'd taken me to the ICU, where I'd stayed, my condition just getting worse and worse.

The surgery had gone on for much longer than expected, Sharon told me later. Five hours, she said, not the two we'd expected. The doc had gone in through the back of my neck, like he said he would, so he didn't have to risk messing with my vocal cords. But what I didn't realise was, to get to my spine, he had to get through my neck muscles – the ones that hold up your head and let you move it from side to side. They're like a clump of rubber bands, those muscles, or that's how it was explained to me. Some of 'em he could just push aside while he worked. Others he had to cut. Which meant he had to sew 'em back together at the end.

The good news, apparently, was that Dr No Socks had got my spinal fluid flowing again – by chiselling around my spinal column to make a bit of extra space. But then he'd gone a step further and put two fuck-off metal plates in my spine, holding 'em in place with screws on either side. And that was on top of all the rods, plates and screws the NHS had already put in there. I had so much metal inside me, I thought, I wouldn't need a burial when I died – the undertaker could just pop me in the recycling bin.

Whatever the doc had done . . . my body couldn't take it. After the surgery, I was supposed to start my recovery. Instead I ended up on life support. And of course being in the ICU so long caused all kinds of other problems. After a couple of weeks, my muscles started to atrophy. That's why my legs hadn't worked when I woke up. I also developed blood clots, which can be fatal if they travel to your lungs. So they put me on pills for the blood clots. But the pills caused my lungs to fill with fluid. So that meant diuretics and oxygen therapy. At one point, I was on sixty-four different medications every day. I'd never taken so many drugs in my life, which was fucking saying something. And of course the medications were all interacting with each other, causing other problems, then those other problems needed to be treated.

It was a domino effect. One thing after another after another. Meanwhile, my neck had swollen up so badly the doc couldn't even see if the surgery had worked.

According to Sharon, one of the only things I said to her during the first few days after the operation was that I'd been visited by Elvis. She didn't think anything of it. She thought I meant my dog Elvis. It made sense that Jack would have brought him over. I mean, I love my four-legged friends – Elvis, Pickles, Wesley and of course my favourite, Rocky, God rest his soul. But after I'd mentioned it a few more times, she got suspicious.

'Ozzy, why do you keep talking about Elvis?' she asked.

'He came to see me.'

'You mean Jack brought him over?'

'No, no . . . he came on his own,' I said. 'Why would Jack know Elvis?'

'We're talking about the *dog* . . . yes?'

'What dog?'

'Oh God.'

'It was nice of him to visit,' I said.

'Yes, it was. *Very* nice of him. Especially since he's been dead for forty-two fucking years.'

Why I was thinking of Elvis, I've no idea. It wasn't like I'd ever been a big fan or anything. When he came out with 'Heartbreak Hotel', I was too young to appreciate it. It was the kids who were five or six years older than me who went nuts for him. That said, I do remember my mum taking me to see *Jailhouse Rock* at the Orient cinema when was about nine or ten. Then on Sabbath's first tour of America – this would have been late November 1970 – we had four nights at the Whisky a Go Go in LA at the same time he did his comeback gig at the Forum. It was his first show in LA in thirteen years, the press were saying, 'cos he'd spent the sixties making movies. So of course me, Tony, Geezer and Bill couldn't resist forking out for tickets and going down there to take a look.

When the warm-up acts were finally done, I remember the band starting up.

Guitar first.

Then drums.

Then the backing singers came dancing in.

And this went on, and on . . . *and on* . . .

We were all looking at each other, going, okay, so when does—

YYYYEEEEEEAAAAAAAAAAEEAARAAAAAG-GGGGGGGGGGGGGGHHHHHHHHHHHHHHH!!!!!!

The crowd just about blew the roof off the place when this distant figure appeared in a white fringed jumpsuit. We were sitting so far back, he could have been an impersonator for all we knew. We could barely even make out his pork-chop sideburns. He had all the moves, though. The hip swivels. The leg shakes. That karate-chop shwooshy thing he'd do, ending up on one knee. At one point he collapsed and lay flat on his back in the middle of the stage like he was too knackered to go on, then he jumped back up, the orchestra came in and he crooned his way through 'Love Me Tender'.

It felt like he'd only just got started when he fucked off again. He couldn't have been on stage for much longer than forty-five minutes. It was unbelievable. And of course the band kept playing even after he'd gone. Then a few minutes later, over the PA system, you heard 'Ladies and gentlemen . . . *Elvis has left the building*' and the whole place went crazy all over again.

What made it all worth it, honestly, was the drummer. Ronnie Tutt, I'm told his name was. He'd have been in his early thirties at the time, so a good ten years older than us. Fucking amazing. If he hadn't been doing 'Polk Salad Annie', he could have kicked some serious arse in a metal band.

Once I stopped hallucinating in the ICU, I became incredibly paranoid. Although I was getting some feeling back in my legs, they kept going cold – like *freezing* cold – which was freaking me out in a major way. Meanwhile, my right arm was so numb I could hardly use it. I was convinced Dr No Socks had messed something up in the operating room, and I was on my deathbed.

'If the surgery was such a success, how come I can't feel my legs?' I kept asking Sharon.

'Because you've been in bed for so long,' she said. 'You need to give it time. The doctor says—'

'They fucked it up, didn't they? *Just tell me!* What happened? *What did they do?*'

'Ozzy! This is a long road, you can't just—'

'I'm dying, aren't I? Why don't you just *tell me*? If I'm gonna be stuck in this bed for the rest of my life, I want you to switch off the fucking machine!'

'Ozzy, stop! *Just stop it.*'

The problem was, there was nothing Sharon or anyone else could say that would make me believe them. I pushed Sharon so hard a couple of times we both ended up in tears, until eventually I realised I needed to back off.

Meanwhile, there was an elephant in the room that no one wanted to talk about. Other than family and close friends – including Zakk and the other guys in my band – no one knew about my fall or my spinal surgery. The only thing we'd said publicly was that I'd come down with the flu. Maybe we'd also mentioned the bronchitis and pneumonia, I don't remember. But that had been in January. Now it was March, when *No More Tours II* was supposed to be starting up again. But there wasn't a snowball's chance in hell of that happening. Not now, not next month, maybe not this year. Maybe not *ever*, if I was being honest with myself.

'People are asking questions,' said Sharon. 'They're not buying you've just got the flu any more. If you believe Reddit, you've been found dead at least six times by now. We need to put out a statement. We don't need to go into any detail, but we should make it clear the tour's off.'

'We ain't cancelling it,' I said.

'Ozzy—'

'I'm gonna finish that fucking tour if it kills me!!' I hadn't meant to shout. But suddenly I just felt so angry, man. Ever since I got over the stupid fingernail infection, it had been one step forward, eight steps back. I didn't wanna be in a hospital bed. I wanted to go for a piss on my own. I wanted my life back.

'The tour almost *did* kill you,' Sharon reminded me.

'Well, I'm still here, aren't I?' I said, and I ain't ashamed to say I had to wipe away a tear.

It fucks with you, being ill, man. You think you're strong right until the moment you break.

That's when I remembered what I'd wanted to say before going into the OR.

'Why didn't we listen to Zakk?' I said. 'Why didn't we get a second opinion?'

Now Sharon also had tears running down her face. 'I

must have asked myself that question a thousand bloody times,' she said. 'I was scared, Ozzy. I thought you'd slip and end up like Christopher Reeve! The thought never occurred to me that we could bring someone else in to take a look at your neck.'

'Me neither,' I admitted.

'We panicked,' groaned Sharon. 'I can't believe we *bloody panicked.*'

For a moment we just sat there, feeling terribly sorry for ourselves. Then I caught Sharon's eye ... and I couldn't help but smile. I mean, what else was there to do? The whole thing was just so fucking ridiculous.

Next thing I knew, I was laughing.

Which hurt. A lot.

It took a moment for Sharon to see the funny side. But I eventually got a smile out of her. And as corny as it is to say, l was just so grateful she was there, y'know? Almost forty years after we met and fell in love, it was still the two of us against the world. And y'know what? We'd got through every kind of accident, fuck-up and tragedy before. We could do it again.

'Okay,' said Sharon, pulling herself together. 'If we're not cancelling the tour, we at least need to tell the fans what's going on. What should we say?'

Between us, we agreed the UK and European shows should be put back to January of the following year – 2020 – while the American shows should be rebooked for that spring and summer.

A few days later, I put out this message on Instagram:

I can't believe I have to reschedule more tour dates. Words cannot express how frustrated, angry and depressed I am not to be able to tour right now. I'm grateful for the love and support I'm getting from my family, my band, friends and fans, it's really what's keeping me going. Just know that I am getting better every day, I will fully recover, I will finish my tour . . . I will be back!

I'd never meant anything so much in my life.

When it was finally time to start physical therapy, Dr No Socks appeared to give me a pep talk. At this point, I've gotta say, the bloke was really starting to get on my tits.

'I'm going to tell it you straight, Mr Osbourne,' he said, 'this isn't going to be easy. But you'll get out of it what you put in. If you're determined, you'll see results. But you've got to do the work, and you've got to stick at it.'

I thought to myself, I'll show you determined.

'How long?' asked Sharon.

'Excuse me?' said the doc.

'Before we know how much movement he'll get back?'

'Oh, I'd say . . . uh . . . well . . . three to four months?'

It sounded like another 'fucked if I know' to me. What I was finally starting to realise is, doctors ain't gods. I mean, don't get me wrong, I have so much respect for everything they do. But they don't have all the answers.

That said, when I heard the doc say three to four months, I was like, fuck that, I'll do it in two. I was so cocky, I even told Sharon to order some new equipment for our gym at home and donate my old stuff to the hospital.

Then the torture sessions began.

We started with neck exercises.

When the brace came off, just trying to hold up my

head was like someone ripping my spine out. It was the most diabolical agony I'd ever felt in my life. I almost puked, it was that bad. I knew it couldn't be possible, but it felt like I was injuring myself all over again, just by trying to lift my chin a couple of inches. As for moving my head from side to side, there was no point in even trying. Without the brace, it just flopped around like I was a rag doll.

When you cut through a muscle, the physiotherapist said, it damages the nerves. And without those nerves, your brain can't tell the muscle what to do. But with time and exercises, she said, the nerves would start to grow back.

'But how *much* will they grow back?' I asked her. 'I can't wear a neck brace for the rest of my life. I feel like I'm walking around in a bomb disposal suit.'

'We just don't know yet,' she said.

Fuck me, I thought, *no one knows anything.*

Trying to walk was a different kind of hell. There was no way I was getting out of bed on my own, so they lifted me into a wheelchair, then rolled me out to the end of this corridor. Then the nurses got hold of my arms, pulled me to my feet and gave me a Zimmer frame to hold on to. 'Just put one foot in front of the other,' they said. 'Take your time, you're doing great.'

Doing great? I thought. *I haven't even started yet . . .*

When I finally got going, it was like trying to push a boulder up a hill. While wearing diving boots. With bricks tied to my legs. I'd never expected it to be easy. But this . . . this was bad, man. For the first time, I found myself thinking, Maybe I should just go back to bed. But in my head, I had Dr No Socks telling me, over and over, '*You'll get out of it what you put in.*'

Eventually I made it to the end of the corridor. It took most of an afternoon. There were continental plates moving faster than I was. Then the next day they opened the fire door and let me shuffle out into the quad.

After God knows how long, with the help of a walker, I could get all the way down the corridor, out of the door, across the quad, then come back around in a loop through an entrance on the other side. When I was done, I felt like I'd been hit by a train, then run over by a truck, but at least it was one small victory.

A few days after that, they said I could go home and continue my treatment there.

On the day I checked out, they wanted to put me in a wheelchair. I was like, fuck no, I ain't going anywhere in that. So they brought out a walker. When I told 'em I didn't want that either, they started freaking out, telling me I could fall and do more damage. But in my mind I needed to break through the pain barrier, keep building strength. 'I can do it, I can do it!' I kept saying.

All I remember is wobbling off down the corridor with about ten doctors running after me, their coats flapping around, ready to grab me in case I fell.

I was so over it by then, man.

I came in here with a sore neck, I remember thinking, and I'm coming out a cripple.

What a load of shit.

I was a prisoner when I got home.

I had nurses with me twenty-four hours a day, even sitting in my room at night. I couldn't scratch my bollocks without one of 'em reaching for the panic button. It was too much. What did they think I was gonna do?

I could barely hold my own dick, never mind try diving into bed again.

The one thing I forced myself to do every day, no matter how bad I was feeling, was walk around the block. One of the nurses would come with me, but other than a cane, I didn't want any help. At first, I could barely do one lap. Then it was two, three, five . . . until eventually I worked my way up to eight.

I'd get so tired, I'd literally crawl across the back-door threshold on my hands and knees. But I kept pushing myself, harder and harder, as the words of Dr No Socks kept repeating in my head, '*You'll get out of it what you put in.*'

Strengthening my neck was another part of my daily routine. A physiotherapist would come and put this rubber band on my head. The idea was, if I nodded my head up and down while wearing the band, the resistance would strengthen my muscles. It hurt so much, I can't even describe it. But I wanted rid of that brace so bad, man. I'd have suffered through anything.

I also had to get my vocal cords back into shape. Before the accident, I used to have singing lessons to stop my Parkinson's weakening the muscles in my throat. But while I was in the ICU, all of that had gone to shit. By the time I came out, it was shocking how much progress had been lost. I felt like I was slurring and mumbling over every single word. So as well as my usual vocal coach, I had a speech therapist come and work with me.

The constant pain was my biggest problem. And it wasn't like any other kind of pain I'd experienced before. I remember asking Dr No Socks about it when I went to see him with Sharon for a follow-up appointment.

'Okay, are you experiencing any numbness?' he asked.

'That's what I've been trying to tell you!' I said. 'I can't feel my right arm!'

'Hmm. Any burning or tingling?'

'Yes and yes.'

'Shooting pains?'

'Yeah, all the fucking— *Arrgh!* There it is again.'

'And does it get worse at night, or when you move?'

'Yes and yes.'

'Any hypersensitivity to touch or changes in temperature?'

'Yes and yes.'

Finally he goes, 'Any spasms, tremors or weakness in your muscles?'

'Are you *seriously* asking me that?' I said.

'Mr Osbourne,' he said, 'what you're experiencing is almost certainly nerve pain, or neuralgia. It's from the damage to your nerves during surgery. We already have you on several medications for it. All I can say is, just keep up the physical therapy. Y'know, what I always tell my patients is, you'll—'

'Get out of it what I put in,' I said. 'I know that, doc. You've told me that a thousand fucking times. But I need something stronger for the pain. It's too much. Can't you give me some more of whatever I was on in the ICU?'

The doc hesitated a moment, then looked at Sharon.

I knew a brick wall when I saw one.

'Ozzy,' said Sharon, 'he can't give you anything stronger. It's just too dangerous. I'm sorry. But I don't have to tell you ... you're the boy who cried wolf.'

The sad thing was, I knew she was right.

When you're an addict, every injury is an opportunity. What you quickly learn is, if you complain of certain types of pain, only a mind-reader could know if you're bullshitting or not. Addicts are some of the best liars out there, man. We're so good at it, we convince *ourselves* we're telling God's honest truth.

For a long time, toothaches were my way of getting my hands on some naughty pills.

I'd know within five minutes of meeting a dentist if he was gonna open up his prescription pad. Some of 'em could sniff out an addict a mile away. Others didn't give a fuck if you lived or died, it was just business to them.

When OxyContin came out at the end of the nineties, it was insane how many 'pain dentists' suddenly popped up in Florida. Whenever I did a gig in the Sunshine State, I'd book one appointment after another. It was like going on a shopping spree. How they got away with it, I've no idea.

Before Oxy, your best bet was to get some minor root canal work done and make friends with the anaesthesiologist. At one point, I had more friends who were dental anaesthesiologists than the average dental anaesthesiologist did. This one guy would hook me up with Vicodin, Percocet, Demerol, shots of morphine, whatever the fuck I wanted. He'd just send 'em to me in the post ... or at least he did until Sharon cottoned on to it.

'I found out what's been causing all your toothaches,' she announced one day.

'Oh yeah?' I said, all innocent, hoping she meant my secret bag of English sweeties.

'Yes,' she said. 'I met him at the dentist's. We had a nice chat about his medical licence, and he reassured me your teeth won't be hurting any more.'

That was the end of that little scam.

Backaches were the next best thing to toothaches, but back surgeons were harder to crack than dentists, and the last thing you wanted was to end up on the operating table for some non-existent pain you'd been complaining about. I hit the jackpot once, though. I had this Learjet at the time, and I was flying into ... okay ... let's just call it Milwaukee, Wisconsin, so I don't get anyone into any trouble. And on the way there, I started talking to the flight attendant, and it turned out her old man was Milwaukee's best-known back surgeon. So of course the second I hear that, I start telling her all about my back problems, how I'm in the most unbearable pain all the time, how I'm gonna have to cancel gigs because of it. And of course she says, oh, you should go and see my dad.

I was in that guy's office almost before we landed.

After checking me out, he says, 'So how much longer are you on tour, Mr Osbourne?'

'Six months?' I said. The real answer was more like three, but I thought I'd better double it in case he was gonna be tight with whatever he was gonna give me.

'Okay,' he says, scribbling on his little pad, 'this should keep you going.'

When I looked at what he'd written down, I could hardly believe my own eyes. He'd given me *five hundred* maximum-strength Vicodin. It was one of them moments when you're like, be careful what you wish for, you might just get it.

When I went to the pharmacy, the woman behind the counter took one look at the prescription, went very pale and called me over for a private chat. She goes, 'Sir, this is ... *an awful lot of pills*. I don't know how you got this prescription, or what it's for, but if you're going to be taking these yourself, may I suggest I dispense just the narcotic, not the mixer?' The mixer was Tylenol, she said. In that quantity, it would rot out my liver in about two seconds. Assuming I hadn't OD'ed on the Vicodin first.

I got through two hundred and fifty of 'em before I freaked out. I flushed the rest down the toilet. But of course a few days later I was out looking for more.

The trick I'd use was, I'd keep an old pill bottle from a year earlier – with four or five pills still rattling around in the bottom – so when I did a gig, I could say to the doctor in that city, 'Look, I'm running low, and I'm out on the road, could you refill me?' The bottle would have a date on it from the pharmacy, which in theory meant you weren't misbehaving. In reality, of course, I'd have been through at least ten other bottles since then. Gig doctors aren't stupid, of course. They know the games rock stars play. But sometimes if you give 'em enough cover, they're happy to play along.

My only lucky break when it came to addiction was that I never, *ever* wanted to shoot up. Which meant street heroin was off the menu. Needles just freak me out, man. Everyone's got their limit. That's mine. If I ever got injected with anything, I had a doctor do it for me. They'd be sitting there with me the whole time, in case anything happened. Given how much I like opioids, it's probably the only reason I'm still here.

Now that I'm sober, I've learned to think of a doctor's appointment as like walking into a pub. The first thing I say is, look, I'm an addict, no matter what I say, don't give me any kind of controlled substance. Better yet, I take Sharon with me, and she puts the fear of God into 'em. Of course, there are times – like in the ICU after the surgery – when they have to put me on *something*. But it's a joke, 'cos I've built up such a tolerance, I need about eight times more than the average person. And that's just the start of my problems. On the way up, it's all sunshine and roses. But coming down again, it ain't so funny. The withdrawal. The cravings. Realising you've gotta slay the dragon all over again.

My addictive nature scares me a lot more now than it ever did before, to be honest with you. I'm older. Not as strong as I used to be. If I ever start climbing the old relapse ladder again, I'm pretty sure it'll be a one-way trip.

By the time spring arrived, something happened I never expected: I lost hope. I was crawling up my back steps at the time, sweating and cursing, and I just thought . . . *who am I kidding? This ain't going nowhere.*

At this point, you've gotta remember, I'd been forced to keep my head in a completely rigid position – other than the times when I was doing the rubber-band exercises – for three months straight. I had no privacy whatsoever. Even when I was taking a shit, I had nurse hovering outside, asking me for the details of my bowel movement. My legs kept going cold. My arm was still numb. And I was in non-stop pain. Even a 'nerve block' procedure – when an anaesthesiologist came over and injected some anti-inflammatory shit into my spine, like an epidural – didn't help much.

Meanwhile, the Parkinson's doc had gone back to my old files, run some extra tests and confirmed that my Parkinsonian syndrome was caused by a dodgy gene called PARK2. I'd inherited a fucked-up copy of it from both my mum and dad, he said. What the mutated gene was doing was, it was killing the dopamine-producing nerve cells in my brain that control my muscles. That's why, when you have Parkinson's caused by PARK2, you get tremors and stiffness, which fucks up your balance and coordination. But of course those are the exact same problems you get from unsuccessful spinal surgery, so it was impossible to tell which was to blame. And because Parkinson's gets worse over time, just 'cos I could walk *before* the surgery this didn't mean it couldn't have progressed since then. I mean, I personally didn't believe it was my Parkinson's fault for one second. But what could I say? It was a catch-22 situation.

More than anything, I just felt so stupid for believing everything the docs had told me. I'd done months of physical therapy by now, but I was still a cripple. Still wearing the neck brace. Still needing around-the-clock care. Before the surgery, I'd been able to walk like a normal human being. Now I had the posture of fucking Gollum.

I just felt so jaded, man. I mean, why the *fuck* had I agreed to the surgery? I didn't understand it. If anyone had said to me, look, Mr Osbourne, the recovery for this operation could involve weeks in the ICU, and oh, by the way, you might end up more or less paralysed from the waist down – with a numb right arm – and if you complain about anything we're gonna blame it on your Parkinson's, I'd have told 'em to fuck off.

I ain't saying the doc did anything dodgy. Or that he didn't believe the operation would be a success. And obviously when you've got Parkinson's, it's gonna make things harder. But when it comes to anything spinal related, when they tell you what's wrong and what's needed, it's an *opinion*. And no two doctors ever seem to say the same thing. It's so frustrating when all you wanna do is get back on your feet and go back to work.

At the same time, after the surgery I couldn't help but think to myself, the American medical profession is all about money. Operations like mine cost hundreds of thousands of dollars, maybe even a million or more, not including all the follow-ups and medication. But if all goes tits up and you end up in worse shape than when you went in, everyone still gets paid.

If anyone should have known that going in, it was me. I mean, I was the one who'd spent decades taking advantage of the same fucked-up system to get doctors and dentists to prescribe me all kinds of pills I didn't need.

The final kick in the bollocks was knowing that Zakk had told me at least twice to get a second opinion. If I'd have listened to him, who knows what would have happened. It's hard to imagine it could have turned out any worse.

The one thing that had kept me going after my surgery was my determination to get back on tour. But my recovery – if it could even be called a recovery – was so slow I was starting to worry that even the tour dates we'd rescheduled for 2020 would end up getting pushed back again. Meanwhile, the fourth season of *Ozzy & Jack's World Detour* had to be called off entirely. I felt like I had nothing to look forward to. Like I was never gonna work again. I was in a dark place, man.

Sharon knew it was serious when I went to bed and just stayed there. All I wanted to do was sleep and forget the last six months had ever happened.

But then came the tiniest glimmer of light.

One morning, when I was close to the lowest I'd ever been, Sharon burst in to tell me they'd named a bridge in Birmingham after Black Sabbath. I thought she was taking the piss. I mean, in my mind, a bridge is a huge thing, like the Golden Gate Bridge or Sydney Harbour Bridge. There wasn't anything like that in Birmingham. Besides, Birmingham had surely moved on from anything Sabbath had ever done. In our day, it was a totally different city. It was all factories and soot-faced blokes trudging off down the pub. Now it's all coffee shops and posh shopping centres. Meanwhile, half the world's moved there. When I last went back to Lodge Road, there was a Muslim bloke with a Brummie accent who lived in one of my old neighbours' houses. Nice bloke, actually. Made me a cuppa and gave me a biscuit. It was weird. But whatever, man, things change. In our day, it was the Irish Catholics who were moving in.

Anyway, it turned out the bridge wasn't some huge suspension deal or anything. According to Sharon, it was a little stretch of Broad Street that crossed over the old canal, in what's now the city centre. They'd even put a little park bench on it with life-size portraits of me, Geezer, Tony and Bill on the backrest, each of us dressed in black, wearing the iron crosses my dad made for us during his tea breaks at the GEC factory. Our names were in bronze letters underneath, along with 'Made in Birmingham'.

It was fucking surreal, lying there in my bed in LA, hearing that piece of news.

And it only got stranger.

'Whose idea was that, then?' I asked Sharon.

'A local promoter, Mike Olley, and another bloke called Mohammed Osama,' she said. 'He's an Egyptian architect.'

'Am I hallucinating again?' I asked. 'Is Elvis about to pay another visit?'

'No, that's what it says here,' said Sharon, looking closer at whatever was on her phone. 'The architect lives in Dubai now. Calls himself a "superfan". Says he's been more to more than fifty gigs since he was eight years old. See, Ozzy. More people around the world are into your music than ever before.'

'We never even played Dubai, did we?'

'No, but you did play Abu Dhabi. And I haven't even told you the best part.'

'What?'

'Because of the order of the portraits on the bench, fans have to sit on Geezer's face if they want to get a photo with their arm around you. *Which they all do.*'

It was the first time I'd burst out laughing in what felt like a thousand years. If felt so, so good, man – even though it made my whole body hurt. And thinking about the bridge sent me right back, y'know?

I was pretty sure I knew exactly which part of Broad Street it was. Me and my mate Patrick Murphy used to ride our bikes for miles and miles down the towpaths. Birmingham has more canals than Venice, if you can believe it. But when we were kids, the coal barges had only just stopped running as haulage was moved to the roads, and the canals were abandoned. Some of 'em were filled in, but most were just left as they were. Which was great for us, 'cos they became our playground.

He was a good guy, Pat. He lived at 30 Lodge Road, a few houses up from ours. He was a Catholic, like me, but a proper one who went to church. I thought he'd go on to big things, and I'd be the one who didn't amount to anything. But as time went on, he kept getting busted for all kinds of shit. Eventually he got into big-time drug dealing. I was like, Pat, what the fuck are you doing, man? Eventually his wife asked for a divorce, 'cos she couldn't stand him going in and out of the nick the whole time. It pushed Pat over the edge, that did. He went into his garage, started up his car and gassed himself to death. It really knocked me about when I heard that. I remember calling his mum, and she told me, 'I just want my Pat back.' She lost three of her six kids in the end. It was fucking heartbreaking.

I used to think about Pat after *Paranoid* came out, 'cos I lived in a houseboat on a canal in London for a while. It was in Little Venice, not that far from Paddington. The boat was owned by our wide-boy manager at the time, Patrick Meehan, who'd taken over from Jim Simpson. Why he'd bought the thing, I've no idea. He was raking in so much cash from our album sales and touring, he was probably running out of things to spend it all on. He certainly had no shortage of Rollers and diamond rings.

I loved that houseboat, man. I'd do coke there all night, and talk so much the bloke in the next boat would come over and bang on the hatch to complain. Richard Branson's barge was just a few boats up, if I'm not mistaken. I know that 'cos after I left Sabbath, me and Sharon sold the rights to *Blizzard of Ozz* and *Diary of a Madman* to him – or to Virgin, anyway – and he insisted on us going there to sign the contract.

This was ten or fifteen years after I'd lived there, and I was expecting Branson's barge to be like Meehan's, which was all cosy with fresh paint and nice little kitchen. But it was the most rinky-dinky piece of shit I'd ever seen in my life. For a start, someone had shot out all the windows with a pellet gun, so there was all this broken glass and bird shit everywhere.

'Is this a joke?' I said to Sharon after we climbed on board and waited for one of England's richest men in this absolute shithole. I honestly thought we'd been pranked, that Jeremy Beadle was about to jump out of a cupboard.

'Ozzy, this is *not* a joke,' Sharon hissed at me, 'and you need to be nice to him, because we're broke and he's about to give us half a million pounds.'

'He should spend it on this fucking boat,' I said, ''cos it looks like it's about to sink—'

'Oh, Richard!' went Sharon as the man himself appeared. 'How lovely to see you . . .'

He was also at that Party at the Palace thing, Branson. I went to shake his hand and he kind of looked down his nose at me like we'd never met before, even though we'd done that deal. I suppose that's what you get with those upper-crust guys. I ain't in his world, and he ain't in mine. At least Sharon was eventually able to get back whatever rights we sold him.

Once my mind finally stopped wandering after hearing about the bridge, my thoughts turned to Tony, Geezer and Bill. All the shit we'd been through together. The great albums we'd made. How much I missed 'em.

In some ways, it felt like only yesterday we'd set up our gear at the Newtown Community Centre – just down the street from the Villa Park football ground – after changing our name from Earth to Black Sabbath. That's when Tony started played that creepy three-note riff, Bill did his free-form jazzy thing on the cymbals, Geezer got stuck in there, his bass notes making the windows rattle, and I started wailing about being the 'chosen one'. What a moment that was. It was *close* to the blues, what we were playing. But it *wasn't* the blues. It was something else. Something no one had done before. Not that we had any idea at the time. All we knew was we had goosebumps and needed to keep playing 'til we finished the song.

The more I thought about it, the more I knew we needed to get together one more time. Even if I had to be wheeled on stage on a stretcher.

We owed it to ourselves. To the fans. To the people who'd named that bridge after us.

There was just one problem.

I hadn't spoken to Bill in almost ten years.

8

A Positive on the S***

When a band breaks up, it's like a divorce. The emotions, the money, custody of the name and the back catalogue, all the legal shit that goes with that – it's ugly, man.

With a divorce, mind you, there's only two people involved. With Sabbath, there were four of us. So when it all fell apart it was twice as fucked up.

We'd been together ten years when we reached the end of the road. The spark had just gone. It was the drugs, it was the booze . . . it was making albums and doing shows not 'cos we were excited, but 'cos we had lawyers and back taxes to pay. Something had to give. No one wanted to admit it, but we'd burned ourselves out, physically and mentally.

I'd already tried to leave the band in a half-arsed way a year earlier. We'd been trying to write new material at Rockfield Studios in the Wye Valley – it's basically a farm with a studio attached, so you're surrounded by all this rolling countryside and an overwhelming smell of manure – and I just got in my car one day and drove home. This would have been around Christmas time, 1977. My dad had just died after finding out he was riddled with cancer, and I was in a bad fucking place. But the album eventually got done and I came back for the tour. It was the last studio album me, Tony, Geezer and Bill ever made together.

The title, *Never Say Die!*, was supposed to sound defiant. But looking back now, it sounds more like four guys desperately trying to convince themselves their hearts were still in it. I mean, we'd been fresh out of school when we started. We were so broke, we could barely afford food. And now there we were in our thirties with wives, ex-wives, kids, houses, you name it, having been around the world so many times we'd lost count.

The thing that really finished us off, in my opinion, was our support act on that tour.

It's funny, 'cos we thought we'd learned our lesson when Kiss had opened for us a couple of years earlier. The problem being, they were just too different to us. I mean, we were the kind of band that went on stage in our jeans and leather jackets, plugged in our gear, played our set and fucked off. Kiss, on the other hand, would squeeze themselves into these spandex jumpsuits with their nipples showing, paint their faces in crazy black-and-white Japanese clown patterns and set off about half a ton of explosives every night. It was nuts, what they did. I mean, they weren't the first to use pyrotechnics, but they took it to a whole new level, and they did it long before any kind of safety standards came in. It's a miracle they didn't burn down every venue we played on that tour. Meanwhile,

Gene Simmons must have been about seven feet tall in his platform boots, and he'd go around waggling his tongue at people just to freak them out. He did it to Geezer once and the poor bloke almost had a heart attack. Then after a gig they'd have all these girls lining up to party the night away in their rooms – while all we got were a bunch of blokes who wanted to drink beer and talk about 'Spiral Architect'. We were a male band, Sabbath, for male audiences. We never had many women at our shows. It was the same with my shows later on.

After Kiss, we were like, *never again*. You wanted your support act to be good, but you didn't want to upstage yourselves. You wanted Status Quo, basically.

We were very clear with our management company when it came to booking the support act for the *Never Say Die!* tour. We said, look, it has to be a band that has the same vibe as us, no studded collars, no high-heeled boots, no flames shooting out of their arses. So off they went to do their homework, then they came back to us and said, 'Okay guys, we've found a great little bar band in LA. Two brothers, one on guitar, one on drums, plus a singer and a bass player. They haven't done much, but their first album's coming out soon, and they do a really great cover of "You Really Got Me" by The Kinks. Oh, and they're cleared to travel to Europe, so we can book them for the whole tour, not just the American dates.'

'Sounds good to us,' I remember Tony saying. 'What's the band called?'

'Oh, er . . . let me check,' said the management guy. 'Ah yes, here they are. Van Halen.'

'Never heard of 'em,' shrugged Tony.

'No one has,' came the reply.

'Perfect,' said Tony.

Next thing we know, it's the first date of the tour. Sheffield City Hall. And we're curious to see what this unknown LA bar band are like, so about halfway through their set, we pop our heads around the door. And it's the moment during the gig when Eddie Van Halen – just twenty-three at the time – walks out on stage alone, gets down on his knees and plays 'Eruption'.

So there we are at the back of the auditorium, and there's Eddie under the spotlight, his hands in places on the fretboard that shouldn't be possible, his fingers seeming to move faster than the speed of light, and he's making these crazy, swoopy dive-bomb noises with his whammy bar – all while barely breaking a sweat – and when we look around us, all we can see are about twenty thousand people with their jaws on the floor.

Then Eddie gets to the end of the solo, playing the notes so fast no one's ears can keep up, Alex comes in on the drums and the crowd wakes up out of its trance and lets out a roar like England just scored in extra time against Germany.

All I remember is us leaving the auditorium in silence, going back to our dressing room in silence and just sitting there, staring at the fucking wall.

Ten or twenty minutes later, we hear another roar as Eddie leaves the stage. Then a few moments after that, there's a *tap-tap* on the door and this guy who looks like a walking movie billboard walks in. 'Hey guys, just wanted to say hi,' he goes, giving us this million-watt smile. 'I'm Dave Lee Roth.'

We all just looked at each other while thinking exactly the same thing.

Fuck.

I mean, look . . . you had to hand it to the guys in Van Halen. It was like they'd found a way to time-travel to the mid-eighties, even though it was still 1978. Eddie totally revolutionised guitar playing. And he made it look so easy. What you've gotta remember is, the electric guitar had been getting boring at that time. It's why synthesisers were becoming so popular. But when Eddie came on the scene, it was like a shot of adrenaline to the heart. Suddenly *everyone* wanted to play the guitar again. And they all wanted to sound like Eddie. But when it came to that finger-tapping thing he did, no one came close, man.

Van Halen couldn't have blown up at a worse time for Sabbath. Every night of that tour, they just slaughtered us. They'd go on stage, steal all our thunder, then you could feel the energy of the crowd dipping when we went on and plodded through our set. I mean, we did some good shows. But metal was evolving, and it felt like we weren't keeping up.

All that aside, we had some fun with the guys on the road. Eddie and Tony became close friends, I believe, and stayed in touch until Eddie very sadly died when he was just sixty-five. What a terrible loss that was. The guy was one of the greats. As for Dave Lee Roth, I never really hit it off with him. He was like Mr Showbiz. Always smiling. Never unhappy. He comes from a well-to-do family, I believe, maybe that's why we had nothing in common. You also never knew if he was spinning you a load of bullshit or telling you something for real. One minute he's saying he's getting his law degree, the next he's saying he's a part-time paramedic. There's a story going around that the two of us had a 'cocaine duel' during that tour – meaning, who could snort the most coke before they keeled over. I mean, it's *possible* it happened. But I doubt it. It just wasn't the kind of thing I did with Dave.

No matter how ugly it was when it ended, there's no doubt Sabbath had an incredible run. I mean, we must have been doing something right during those ten years we were making albums together, 'cos people are still streaming 'em and buying 'em on vinyl today. In my mind, we were a band that was just meant to be. And even though I've been a solo artist for much longer than I was ever in Sabbath, it'll always be a huge part of who I am.

I vividly remember the moment I realised Sabbath was going somewhere. I was in a club in Birmingham – Henry's Blues House, probably – and I had a pack of cigarettes in one hand and a beer in the other. Our first album had been released a few days earlier. And through the crowd comes Jim Simpson, our first manager. He was also the owner of the club, which was on the floor above the Crown pub on Station Street and had this trippy blue dog as its logo. 'You're in the charts!' he said, a huge grin on his face. I was confused, 'cos the charts weren't even out yet. But he'd seen 'em in advance. 'You're at *number seventeen*!!'

It was one of those moments when you've wanted something so bad for so long, when it finally happens you're scared to believe it's even real.

But it was real. I mean, okay, *Black Sabbath* wasn't selling in *Bridge Over Troubled Water* numbers. But it was doing well enough that our label, Vertigo Records, wanted another album as soon as we could write the material. Meanwhile, they'd already been promoting us in America by taking out an advert in *Rolling Stone*. 'LOUDER THAN LED ZEPPELIN' was all it said.

We worked our arses off to promote that first album. But it still felt like a one-off thing. It was only when our second album came out, *Paranoid*, that I remember thinking, *okay . . . this might actually keep me going for a few years*. It ended up selling more than twelve million copies, that record . . . and it's still going. What I have a hard time wrapping my head around is that we wrote and recorded it in just a few days. We were flying, man. We finished the song 'Paranoid' in about twenty-five minutes flat.

I've thought a lot over the years about why our music has lasted and others' hasn't.

As with any band, it's never down to just one person or one thing. You're a part of this jigsaw puzzle, and when the pieces all click into place, it's the best feeling in the world. It's totally different than when you're solo. If someone starts getting up my nose in my own band, I'll get rid of 'em. Or if I don't like the way something sounds, I'll say, that's crap, I don't like it. But that don't fly when you're all equals, and you've all started out together.

Although Tony was our unofficial leader, the way we wrote music was, we each did our own thing, and our territory was our territory. No one would tell Bill where to put a drum fill, or say to Geezer, here's what the bass line should be. They'd tell you fuck off – if you were lucky. On a bad day you'd walk away with a black eye. For me, that meant when Tony gave me a riff to put a vocal on, I could do whatever melody I wanted. At the same time, if it was out of my range, there was no going back and asking for a different key. Until I met Randy,

I didn't even know you could *do* that. No one had ever taught me how to speak in those musical terms.

Another thing about the way we worked was – in the early days at least – we never had a rehearsal space of our own, or a studio with our own recording equipment. We just had to sneak into church halls or community centres, go wherever we could set up our gear and play for long enough to come up with a song. Then we'd test it out live that same night at a gig. That's how most of *Black Sabbath* was written. It forced us to be spontaneous. And 'cos there was no studio meter running, we could afford to take more risks. If anything wasn't working, we'd find out soon enough, 'cos we'd see the fans getting restless.

When it came to the lyrics, they usually started out improvised. There's an old video on YouTube of us playing in Paris early on, around Christmas time 1970. It was at L'Olympia, where The Beatles had done a residency before going to America. When I watch the show back, I can tell I'm making up the words as I'm going along. With 'Fairies Wear Boots', a lot of the lines that popped into my head on the mic made it into the final song. Most of the time, though, once I got the melody down with whatever words I could come up with on the spot, Geezer would go away and write something much more serious, turning them into these incredible poems. Which was just as well, otherwise the opening of 'War Pigs' would still be 'Satan's looking for his sinners / After eating bad school dinners.'

People have asked me over the years, why not do the lyrics first? But it's much easier to fit words to a melody than it is the other way around. To me, when someone writes a novel then tries to fit a tune around it, you can tell. It sounds awkward, or like you're trying too hard to sound clever. Geezer's words always sounded natural, which is also why they never aged.

I was always in absolute awe of the abstract colours and moods Geezer could create with his words. The opening lines of 'Behind the Wall of Sleep' give me chills every time. He'd sometimes read me his lyrics over the phone, and I'd be like, Geezer, *what the fuck are you smoking?*

The way we judged a song was, if you got a tickle up your spine while you were playing it, you knew you were on to a winner. And time after time, Tony kept coming up with riffs that did exactly that. After he played us 'Iron Man', I remember us saying, okay, there's absolutely no fucking way he's ever gonna beat that one. Then the next day it was 'War Pigs' . . . then 'Hand of Doom' . . . and he kept 'em coming, album after album.

Bill's drumming was also a big part of what made us special. When he was a kid, I believe, he'd play along to big-band records – Count Basie, that kind of thing – and he kept those influences going in Sabbath. You can hear it on 'Wicked World', when he's on the hi-hats before the opening riff. People think of jazz and Sabbath as having nothing in common, but if you pay attention, it's there. There's even a jazz band that does Sabbath covers now. I ain't joking. Jazz Sabbath, they're called.

The only other thing I'll say about Sabbath's music is that we never had a formula. There was no verse-chorus, verse-chorus. When we got in a room together, we went wherever the feeling took us. We'd go heavier than anyone had ever gone before. We'd have acoustic bits, trippy bits, orchestras, piano, a bit of synth. We'd start a song one way, move on to something totally different, then come back to the original riff ten minutes later.

And it worked, man. It just worked.

Well . . . until it didn't any more.

I don't want to spend a lot of time talking about how I got fired from Sabbath. It was a long time ago, we were all fucked up, we all have our own versions of what went down, and we had some great times, so why dwell on the bad?

All I remember of those final days is flying from London to New York, getting held up at customs 'cos I was shitfaced, missing some sessions, talking too honestly to a journalist about being pissed off with the band, then finally getting to this big house in LA where we were working on the next album.

There was a weird atmosphere as soon as I walked in the door. Then for the next few days, even though I was getting up early and working hard, whatever I did, they wouldn't like it . . . until finally Bill came in and told me I was fired. The reason being that I was drinking too much and taking too many drugs – which was pretty fucking rich given the state of everyone else. It all felt very pre-arranged, as if I'd walked straight into a trap. I was like, fine, fuck it, I'm out of here. I hadn't been feeling the music anyway. They were taking the jazzy stuff too far, in my opinion, and it was leaving me cold. But the truth was, I was just over it, and desperate to go in a new direction on my own.

Although it was Bill who fired me, it was obvious he'd been put up to it. The sad thing was, of all the guys in the band, I'd spent the most time with Bill. Whenever we toured America, Tony and Geezer would fly everywhere, while me and Bill would rent one of them GMC motor-homes and drive it between gigs. It wasn't really a tour bus, more like the kind of thing a family would rent for a cross-country road trip. We had so much fun in those things, man. They were some of the most carefree days of my life. It wasn't exactly glamorous, mind you. One of the GMCs we rented had a hole in the petrol tank and the chemical toilet wouldn't flush properly. It was hard to know what was worse, the smell of the fuel or the smell of the Brummie turds marinating for weeks.

Every morning, Bill's ritual was the same. He'd have a cup of coffee, a glass of orange juice, a pint of milk, then a beer. Always in that order. He said the coffee was to wake him up. The orange juice gave him his vitamins for the day. The milk lined his stomach for all the drinking that would come later. And the beer was to put him to sleep again. He wasn't joking about the beer. He'd drink it in a couple of gulps after breakfast, climb back into his bunk, and that would be him out until we got to the next gig. Unless the GMC broke down. Which was about every other day.

The worst time was in the middle of winter. We must have been up near the Canadian border somewhere. There'd been a blizzard earlier in the day, and it had turned into freezing rain. I'd never been so cold and wet in my life. So there we are, shivering by the side of the road, trying to get the GMC started, and this older guy stops in a Jeep and he says, 'Looks like I'm going your way, do you boys wanna ride?' So of course we jump in, thinking it'll just be an hour or whatever to the gig. But it turns out it's four or five hours. Meanwhile, the Jeep has this leaky canvas roof, so it's like being outside. By the time we got there, we just about had hypothermia. How we managed to get through that show, I've no idea.

Another time, we were in this bar before a show, and Bill decided it was time to leave. So he starts punching me in the back of the head, going, 'Let's go, Ozzy, *let's go!*' But I was enjoying my beer and wanted to stay, so it turned into a bit of a fist fight. And of course the second the barman sees us tussling, he breaks it up and throws us both out. But the fight just continues in the car park. And Bill's so drunk, as I'm swinging punches at him he starts doing this ridiculous Harry Carpenter voice: 'AND HERE WE ARE IN ... WHEREVER THE FUCK WE ARE ... WITH THE UNDEFEATED WILLIAM WARD FACING CHALLENGER JOHN OSBOURNE!'

Eventually I landed a right hook, but Bill barely flinched. He just kept bobbing and weaving with all this blood running down his face, going, 'AND OSBOURNE LANDS A JAB BUT MISSES A STRAIGHT RIGHT CROSS, AND WARD IS STILL ON HIS FEET. THIS REALLY IS A NAIL-BITER HERE IN WHER—'

Thwump.

That time, Bill went down hard.

Finally, I thought, I got the fucker to shut up. But then he jumped back to his feet.

'AND WARD IS STILL IN THE FIGHT!!!' he screams. 'BUT CAN HE GO THE DISTAN—'

Thwump.

There was no getting up from that one.

An hour later, we were playing the gig, both of us with black eyes and teeth missing.

We were nuts, the two of us. Absolutely off our rockers.

My final memory of the GMC was when I finally convinced Bill we needed to empty the shit tank. We were at one of those motor-home parks and I refused to get back on the thing 'til we did something about the smell. I was getting sores on my face from it. Besides, we were close to the end of the tour and the rental company had been very clear they wanted us to return the GMC in mint condition. They'd even given us a little lesson on how to use the septic pump, but of course neither of us had been paying attention.

Bill was off his trolley as usual, and his brother Jim was there, 'cos he'd been helping out with the driving. The park was empty with no one around to help, but we found the 'dump station' and the industrial-grade hose we needed to suck out the turds. The problem was, we didn't know where the hook-up was. Was it in the cabin? Under the bonnet? By the petrol tank?

'Where the fuck does the shit come out of?' I kept asking.

'Where's Bill?' was all Jim kept replying. 'He was here just a minute ago . . .'

Eventually, we found what we thought was the hook-up on the floor of the GMC. So we unscrew the cap and force the hose into it, then Jim jumps into the driver's seat, starts up the engine and pulls the 'empty septic' lever. Suddenly the engine revs like crazy and we hear this *NNNNNEEEEE!!* as the pump activates. But it's very clear nothing's coming out of the hose. So Jim kills the engine and we sit there scratching our heads.

Then from somewhere under the GMC we hear this muffled, gargly-sounding voice.

It's Bill.

'Ozzy!' he says. 'Tell Jim . . . I've got a positive on the shit!'

It turned out Bill had crawled *under* the GMC to find the shit-emptying outlet. That's where he'd been this whole time. And he'd found it. So he unscrewed the cap, ready to connect the hose. But *we* had the hose, not him. And 'cos he was arseholed, he must have nodded off for a moment. Meanwhile, we'd hooked up the hose to the windscreen-washer tank or something. So when we emptied the septic, we emptied it on Bill.

When Bill finally emerged, he was covered head to foot in this blue chemical-toilet shit, spitting out bits of God knows what. But he didn't seem all that bothered. He just washed himself off under an outdoor tap.

At least we'd finally emptied the shit tank, I thought.

When we pulled away and looked back, there was a blue outline of where Bill had been lying, surrounded by this horrible lumpy blue lake.

He must be forty years sober now, Bill, God bless him. But fucking hell, man. The times we had.

Bill didn't last much longer than I did in Sabbath. He was in a bad place with his drinking, from what I understand, and he just disappeared one day before a gig.

For a long time, it bothered me that they kept going with the same name but a different singer. I wished they'd called it Black Sabbath II. To me, the singer is just the most obvious part of a band's sound, so it's a whole different thing than when you replace anyone else. I mean, okay, *sometimes* it works. Brian Johnson did a great job taking over from Bon Scott in AC/DC. But it's never the same. If you've been a fan of a band from the beginning, chances are you're gonna prefer the original singer.

Even when a band *does* change their name after ditching their singer, it can feel weird.

I remember when Slash and the guys from Guns N' Roses split with Axl Rose and formed Velvet Revolver with Scott Weiland from the Stone Temple Pilots. It must have been in the early two thousands, just as *The Osbournes* was taking off. I walked into the Polo Lounge in Beverly Hills one day and they were all there. I didn't know Slash all that well at the time, and I was just so upset that one of my favourite bands had broken up, I really put my foot in my mouth. I said to them, 'Do you know, in my career, there's only been a handful of bands that ever reached the level of Guns N' Roses? The Beatles, the Stones, Led Zeppelin . . . and that's about it. Couldn't you guys have worked something out?'

I didn't win any diplomatic medals for that comment, that's for sure. I just loved *Appetite for Destruction* so much, y'know? To me, it was just one of them perfect albums that come around only a few times in a generation. I remember listening to it for the first time and thinking, okay, this has got everything you need. When they broke up, I thought that was it, they'd never get back together. I was amazed when they came back with *Chinese Democracy*, twenty years later or something. It was the most expensive album ever made, apparently. But when you leave it that long, it's hard to get the old spark back. People's heads are in a different place.

Come to think of it, Axl Rose also switched bands later on, taking over from Brian Johnson in AC/DC for a few gigs. I take my hat off to him for that. To replace Brian, you've gotta put your balls in a vice and put a rocket up your arse. To sing like that, night after night . . . it's gotta be torture, man. You're gonna need protective clothing and breathing apparatus.

The only time I was asked to replace another singer was around the same time I lectured Slash about Guns N' Roses breaking up. I was at home in the kitchen, and the phone rings. So I pick it up and this voice goes, 'Who's thishh?!' Whoever it was, it sounded like they'd been drinking.

'Who the fuck do you think it is?' I said. 'And who the fuck are you?'

'Oh, hey Ozzy,' he goes. 'It's . . . Eddie. Want a sing a few tunes for us?'

'Eddie?' I said. 'I don't know any Eddies—'

'Yeah you do, man. It's *Eddie*. Eddie Van Halen!'

I couldn't believe it. It had been *years* since I'd last seen him. So we get chatting, and it turns out Dave Lee Roth has left the band – or maybe it was Sammy Hagar on vocals at that point, I don't remember – and Eddie wants me to take over. I thought he was joking. I mean, he was halfway out of his fucking tree on the call. Anyway, the second Sharon heard about it, she jumped in the car and went straight over to his house. And she told him very nicely that I couldn't do it, 'cos I had my own career.

What I'm trying to say, I suppose, is that in the years since I got kicked out of Sabbath, I've come to learn that shit happens if you stick around long enough in the music game. And on reflection, getting fired from Sabbath was the best thing that ever happened to me – and it was certainly the best thing that ever happened to *them*. When they hired Ronnie James Dio to take over from me, they had something to prove. And I had something to prove. And that re-lit the fire inside all of us at time when we all badly needed to feel that hunger again. I mean, okay, I've said a lot of shit about Dio over the years, and I've never been able to bring myself to listen to any of the records the guys made with him. Sabbath is just too close to my heart, y'know? But the truth is, he was a good singer. He wasn't me, and I wasn't him. But it wasn't like they suddenly lost it after I left – they didn't. And the fact is, some people discover Sabbath through the Dio albums, then they work their way back to *Paranoid* and *Black Sabbath*. So yeah . . . it's taken a while. But at the grand old age of seventy-six, I think I've finally made some kind of peace with it all.

It always bugged me that *Never Say Die!* was my last album with Sabbath. That's why getting back together with them to make *13* felt like something I had to do. I knew we had one more killer album left in us. And by 2011, it felt like now or never. None of us were getting any younger.

We'd had a few reunions over the years, of course. Some more successful than others. The first was for the Philadelphia part of Live Aid in 1985. I'm glad we did it, 'cos it was for a good cause. But it wasn't exactly the happiest of get-togethers. They put us on at ten o'clock in the morning between Billy Ocean and the Four Tops, for a start. And those were my full-blown alcoholic days, so I wasn't on my best behaviour, and I was grossly overweight. I also got served by Sharon's father as I was walking into the place. I mean, who the fuck does that? *At a charity gig?* It was something to do with me leaving

Jet Records, I don't remember the details. Some bloke just jumped out of nowhere and shoved a lawsuit in my face. Don and Sharon had been fighting about it for years.

We had a much happier reunion in the late nineties, when we got together to do some shows at the NEC in Birmingham, which we put out on the *Reunion* double album. We also did a few Ozzfests during *The Osbournes* period.

When it came to making a new album, though, it just never happened. We tried once after *Reunion*, but during one of the early sessions at Rockfield Studios – the same studio I'd walked out of in 1977, before coming back for *Never Day Die!* – Bill suffered a serious heart issue. We'd all been giving him shit for his health, and Bill had always been a bit of a practical joker, so when he started complaining about his hand feeling funny – at one point he asked me to massage it – we all thought he was winding us up. Then when an ambulance showed up – it raced past us with its siren blaring as we were having a fag break in the rain – we were like, fucking hell, he's really taking this to the next level. But it was deadly serious. We almost lost him.

When Bill finally got out of hospital, the docs told him he couldn't work for a year. And by the time we got around to trying again with the album, we'd all become busy with other projects, so it just kind of petered out.

As strange as it sounds, the album that became *13* actually got its start in the late eighties, when the big-time producer Rick Rubin called me out of the blue one day. He didn't mention an album, he just invited me up to his house in Laurel Canyon, up in the Hollywood Hills, to hang out.

I didn't know all that much about Rick, to be honest with you, other than he was the guy who'd produced 'Walk This Way' by Run-D.M.C. and Aerosmith, and also that first Beastie Boys album. They'd both been massive hits, so Rick was hot shit at the time. *Everyone* wanted to work with him.

Rick was obsessed with Sabbath, I found out. I remember walking into his Spanish-style mansion, hidden away on some narrow street, with epic views over LA. He had these huge speakers, like a full PA system, and he was playing tracks off our first album. The weird thing was, there were also all these Buddha statues everywhere, and a sign that said 'Quiet Please: Meditation in Progress'. The bloke must have a screw loose, I thought.

He was heavy then, Rick, like a sumo wrestler, and had the long hair and the beard, only they weren't all silvery like they are now. And he was barefoot, like he always is. I've not once seen him in shoes. The first thing I said to him – I remember this very clearly – was 'Hi Rick, wanna do some blow?'

This was the late eighties, you've gotta remember. Whenever I met anyone, no matter what the circumstances, I just assumed they were either on coke, about to do coke, or coming down from coke . . . which meant they were out of coke and needed more coke. But Rick was different. 'You should stop doing that shit, man, it'll kill you,' he told me.

'Oh . . . okay then,' I said, trying hard not to sniff, even though my nose was dripping like a leaky tap thanks to all the powder I'd been blasting up there. 'Quick question, though, Rick. Where's the nearest bog?'

'Just up the hall.'

'Back in a sec.'

Off I went, sniffing all the way.

I'd never met anyone like Rick before. He didn't smoke. Didn't drink. Didn't do *any* kind of drugs, not just cocaine. He must have liked the occasional Big Mac, though. I mean, for a working-class guy like me, it was hard to wrap my head around. Other than listening to music, what did he do for *fun*?

There was a much bigger problem between us, though. Rick wanted Sabbath to get together so he could make a new album with us. But I still had a bit of a bee up my arse about getting fired, even though that had been close to a decade ago. 'Ozzy, you gotta tell me,' said Rick, 'is there *any* chance you guys might work something out?'

'No fucking chance,' I said.

'Okay,' he said, 'then can you do me a favour?'

'Sure.'

'If you guys ever *do* get back together, can you call me?'

'Rick,' I said, 'it just ain't gonna—'

'Ozzy, I get it, I totally get it,' he said. 'But *if* it does happen, can you call me?'

'Okay ... but like I said—'

'That's all I need.'

Every time I saw Rick after that, he'd pull me aside and whisper, *'Don't forget our deal!'* Literally every fucking time, for the next twenty-five or something years. We had a couple of false starts along the way, like when we got together in the studio before and after Bill's heart attack, but otherwise it seemed like it would never happen. But then once *The Osbournes* had wrapped its final season, and

Tony had done his last tour with Dio and their Heaven & Hell band, it seemed like the time had arrived. It also helped that we'd finally settled who controlled the Black Sabbath name, with me and Tony splitting it fifty-fifty between us.

Of course, it took about four seconds for the first cracks to appear.

The first problem was that my ego was out of control, and I was starting to fall back into my bad old ways. The second problem was that because we all got so badly ripped off back in the day, Bill takes a long time to agree to any kind of deal. And he wanted an equal cut, which I thought was a bit naughty, because he hadn't been playing on the road for a very long time. Then I made some comment about it in the press, there was a blow-up with Sharon, it all got ugly and we just ended up going ahead without him. It did a lot of damage to my relationship with Bill and we stopped speaking to each other. I came to deeply regret that.

The thing is, when we started arguing, Bill took it personally. It was understandable. Feelings run deep in bands. Especially when you started out basically as kids. But with Tony, he'd just call me out on my shit. He'd go, 'Ozzy, it's not your fucking band.' And that shut me down. Although Sabbath never had an official leader, unofficially it was always Tony. As for Geezer, I honestly have no idea what happened with his deal, but he worked something out. He must have just left it to his management.

The thing is, over the years I've gone off Tony, and he's gone off me. Same with Geezer and Bill. But we've always come back to each other. We always will.

With *13*, though, Bill got left behind.

It was very sad for all of us, and I think we all wish it hadn't happened that way.

Once our deals were done, and Bill was officially out, it was time to start writing the material. Luckily my good friend Tommy Clufetos was available at the time, so he stood in on drums while we jammed and put together our ideas. We started out at my home studio in LA. I was living in a place called Hidden Hills at the time, a gated suburb near Calabasas, way out in the rolling hills west of the city, just over the mountain from Malibu. One of the first things I noticed about Tony when he flew in was how thin he looked. He said it was nothing. But I said to him, 'Tony, you *really* need to go and see a doctor when you get back to England.' So he did, and that's when he found out he had lymphoma. But you can't keep Tony down, man. He's a fighter, like we all are. We just moved the rehearsals to England as he went through his chemotherapy and radiation treatment. If anything, it made us even more determined to get the album done and make it fucking great.

Once Rick started to get heavily involved, he said he wanted to try a different drummer, someone who wasn't 'straight-up rock', in his words. He kept suggesting Ginger Baker, who'd obviously been in Cream and also Hawkwind for a while with my great friend Lemmy Kilmister, God rest his soul. But Baker was crazier than *me*. I mean, there was a documentary about him, *Beware of Mr. Baker*, where he broke the director's nose with a metal cane at his house in South Africa. And that was *after* the guy had been thrown out of every other country. Not that he would have taken the job anyway. He was nuts. He'd have been a liability on tour.

In the end, we went with Brad Wilk from Rage Against the Machine. Now, to me, Brad's about as rock as you can get. But Rick thought he had more of a jazzy, swingy feel. I was never comfortable with that decision. Everyone had been fine with Tommy until Rick came on board and had other ideas, so I was kind of pissed off about that for a while.

The recording sessions for *13* began in August 2012 at Shangri-La Studios, off the Pacific Coast Highway in Malibu.

Rick had just bought the place, or so I heard, and he'd painted every room white before we arrived, so it would feel like we were starting fresh. Apparently, it had once been Bob Dylan's studio, and before that, a brothel. The bedrooms still had mirrored walls. It also still had the leather-upholstered bar where the punters would choose which girl they wanted. Meanwhile, Dylan's old tour bus was parked on the lawn in front. He'd left it there after a tour in the sixties, said Rick. It was now the studio's control room, which was pretty cool. There was even a little padded listening area at the back. Behind the property, I also found out, there was an old barn where the retired sitcom star Mister Ed used to live. I remember thinking the poor guy must have been pretty down on his luck to end up in a barn. Then someone explained that Mister Ed was a horse. We mustn't have ever got that show in England.

Once we'd fully moved in and started recording, Rick was like the resident guru. He'd always be padding around barefoot in his white T-shirt and black shorts. The whole thing was fucking weird, man. When we were trying to work stuff out, Rick would just be lying in the corner, going, 'I like this . . . I don't like that.' He'd never mince his words. I was a bit worried about Tony's reaction at times. Tony doesn't like being told what to do. He certainly doesn't like anyone fucking around with his guitar. I've seen people try over the years, and they usually end up getting a left hook from him.

Rick kept saying he wanted us to go back to the first Black Sabbath album. But both *Black Sabbath* and *Paranoid* were basically live albums. They had that looseness to them. We just set up our gear and hit 'record'. He also kept saying, 'I don't want you to write anything *happy*.' That got under my skin a bit. It reminded me of the days when people got Black Sabbath all wrong, and they thought we were some kind of Halloween band.

The thing is, there are only so many 'Iron Man's you can do. The mistake a lot of bands make is, they go, oh, that last album, *Smoke on the Water*, was a big hit, let's do another one that's basically exactly the same, but with a slightly different riff. It gets old. Really fucking fast. You've gotta move on.

Tony's cancer didn't make things easier. But he kept going, even through all his treatments, which ended up lasting a few years until he was officially in remission. Meanwhile, Geezer hammered out the lyrics, working day and night. And he delivered. He hadn't lost any of his genius for words.

The first time I took the rough mixes home with me, I thought, *Rick's out of his mind*. It didn't sound very good at all. I was like, I need to speak up more, we need a change of direction here. But after a while, I realised what I needed to do was leave my ego at the fucking door. The thing is, albums are such a personal thing. They're like your children in some ways. When you have a vision in your head, you can drive yourself crazy trying to get it exactly how you want. It's so demanding on your person. It absolutely drains you. I had to let it go in the end, especially since it was a Sabbath album, and there were others involved.

I was in the booth *all the time*. I'd go through a song five hundred times, and Rick would go, 'That last one was great, Ozzy. Give me one more.' And I was like, how can it be great if you still need one more? But that's Rick. It got to the point where I decided to stop fighting it. I just said, 'Okay, Rick, I'm here for you. If you want one more, you'll get one more.'

No one could argue with how well *13* did. It was the first album in our career that went straight to number one in both Britain and America, and a whole host of other countries. We won a Grammy. Even the reviews were amazing . . . not that I read them. But when we took the album out on tour, it was all business, not like in the old days. We'd go to the venue, do the tune-up, then each of us would go off to our own dressing room. I had my little crowd with me. They had theirs. We wouldn't have meals together or do any kind of fun band stuff. You felt like a hired gun. There was no camaraderie. Geezer, you just wouldn't see at all. His wife had some kind of beef with Sharon, so Geezer was very cold to me for most of the tour. You'd see Tony out and about now and again. But a lot of times, it felt like everyone just wanted to get it over with.

I suppose it didn't help that once the album was done, I said, if Tommy ain't on drums for the tour, I ain't doing the tour. It caused a lot of resentment when I pulled that move. Brad even called me up and said,

'Why don't you want me to do this gig?' All I could say was, 'Brad, if you were Tommy, and you'd been there for all the writing, and Rick had wanted you gone, how would *you* feel?' He had no answer to that. There wasn't an answer. The truth was, Brad did good work on the album. But in my mind, Tommy should have been there all along, and he deserved to be on the tour. At the same time, I'll admit I was just so used to doing my own thing and having my own band it was really hard to not be in control. Maybe that's why the atmosphere on stage never felt that great.

Looking back now, the way I was behaving was also a result of my old insecurities coming back to bite me. Because I'd never had the patience to learn how to play an instrument – other than the harmonica – I'd always felt less than, y'know? It was like, I was just the singer, and Tony, Geezer and Bill were the *real* musicians, so I didn't have much to say about what went down. That wasn't true – or not always, anyway – but it was how I'd felt since I was twenty years old. When I got fired from Sabbath and went solo, I escaped that. But now we were back together, it felt like I'd never left, with all those old tensions coming back.

I don't mean to sound like I regret doing any of it. I don't. The album and the tour were successful beyond what any of us could ever have dreamed of. But it would have been so much better if it had been friendly, and if we'd had Bill there. Tommy did a great job on the drums, don't get me wrong. But he'd be the first to admit he ain't Bill and never could be.

9

Dead by Christmas

When I gave up on my recovery, it was Kelly who realised what needed to be done. I needed to get off my arse and get back to work. And if I couldn't go back on tour, that meant going into the studio. Singing would also help with my vocal cords. And it would be a lot more fun than going 'ba, ba, ba' and 'la, la, la' with my speech therapist a thousand and one times a day. But I wasn't interested. 'If I ain't making an album, what the point?' I said to her. 'I'd just be wasting everyone's time.'

'Actually,' said Kelly, 'I know a guy who really wants to sing with you.'

'Really? Who's that then?'

'Post Malone.'

I thought about it a second. 'That's very interesting,' I said. 'I've just got one question.'

'Okay . . .'

'Who the fuck's Post Malone?'

'Oh, for God's sake, Dad!' She pulled out her phone and started playing me 'Sunflower'. Okay, now I knew who he was. I liked that song a lot. Like everyone else, I'd heard it on the *Spider-Man: Into the Spider-Verse* soundtrack. It was one of them massive hits, like 'Sweet Child o' Mine', that you couldn't avoid for about two years straight. It sold twenty million copies or something. Post was obviously a very talented bloke, and one of the biggest deals out there. But I was in such a bad way, I didn't believe he really wanted to do it. 'He *seriously* wants to sing with me?' I asked.

'Yes! He's been a huge fan of yours since he was a kid, everything from Sabbath to *Blizzard of Ozz*. We have a friend in common who's a producer, and everyone thinks this would be amazing. Dad, *you've got to do this.*'

'Okay then,' I said, warming up to the idea. 'But don't we need to write a—'

I couldn't finish my sentence 'cos Kelly was hugging me and jumping up and down at the same time with tears running down her face.

It was a weird role reversal, Kelly looking after *me*. I mean, okay, I'd been a pretty absent father in many ways. But when Kelly was a teenager, she gave me and Sharon a run for our money. I remember there was a time when I kept getting these bills from the Beverly Hills Hotel for like thirty-five, forty thousand dollars. Every month they'd arrive, and I'd just pay them. Until eventually I was like, *this can't be right for the occasional lunch with Sharon at the Polo Lounge.* So I went down there and talked to the manager, and he was like, 'Oh yeah, Kelly brings all her friends here after school and buys them all dinner on your account.' And I was like, 'What the fuck are they eating, gold bars?'

Yeah, she's a chip off the old block, is Kelly. I can't imagine how much grief I must have given my own mum and dad, especially when I went to prison.

But now here I was, stuck at home, either in bed or getting stretched out on a traction table, while Kelly, Jack and Aimee were out earning a living and basically acting as my carers. Sharon too. She was doing that TV show of hers – *The Talk* – five days a week, which was a crazy schedule to keep up. She was wiped out come the weekend. But she still made time to organise all my treatments.

I felt so guilty, y'know? Like I wasn't doing my job, which was providing for my family as I'd always done, no matter what state I was in. Like I was letting everyone down. My family. My band. The crew. Most of all, the fans. Above all, I felt like I was a burden to everyone around me. When you're a working-class guy, if you're not clocking in, you feel like you're making everyone else work double shifts to cover your lazy arse.

Meanwhile, my round-the-clock care was straining the old bank account like never before. And we still hadn't told the fans what the fuck was going on with my health. As strange as it might sound coming from a guy who's lied about his addictions his whole life, I *hate* secrets. They weigh you down, man. And the truth was, I was running out of excuses to not be on tour. That's why half the internet seemed convinced I was dead.

I couldn't believe how quickly the song with Post Malone came together.

The first thing that happened was, Kelly introduced me to her producer friend, Andrew Watt. He was still in his twenties then, Andrew, but he'd already been in a band with Glenn Hughes from Deep Purple. He'd also worked with Lana Del Rey, and with Post on his *Beerbongs & Bentleys* album. How he and Kelly became friends, I've no idea. I think they just bumped into each other once at a party. And 'cos Andrew knew Post was a big metalhead, and he obviously knew Kelly was my daughter, he called her one day and said, 'Ozzy and Post should work together!'

I hit it off with Andrew immediately. He just loves music, y'know? And the guy can shred with the best of 'em. At the same time, I ain't gonna pretend he didn't seem like a kid. I mean, he was born in 1990. I've got socks down the back of the sofa that are older than him. He's also got an attention span that makes me seem like the world's most patient man. When I went over to his home studio in Beverly Hills – it was in his basement, with these heavy Persian rugs on the floor, guitars on the wall, all kinds of vintage keyboards and computer monitors everywhere – he was whizzing around all over the place, air drumming, headbanging, the guy couldn't sit down for two minutes straight. For a moment I was worried he might be some kind of whack job. And when he did sit, his face was glued to his phone, like everyone else his age. I've gotta tell you, man, I'm so happy I grew up without those things. Life might have moved slower in our day, but at least we got to stop and smell the roses once in a while, instead of constantly checking some glowing screen. Not that there were many roses in Aston, mind you. Mostly what we were smelling was coal dust and ammonia.

At some point, Andrew sent me the rough version of the song over email. I loved the vibe of it right away. It was like this dark break-up song with a massive chorus and proper rock-god guitar solo. 'Take What You Want' was the title. Andrew had been working on it for a while with Post and another guy called Billy Walsh, I believe. All it needed were the vocal melodies added. Andrew also mentioned they were gonna try and get the rapper Travis Scott to do a verse. As with Post, I didn't know much about Travis at the time, and obviously hip-hop ain't exactly my thing. But when I looked him up, I realised he's more than just a rapper. He has this dark, futuristic sound, with a kind of crazy mosh-pit energy to it. Kelly told me his video for 'Sicko Mode' got more than a billion views.

When it was time to do the recording, Post couldn't be there in person, 'cos he'd just come off a tour, but he was on FaceTime with Andrew while we worked. And of course, me being me, I started taking the piss, calling him 'the postman' at every opportunity. We had a good laugh, actually. I must have been there four or five hours. The thing with Andrew was, once we finished nailing down the vocal melody, he didn't need me to do fifty takes like Rick Rubin would. If you know what you want, that's just not necessary. We got it done in just two or three takes, I believe.

Afterwards, or maybe it was another night, me and Kelly took Andrew out to celebrate at this Italian place. For some reason Andrew wanted to order the same thing as me, so I got him some real rock star food – spaghetti with this ridiculously heavy cream sauce and two scoops of caviar.

'So why is this rock star food?' he asked when he was halfway through.

''Cos it costs a fortune and it'll kill you,' I told him.

Seriously, though, I'll forever be thankful to

Andrew – and to Post – for lifting my head above the clouds at one of the lowest points of my life. I'd been lying in my own self-pity for so long, but the second I started working again, I felt the darkness start to lift. I mean, I was still in pain. I still couldn't really walk on my own. My neck still needed support. But now that I had a distraction, some kind of purpose, it was night and day. I'd even motivated myself to start doing Pilates three times a week. Meanwhile, I was sleeping much better thanks to some CBD oil.

'I can't believe you just did that,' said Kelly on our way home from the restaurant.

'Did what?' I said.

'Smiled.'

'What are you talking about?'

'Dad,' she said, 'that's first time I've seen you smile in at least six months.' Then her face lit up. 'Y'know what? You and Andrew should do an album!'

I wasn't gonna argue.

If you're on a roll, why stop?

Once the album plan was official, Andrew got together with Duff McKagan from Guns N' Roses and Chad Smith from the Chili Peppers to jam out twelve song ideas. They'd all just played a benefit together, apparently, so they had a bit of chemistry going. Even so, I couldn't believe it when they came back just four days later and said they'd written the bones of the material. I mean, I've been holed up in country houses where nothing's happened for months before *bang*, the first good idea comes out.

So off I went back to Andrew's studio to finish the

writing and do the recording. We were there for about three weeks. 'Cos I had to sit most of the time, Andrew bought me this fabulous crushed-velvet wingback chair with a psychedelic flower pattern on it. In return, I brought along my old ARP 2600 synth, the same one we used on the Sabbath albums *Vol. 4* and *Sabotage*. The thing's about the size of a semi-detached house, with all these patch cables coming out of it, and it's got an original Black Sabbath sticker on the back. I've no idea how the fuck it works. I didn't even know how it worked in the seventies – I was on acid every time I played it.

I'd honestly never felt so excited about making a record since *Blizzard of Ozz*. Andrew really understood that balance of heaviness and melody I was going for. He called it 'evil Beatles'. And the crazy thing is, after our first day in the studio, before we had any song titles, lyrics or even finished music, me and Andrew both went away and jotted down some ideas for concepts while we were at home. When we came back into the studio the next day, I'd written down the line 'I'm just an ordinary man', while Andrew had written down 'I don't want to die an ordinary man'.

Talk about a song that was meant to be.

As we started working on it more, we got this idea about a guy like me who'd come from a working-class background, he'd become famous very quickly, and he's singing the song at the end of his life, looking back, not sure how or why he's still alive, and he's hoping he won't die penniless and unknown, like how he started out. Meanwhile, the melody was based around this very stately, very seventies-sounding piano riff. As Andrew was playing it, I was like, 'Y'know who'd be perfect on this?

The rocket man – Elton John.' I mean, the song could have been about either of our lives. We'd both grown up in piss-poor parts of England after the war, and we'd both gone from absolutely nothing to more than you could ever imagine in a very short space of time. It's a pretty small club, the people who've seen those extremes in their lives.

When I mentioned it to Sharon, she just said, 'Why don't you ask him?'

A few days later, Elton was in a studio in Atlanta with Andrew, Slash was doing the guitar solo and I was pinching myself. I can't even put into words how much it meant to me to do a song with Elton. The guy's a living fucking legend. When the final version was done – the last step was Andrew flying over to Abbey Road to add an orchestra – everyone I played it to would just start sobbing. I was like, 'It's not *that* bad, is it?'

The title of the song – 'Ordinary Man' – also became the title of the album.

I'm so grateful to everyone who appeared on *Ordinary Man*. My old friend Tom Morello from Rage Against the Machine was on there, doing guitar on 'Scary Little Green Men' and 'It's a Raid', another song with Post Malone.

Since Post was such a big Sabbath fan – and we'd put the trusty old ARP 2600 back into service – 'It's a Raid' was inspired by the making of *Vol. 4* in Bel Air. This would have been the summer of 1972 – the absolute height of our coked-up period, when we were getting wax-sealed vials of the stuff from Pablo Escobar via some bent LA customs officer. Anyway, one afternoon, I was sitting there in this mansion we were renting, I had a spliff in one hand, a beer in the other, and there was this huge glass bowl of coke on the coffee table. And it was getting a bit hot, so

I got up to adjust the air-conditioning. But just as I'm sitting back down, I hear the unmistakable wail of sirens echoing through the canyon, and next thing I know, five cop cars are screeching into the driveway. I'm like, *fuck, we're being busted.*

'It's a raid! It's a raid!' I start screaming, and suddenly everyone's running around in their underpants, hair on end, trying to hide all our shit. Tony legs it upstairs. Bill and Geezer bolt out the back door. And me and this roadie grab the bowl of coke and lock ourselves in the downstairs bog. But as we're trying to flush the stash down the toilet, the pipe backs up, and the only thing left to do is get down on all fours and snort the evidence.

Meanwhile, the cops are banging on the door, screaming at us to open up, and a few moments later the maid answers, and I hear this officer say, 'Is everything okay, ma'am? Someone pressed the emergency call button.'

At this point my nose was bleeding and my eyeballs were throbbing so hard I thought they were gonna pop. But when I heard the words 'emergency call button', I froze. Suddenly I knew exactly what had happened. Instead of adjusting the air-conditioning, I'd accidentally hit the panic button on the wall, which had automatically called the cops. They thought we were in the middle of a robbery or something.

I remember standing there, frozen – my face a mask of white powder, like the roadie's – until I heard the officer apologise to the maid for disturbing her, followed by the sound of the cop cars leaving.

How much of the coke we got through, I've no idea.

But I didn't sleep for what felt like a year.

*

It was an education, being back in the studio. Even compared with the way we made *13* back in 2012, holy shit, it was completely different. Everything's done on this one app now, Pro Tools. It's wham-bam-thank-you-ma'am. It's McDonald's music. I saw Andrew do things in a few seconds that would have taken Sabbath three years, a million quid and a pound of cocaine to do. And even then we probably wouldn't have got it done, 'cos we'd have been too busy fucking around, trying to spray-paint each other's dicks blue or whatever.

It made me think back to all the other times I'd been in the studio over the years – what I'd done right, what I'd fucked up, what I'd do again if I could.

The albums I made the fastest, *Blizzard of Ozz* and *Diary of a Madman*, were also my best, I think. *Bark at the Moon* was also okay, and gave me a couple of hits. The thing I remember most about *Bark at the Moon*, though, was being in training for the tour. I was running every day, getting fit, eating better, not drinking so much. It was fun, being a health freak for a while. And when I look back at the tapes of those shows, I was in amazing shape. For the first three or four gigs, anyway. The problem is, you can't keep that up. Or at least I can't. I'll set myself a goal, then I'll reach it, then I'll be like, okay . . . *what do I do now?* In the case of *Bark at the Moon*, the answer was get shitfaced and eat pizza. Which was exactly what I did. By the end of the tour, I was in Betty Ford.

There's a limit to how quickly you can work in the studio, of course. Go too fast, and you'll fuck it up. I learned that lesson the hard way with 'S.A.T.O.' on *Diary of a Madman*.

I was just being lazy the day we recorded 'S.A.T.O.' I

can't remember why I was so desperate to get out of the studio. I probably just wanted to go back to the Plough, the cosy old English pub around the corner. So I did a couple of takes and called it a day, even though I was singing a bit behind the riff. What I didn't realise, of course, is when you do a half-arsed take like that, every time you hear that song, *for the rest of your life*, you're gonna say to yourself, fuck, I could have done a better job of that. Which is very much the case with 'S.A.T.O.' I wince every time it comes on.

Ever since, I've always been very conscious not to leave the studio too quickly when I'm making an album. I'll say to the producer, I'm here, I ain't going anywhere, and I'll keep doing this until you tell me you've got it.

That said, sometimes the vocal ain't the problem. Sometimes no matter how many hours you spend in the booth, it won't make any difference. I feel that way about *The Ultimate Sin*, which had 'Shot in the Dark' on it. Ron Nevison produced that, right after he'd done Heart's comeback album. It could have been a good record, too, but it just didn't have any personality. It wasn't meaty enough. Every track had that same late-eighties treatment – it needed more imagination. I also felt like Ron was producing it between other artists. The one good thing about it was Jake E. Lee, who played some great guitar on there. It also did well commercially, or so I'm told. But to me, it's hands down the worst album I ever made.

As for the most difficult album – or the most irritating – that was *Ozzmosis*. It was the follow-up to *No More Tears*, which had come out in 1991 and been a huge hit. So there was a lot of pressure to live up to that. It was also my 'coming out of retirement' album, which added to the importance of making sure it didn't go down like a wet turd.

The producer was Michael Beinhorn, who was known at the time for his work with the Chili Peppers and Soundgarden. It was like working with a torturer. I remember he had this line of mics, and he'd say, okay Ozzy, sing in that one, then that one, then that one. For every line. Of every song.

This would have been at Electric Lady Studios in Greenwich Village, then up at Bearsville in Woodstock. The demands the guy would make were unbelievable. At the very end of a day's work, he'd convince you to do ten more takes, then he'd go, y'know what, your voice sounds tired, let's try again tomorrow. But you already knew that the next day, he'd be like, Ozzy, your voice doesn't sound the same as it did yesterday, we need to start over. By the end of it, I was ready to retire again.

To be fair, I do like *Ozzmosis*. Geezer was on there playing bass – the only time he ever appeared on any of my solo albums, I'm pretty sure. And it's got 'See You on the Other Side' on it, with lyrics by Lemmy. It did well, too, selling a few million copies. Which was just as well, 'cos there came a point during the recording, no kidding, when it nearly killed me.

The problem was, I'd been sipping neat vodka to get through Beinhorn's torture sessions. And as they dragged on, I was getting through more and more of the stuff, maybe a bottle a day. Then once I got back to my hotel – I was staying at my usual haunt, the Peninsula in Midtown – I was getting stuck into this bottle of pure liquid codeine I'd scammed off an ear, nose and throat doctor. I'd convinced myself it was the only way I could calm my mind and get myself to sleep.

Now, obviously, it ain't a very clever combination, vodka and codeine. But like all addicts, I thought I could handle it . . . until one night, when I was lying there in my bed I suddenly realised I couldn't breathe.

It was absolutely terrifying. There I was, gasping and gurgling, my heart beating so fast, while in my head I was saying, *God, if you exist, please don't let me suffocate, please don't let this be the way I leave this world.* I knew that suppressed breathing could be a side effect of codeine. But it had never happened to me before, so I'd just assumed it never would.

I came *that* close, man.

It scared the living shit out of me.

If Sharon was with me that day, I don't remember. But my old assistant was there. When he realised what was happening − I'd asked him to come and check on me every so often − he called the doctor who'd given me the codeine and kept him on the line most of the night. Whether the guy came over and shot me up with something to wake me up, I don't know. But I do know I never did vodka and codeine again.

The truth is, every day I was abusing opioids, I could have died. At one point I'd built up such a tolerance I was taking nine Lorcets at once to get a buzz. I mean . . . that'll do it. Meanwhile, after the near miss with the codeine, I switched to barbiturates 'cos I thought they were safer. Those are the same drugs they use for euthanasia and lethal injections, which goes to show how fucked up my definition of 'safer' was. Especially since my tolerance to barbiturates was almost as high as it was to opioids.

By the time we finished *Ozzmosis*, I'd reached the point

where even the dodgiest doctors were reluctant to give me the quantities of pills I was asking for. They didn't think I was trying to get high. They thought I was trying to kill myself. I remember this one guy looking me in the eye and going, 'Mr Osbourne, you're asking me for one hundred Seconals. You need to tell me honestly, are you trying to commit suicide?'

'If I wanted to kill myself, I'd be dead already,' I said. 'What I'm trying to do is *relax*.'

'Take What You Want' dropped at the end of October. I already knew it was a great song. But you can never tell how a single's gonna do once it's out there. I shouldn't have worried, though. It was a proper hit, getting to number eight on the US chart and selling two million copies, whatever they count as a sale these days, now that everyone just streams music straight into their frontal lobes. According to Sharon, it was my first American top-ten hit in thirty years, which broke some kind of record. The last time was with 'Close My Eyes Forever', the duet I did with Lita Ford. Back home in the UK, meanwhile, the song made it to number twenty-two.

While the song was everywhere, it seemed like the right time to give an update to the fans. This time, though, I put out a video message, not a press release. 'As you probably know, or you may not know, at the beginning of this year, I had a bad fall,' I said. 'I screwed all the vertebrae in my neck and had to have surgery. I'm not dying, I'm recovering – it's just taking a little bit longer than everyone thought it would. I'm bored stiff of being stuck on a fucking bed all day. I can't wait to get off my arse and get going again. But you're just gonna have to be a little bit more patient. I'm not retiring – I've still got gigs to do – but when I do come back on tour, I wanna be one hundred per cent ready to come out and knock your fucking socks off. Also . . . there's a new album on the way.'

I ended it by thanking my band, my crew, our promoters Live Nation, and Judas Priest, who'd been incredibly understanding about the endless delays. The North American shows were still set for May of 2020, I said – just a few months away – but the European leg would be put back from January to October. I signed off by saying, 'I just wanna say one thing to the fans. I sincerely thank you for your patience and your loyalty. I love you. Now . . . will you fuck off and let me get better.'

The best part of releasing 'Take What You Want' was going back on stage for the first time since my New Year's Eve show at the Forum – even if it was just for a few minutes. That was thanks to Post, who asked if I wanted to make a guest appearance when he played there at the end of November.

It was weird going back to the Forum as a different man than the one I'd been ten months earlier. As I stumbled in there with my cane and my nurse by my side, trying so hard just to put one foot in front of another, it was hard not to think about all the things I'd lost in such a short space of time. But it was an honour to be invited, it really was. And I knew it was gonna give us some killer footage for the official music video.

It was wild being back in the action after spending so long either at home or in a hospital bed. I'd forgotten how much noise and chaos there is backstage at a show. There must have been a thousand and one people milling around. I was like, why the fuck does anyone want a backstage pass when they could be out front with a nice seat and a bar right next to 'em?

Post came to say hello after I arrived. We'd only seen each other on FaceTime before. His real name's Austin, I learned. Andrew was there too.

He's actually a very quiet man, Austin, very respectful, very easy to be around. I mean, his face tattoos are a bit over the top, but everyone's doing that shit now. Like I said before, an arm tattoo just ain't cutting it any more. Everyone wants the next outrageous thing. There's no mistaking the guy for anyone else, that's for sure. He was also wearing this bright pink short-sleeved suit with bats on it, which was a nice touch.

I got a bad case of the old stage fright before I went on, but it couldn't have gone better. I was wearing my neck brace, but it was carefully hidden, and they put me on this giant wheeled throne thing, so I wouldn't have to walk. But I managed to get to my feet a couple of times.

It was a great night. I was moved to be up there, actually. I think it meant a lot to Post, too. And of course Andrew's guitar solo was phenomenal. Then at the end they both gave me a hug as all these pyrotechnics went off.

A few days later, we did the same thing again, but for the American Music Awards. Travis Scott was there for that one, but we didn't get to hang out. Unlike the show with Post, it was lip-synched, which I don't love.

The funny thing is, when people realised I'd done a song with Post and Travis – who are both forty years younger than me – they kept asking what kind of life advice I'd given 'em. I suppose it's 'cos they've both had their fair share of controversies to deal with in the press, like I have over the years.

But here's the thing, man. Why would anyone want life advice from *me*? Also, people are gonna do what they're gonna do, no matter what you tell 'em. When you're feeling all right and having a good time with your mates, and someone says, 'If I were you, son, I wouldn't do all those drugs and smoke those cigarettes,' you're never gonna go, 'Oh, okay then.'

I don't know much about Travis, but I've seen photographs of Post out on the town, and he looks like he's enjoying himself. If I were him, I'd be doing exactly the same thing. I mean, to be honest with you, until I was seventy I had the best life in the world. I can't complain. I had seventy great fucking years – which is a lot longer than I ever expected or probably deserved.

Which is my way of saying, people should do what they've gotta do, man. And more important than that, they should make sure to have some fun while they're at it – 'cos you never know when or how your ride's gonna end.

By the time the new year came around – it was now January 2020 – I knew I had to explain myself properly to the fans. Even after my appearance at the Forum, the rumours about my health were getting crazier and crazier. The website RadarOnline was saying I was on a 'crazy train to death' while the good old *National Enquirer*, not exactly known for its subtle headlines, had declared I'd be 'dead by Christmas'.

I suppose part of me had hoped I'd have a miracle recovery, and I'd just pop back up, fitter than ever. But it was clear by now that wasn't gonna happen. Even my physiotherapist had told me there wasn't much more she could do. My floppy neck could be hidden, to some extent, with a smaller brace. But I still couldn't lift my head properly 'cos the pain was too much. And there was no hiding the fact I could barely walk more than a couple of steps. Especially not since I'd be going to the Grammys with Sharon to announce one of the winners, then promoting *Ordinary Man* when it came out a month later. The launch campaign would include a party at the Rainbow Bar and Grill on the Sunset Strip, then a signing at Amoeba Records, the massive record shop on Hollywood Boulevard.

It was time to come clean. Or clean-ish, anyway, 'cos I didn't wanna get into the details of my failed stage-dive onto the bed in the middle of the night.

I suppose another thing I wanted to get on the record was that I have Parkinson's disease. Although I'd talked about having Parkinsonian syndrome before, a lot of people still didn't know. They just assumed the way I walked and talked was all down to the booze and the drugs. Which was fair enough, I suppose. But it wasn't the truth. And there were times when people thought I was fucked up or half senile when I wasn't.

The worst case of that was at the Grammys back in 2014, when Sabbath won best metal performance. It meant a lot to us, that award, 'cos we'd been looked down on and shit on by the critics since *Black Sabbath* came out, and now finally we were getting some recognition. So me, Tony and Geezer agreed we'd get up there on stage together to accept it. And 'cos we were there, the Grammys people asked if the three of us would introduce a live performance of Ringo Starr singing 'Photograph', the big seventies hit he wrote with George Harrison.

The idea was, I'd say a line, Geezer would say a line and Tony would say a line. But I said mine three times without even knowing it, which made Geezer fall about laughing. When I watched it back, I looked like a fucking halfwit. What made it so much worse was I was introducing a Beatle, one of my heroes.

It wasn't the Parkinson's that made me blank out, it was the drugs I take for it. They're very good at controlling tremors, but the main side effect is short-term memory loss. When I was up there on stage, I ain't kidding, I had no idea what Geezer was laughing about. If you look closely, you can see this moment of total confusion on my face. That's what happens. I'll forget what I'm saying when I'm halfway through saying it. It makes me seem like I'm nuts. Which, okay, I am. But not in *that* way.

I was so embarrassed when I came off stage. And pissed off too, 'cos I *knew* it was gonna happen. I'd said to Sharon before I went up there, 'I can't make speeches any more, I can't do this.' And she went, 'Of course you can, it's only one line, you'll be fine.' I think she was expecting me to go ballistic when it was over. But I didn't say a word. The clip that went viral the next day spoke for itself, y'know? And she must have got the message, 'cos she never tried to convince me to make a speech again.

Anyway ... it had now been six years since that fuck-up, and 'cos I was going back to the Grammys, Sharon thought we should make the announcement about my health a few days before. So the two of us went to the set of *Good Morning America* in New York's Times Square to be interviewed by Robin Roberts about my spine problems and dodgy PARK2 gene.

'A year ago this month, I was in a shocking state,' I told Robin once the cameras were rolling. 'I'd had a bad fall.

Then I had to have surgery on my neck, and that screwed my nerves up. I also found out I have a mild case of—'

'PARKINSON'S DISEASE IS A NEURODEGENER-ATIVE DISORDER THAT PROGRESSES SLOWLY IN MOST PEOPLE, BUT, AS OF NOW, HAS NO CURE,' went this booming voiceover. I was like, yeah, cheers.

I was happy Sharon was there, 'cos she could go into more detail. She explained that research on the PARK2 mutation I've got is limited, 'cos everyone has a different experience with the disease, and it's a pretty rare thing, so drug companies don't want to spend a lot of dough on research for new treatments. 'There are so many different types of Parkinson's,' she said. 'It's not a death sentence by any stretch of the imagination, but it does affect certain nerves in your body. It's like you have a good day, a good day ... then a really bad day.' With that, she suddenly welled up and got very emotional. 'Ozzy loves to perform,' she said. 'It's the air that he breathes. And this is the longest he's ever been home. And it's time for him to get back on the road ... because he's driving me *mad*.'

That part made her laugh, at least. 'He needs to get out now,' she said, 'he *really* does.'

We don't always agree, my wife and I.

But believe you me, we did on that.

The day of the Grammys started with some seriously fucked-up news. A helicopter carrying the basketball player Kobe Bryant had crashed in the hills near my old house in Hidden Hills. Nine people were missing, including Kobe's thirteen-year-old daughter. The helicopter had come down in thick fog, setting half the mountain on fire. The only way the rescue crew could get to the wreckage was to hike there, or so the local news was saying. Later on, the LA Fire Department said no survivors had been found.

It was so sad, man. Kobe was like the face of LA, 'cos he'd been the star player of the LA Lakers for so long. The whole city was in shock. Even today, whenever a police chopper goes over my house, the first thing I think of is Kobe.

By the time we got down to the Staples Center at about four o'clock for the red-carpet thing, the crash was all anyone was talking about. It was crazy that it had happened just a few hours before. Even crazier, the Staples Center – or the Crypto.com Arena, as it is now – was where Kobe had played for more than twenty years. When Alicia Keys started the show by coming out and saying everyone was 'heartbroken in the house that Kobe built', there wasn't a dry eye in the house. Meanwhile, quite a few people wore his number twenty-four jersey when they got up on stage.

But then the ceremony went from sad to weird.

Me and Sharon had been asked to announce the winner of the Best Rap/Sung Performance. Why the fuck they'd given us that category, I've no idea – maybe 'cos I'd just done the song with Post and Travis Scott. Or maybe they just wanted to hear Sharon read out all these rappers' names in her very prim and proper English accent. All I had to do was stand there and not embarrass myself. I hadn't heard of most of the nominees. Lil Baby? Young Thug? Mustard? I'd heard of the winners, though – DJ Khaled with John Legend and a rapper called Nipsey Hussle, who'd been murdered in LA the previous year, according to Sharon.

I was happy to see Legend when he came up on stage. I knew Kelly was friends with him. He'd sent me a seventieth birthday message. But the strangest thing was, he just kind of blanked us. I was baffled.

It turned out he was pissed off with Sharon 'cos she'd criticised him for rewriting the lyrics to that Dean Martin Christmas song, 'Baby, It's Cold Outside'. In the original version – which I'm told was written by the old Tin Pan Alley guy Frank Loesser – it's a bloke flirting with a girl at the end of the night, trying to get her to stay, and she's playing along with it. But the way Legend had rewritten it, inspired by the whole MeToo thing, the bloke's basically offering to call her an Uber home instead.

Now, personally speaking, I couldn't give a fuck that he rewrote the lyrics. Who cares? It's a Christmas song, they're all hokey. When Busta Rhymes told me he'd changed the lyrics to 'Iron Man', I didn't walk out of the studio, I sang the new chorus with him. Although I suppose that was a bit different, 'cos I was the original singer and he'd asked for my permission.

But whatever, Sharon didn't like the idea of someone messing with a classic when the guy who wrote it was fifty years in his grave. She was entitled to her opinion. She was also on a TV show where her *job* was to have an opinion. So when I realised Legend was giving us the cold shoulder for that, I was like . . . *seriously*? If he had something to say to Sharon, why didn't he just have the balls to say it? The thing is, I've been in this game longer than him, and I've seen a lot of people become Mr Celebrity of the Month and start giving people the deep-freeze treatment. But I learned the hard way you should never forget the old rule:

be nice to people on your way up, 'cos you'll meet 'em
again on your way back down.

What you realise when you get to a certain age is, every
few years, like clockwork, the mood of the planet changes.
You can never tell exactly when or how it's gonna happen,
but it always does. Next thing you know, a song that was
perfectly okay for sixty years – like the Dean Martin version of 'Baby, It's Cold Outside' – is suddenly the worst
thing ever made.

I've gotta say, though, I'm glad I'm not young and
dating in 2025. It's a different ball game now. I don't know
how people fall in love and get married any more, to be
honest with you. There are so many rules. You've gotta be
careful what you say, when you say it, how you say it. And
if you hit on anyone, God help you, especially if you're a
well-known name. One wrong move and it's game over.

On the other hand, it's good that a few monsters got
exposed. Take Jimmy Savile. Back in the old days, you
were just supposed to look the other way while he was
making his stupid yodelling noises and licking people's
arms, or whatever the fuck he was doing to get his thrills.
I can't even look at pictures of Savile now. Just the sight
of the guy makes my skin crawl. And to think Margaret
Thatcher had lunch with him at Chequers – and apparently invited him over for Christmas dinner every year.
And all those royal functions he went to when no one
knew what he was doing under the table. *Jim'll Fix It*? Oh,
he'll fucking fix it all right.

What a creep.

But then of course the police went nuts for a while, ar-
resting people all over the place. It's always one extreme or

the other. Poor old Freddie Starr was destroyed by it. The case against him got dropped, I believe. But he was never the same again. Eventually he was found dead at his house in Spain from a heart attack. I'm told he was so broke, there was no money to bring his body back home. A fan who was an undertaker eventually paid for it. But he kept his sense of humour until the end. His coffin had 'Return to Sender' on it. Meanwhile, the BBC had to apologise to Cliff Richard and pay him damages 'cos of the way they treated *him*, which was also unbelievable. I met Cliff once, at that Party at the Palace thing. It was one of them full-circle moments for me, 'cos the first song I ever performed was 'Living Doll'. I can't remember whether I told him that or not, I just remember him being an incredibly nice guy.

In the world of metal, it was definitely harder for some than others when all that sexist shit went out of style. Personally, I just never did any of that stuff. I wasn't singing about trying to get my end away with strippers, I was singing about Aleister Crowley and suicide and nuclear war. The closest I got to a sexy album cover was me in a werewolf costume.

There was temptation out there, of course. Some women would come up to you and be like, 'I wanna go with a rock star.' But you've gotta remember, I was a drunk. Women would run away from me. I ain't trying to cover my tracks. When I was fucked up, I was frightening. Besides, Sharon was on the road with me most of the time, so there weren't exactly many opportunities. Most nights, my only lover was the bottle.

The only other thing I'll say about the way times have changed is that the kind of people who start wagging their finger at you tend to be the biggest hypocrites.

At the height of *The Osbournes*, for example, Bill Cosby
went on *Access Hollywood* and said, 'Let me tell you something about Ozzy Osbourne. This is a sad, sad family. It's
a sad case. The children are sad and the parents are sad.
And this is not entertainment.' Then he said laughing at
The Osbournes was like laughing at Tiny Tim, the crippled
kid from *Scrooge*. He even wrote us a letter, saying our
foul language set a bad example to children. I mean ...
this was *Bill Cosby*! That he had the balls to lecture us
about profanity while he was doping half of America is
unbelievable.

The way I look at it, if you're in the music game for long
enough, the best way to survive is, one, keep your sense of
humour, and two, never, *ever* fall into the trap of believing
your own bullshit. Because that's fatal, every time.

For me, the *Spinal Tap* movie was a wake-up call. It
came out in 1984, I believe, right after *Bark at the Moon*.
I don't remember *where* I saw it, but I remember thinking
to myself, wow, this is the most interesting and relatable
documentary I've ever seen. Then when someone said
they were taking the piss, I was like ... *what? But why's
any of this funny?*

It was so well done, man.

Honest to God, I've lived basically every scene in that
movie.

The thing is, if you grew up in a council house in
England, didn't get much of an education, and you're
thrown into that world when you're young, you think
you know it all. But of course you ain't got a fucking clue.

Take stage props. Right after I left Sabbath, Tony and
the guys came up with the idea of taking a model of
Stonehenge out on the road with them. But their manager

gave the set builders the dimensions in metres, not feet. And no one checked, 'cos no one had a PhD in set building, like they do today. In the end, their Stonehenge came out so big – fifty feet tall, apparently – they could barely get it through the doors of even the biggest arenas. Whoever wrote *Spinal Tap* basically took that story but turned it upside down, so the model Stonehenge in the movie came out in miniature.

Meanwhile, the amps that go to eleven reminded me of the first time Sabbath ever went to America. For some reason, we didn't think they'd have PAs like they did in England, so we took about fifty speaker columns with us. We didn't even put 'em in flight cases. We just checked 'em in as excess baggage. And of course half of 'em ended up in the wrong cities, while the other half arrived in New York in lots of very small pieces. Not that it mattered, 'cos when we got to the first gig and plugged in our amps . . . nothing happened. That's when we realised the electricity in America runs at half the voltage that it does in England. We didn't get past the first note before we had to go out and rent a whole new system.

Of all the scenes in *Spinal Tap*, though, the one that really hit home was the 'Hello Cleveland' bit. That bit when the band walks through this maze of tunnels, making wrong turn after wrong turn, hitting dead ends, ending up on a building site, all while trying to find the stage. Believe you me, there's *nothing* like that panic when you realise you're lost under some arena, and you're jogging up and down corridors, all sweaty and out of breath, while the crowd's out there wondering if you're ever gonna show up. I've been there so many times, man. I've also been stuck inside malfunctioning equipment. I've been lost in dry ice. Pretty much every scene in *Spinal Tap* was just another day at work for me.

So yeah, for a lot of us in metal, it took a while to get the joke with *Spinal Tap*. Especially since the whole fake-documentary thing was pretty new at the time. But you've gotta laugh, man, you really have. Because if you take yourself too seriously in this game, you're gonna end up losing the plot.

Three days before the release of *Ordinary Man*, we officially cancelled the North American leg of *No More Tours II*. Not postponed. Cancelled. I can't tell you how much I hated the fact we had to do it. But if we'd pushed back the shows, it would have been the third time in a row. That didn't seem fair on the fans. As much as I didn't want to believe my touring career was over, I also didn't want people to feel like they were being strung along.

After my guest appearance at Post's show, and how knackered I was after my night at the Grammys with Sharon, it was obvious I wasn't in any state to be doing a two-hour gig every night for weeks or months on end. My movement was still too limited. I was still in too much pain. And my physical therapy just didn't seem to be working. There were days it felt like I was getting worse, not better. Whenever I tried to move my head, I still had the horrible feeling I was somehow *re-injuring* myself, not making the muscles stronger.

The way I saw it, the cancelled North American dates gave me eight months, give or take, to get back on track before the European leg of the tour, which was still due to start in October. The idea was, I'd use the break to get the second opinion on my spine I should have asked for a year earlier. Then, if any corrective surgery was needed, I'd have time to get it done and go through whatever new physical therapy was needed. In the meantime, I could work on managing my Parkinson's. Sharon had booked me into some high-tech clinic in Panama to get stem cell treatment. After that, in April, I'd be seeing a professor in Switzerland who'd invented a kind of immunotherapy for people with the mutated PARK2 gene. It would take six to eight weeks, apparently, and involve using an IV drip to flood my system with special antibodies they'd made in a lab.

It was a relief, honestly, to finally have a plan. And although I felt terrible about cancelling an entire leg of a tour, at least I wasn't pretending any more. From here on, there'd be no more secrets about my health.

On Instagram, I wrote:

I'm so thankful that everyone has been patient because I've had a shit year. But I don't want to start a tour and then cancel shows at the last minute. I'd rather people get a refund now and when I do the tour down the road, everyone who bought a ticket for these shows will be the first ones in line to purchase tickets at that time.

Within moments of the statement going out, the support from the fans was just overwhelming. It meant the world to me, it really did. And it made me even more determined to recover by October, so I could play the nineteen gigs we had planned for Europe, including a night at the O2 in London I'd been looking forward to since *No More Tours II* began.

I also thought, fuck it, since *Ordinary Man* had come

out so well, why not do another one? People say they write the best material when they're unhappy, and that had certainly been true for me. The last year had been the unhappiest I'd ever been, and *Ordinary Man* had been my best album in ages. So I asked Andrew if he was up for it – he was – and that was it, deal done. We had so much momentum from the last album – and so many ideas left over for new songs – we just carried on where we'd left off.

The one thing that really took me by surprise about the cancelled shows was how much the press picked up on it. CNN were doing breaking news on it, it was all over the BBC back home, even *Variety* and the *Hollywood Reporter* ran stories. And of course all the music sites were doing stories too, with everyone and their mother weighing in. It was crazy. I mean, as much as it sucked to see 'Ozzy cancels tour' splashed all over the news, it was good to know people still cared.

Meanwhile, it hadn't occurred to me that the guys in Sabbath were totally in the dark about everything until the *Good Morning America* interview and the news about the tour. Like everyone else, they thought I'd just had a bad case of the flu after the New Year's Eve Ozzfest. But now they were seeing all these stories about my Parkinson's and my fall at home, not to mention all the cancelled gigs, and they were like, *what the fuck's going on with Ozzy?* So, one by one, they reached out. I don't re-member the order. But Tony called. Geezer got in touch via the accountant we share in London, although it took a while for his messages to get through. And best of all, I got a text from Bill.

It had been years since me and Bill had last talked.

Almost a decade. The blow-up over the *13* album had been the biggest falling-out we'd ever had.

It was the greatest feeling in the world, hearing from my old bandmates. In a crazy way, I care about those guys more than I care about my own brothers and sisters. Whenever there's trouble, we circle the wagons. After they fired me, we didn't speak for the longest time. But then there was a medical emergency in Geezer's family, and suddenly all the arguments were forgotten and we were there for him, like brothers again. Whenever we think any of us need each other for any reason, we have this camaraderie that just kicks in automatically. None of us gets special treatment. We're all equals in this club. And we're all in it until the end. To be in your seventies and have that kind of unbreakable bond with people you've known since you were a kid, it's a very special thing.

I ain't ashamed to say I shed a tear when I spoke to Bill. 'We may have all got ripped off, Bill,' I said, 'but our lives were forever changed by what we did.'

'I know, Ozzy, I know,' he said. 'We're lucky guys. We can't complain.'

'I love you, y'know,' I told him.

It went very quiet for a moment on the line.

'I love you too, Ozzy, you fucking lunatic.'

That's one of the great things about getting older. Even if you're a working-class guy from Aston, you stop being as scared of showing your emotions. Because you know that if you wait too long to tell someone how much they mean to you, the chance might never come around again.

We talk all the time now, me and Bill.

And we tell each other 'I love you' at the end of every call.

10

Bang v. Whimper

A global pandemic.

Of course there was a global pandemic.

With a travel ban and a ten-month lockdown to go with it.

And all because someone in the town of Wuhan, China, supposedly ate a . . .

Fucking hell, man. Of all the bullets I've ever dodged, not catching some mutant virus from that bat in Des Moines has gotta be right up there. Until Covid came along, I had no idea that was even *possible*. I thought rabies was the biggest risk. My blood runs cold just thinking about it. Could you imagine? If I'd caused a worldwide outbreak in 1982? People would be burning effigies of me instead of Guy Fawkes.

Having said that, I have a hard time believing the pandemic really *was* started by someone eating a bat. I mean, okay, there was a 'wet market' in Wuhan, where people *supposedly* bought live bats and pangolins and whatever to make dodgy soup out of. But there was also a virus lab in the same town, just across the river. And you're seriously telling me it's the wet market that's to blame? Yeah, right. Then again, what do I know?

The first stay at home order in LA came seven days after we got back from the clinic in Panama. Like everyone else, we thought it would maybe last a week or two. Next thing we knew, all the supermarkets had been cleaned out, and the whole world had shut down. It was weirdly exciting for a minute, like living in an apocalypse movie. But when the news started coming in of people dying everywhere, the vibe in the house turned grim. What I couldn't wrap my head around was why people were panic-buying toilet paper, not food. 'Do they think we're being attacked by an army of arseholes?' I said to Sharon. It didn't make any sense.

Thanks to my Parkinson's, I was considered at high risk of Covid in those early days. If I'd caught the original strain, which went straight for your lungs, there's a good chance I would have ended up on a ventilator, or worse. That's 'cos Parkinson's affects your breathing muscles – along with all of your other muscles – which makes you more likely to come down with pneumonia, even in normal times. I've also got a bit of emphysema from my smoking days, which didn't exactly help. And of course there were no vaccines back then, and no one had any kind of natural immunity. Nowadays, Covid is weaker but more easily spread, or so I'm told, and it tends to go for your upper airways, making it less dangerous.

Our house became like the set of *The Andromeda Strain* once we got our hands on some protective gear. People were walking around wearing masks and gloves, even full-on face shields. Thanks to the constant swabbing and testing, I was putting more shit up my nose than I had since the making of *Vol. 4*. Early on, I got a false positive that said I had the virus, then ten minutes later another test said I was in the clear.

I'd had better mornings, I'll say that much.

As the weeks went by, it became horribly clear just how devastating the lockdowns were for venues, musicians and crew. People were going broke all over the place, on top of getting the virus. I tried to do my bit to help out, working with a group called Sweet Relief to raise cash for people in the music game who were struggling. I can't tell you how lucky I felt that I wasn't still out on the road, trying to make ends meet. If the pandemic had happened during the early days of Sabbath, before we made any money, we'd have been fucked.

Obviously, there was no way I was gonna fly to Switzerland for the immunotherapy thing. Even if we'd been allowed to go, we didn't wanna run the risk of getting Covid while we were away and not being allowed back in the country. Getting the second opinion on my spine also had to be postponed. Anything medical-related that wasn't urgent, you could forget about it. It was all hands on deck. I remember watching the telly with Sharon and seeing all these refrigerated trucks outside a hospital in New York, 'cos they had nowhere to put the bodies. It's easy to forget just how freaky that was. Those were some dark days, man.

By early summer, we'd sort of settled into a pandemic routine. I've gotta admit, I kind of enjoyed the silence that descended over LA. For the first time ever, you could see the stars at night. The smog disappeared. You couldn't hear any cars. Even the planes stopped flying overhead.

At some point, me and Andrew got back to work on the follow-up to *Ordinary Man*. The title we came up with was *Patient Number 9*. We were going for a mental hospital vibe, 'cos I've always been fascinated by those places. I've also been in and out of a few institutions over the years. And of course my spine injury and Parkinson's made me feel like a walking medical experiment, which also played into it.

I got really comfortable working with Andrew. He even started calling me and Sharon Mum and Dad, which was a bit cheeky. But at least he could keep his sense of humour through it all. Apart from the times he and Sharon had screaming arguments, that is – and they had a few. Although they always made up after. The pandemic was a big strain on all of us. It was easy to get dragged down, especially if you watched the news.

Meanwhile, Sharon's TV show moved to Instagram Live, so she was working again. Then after a few weeks she started using the Zoom app, and did every episode from home. By September, she was back in the studio.

In a weird way, the lockdowns didn't change much for me. I'd been in a kind of lockdown for a year already thanks to all that time in the ICU, then in bed at home. And, very selfishly, it made feel me less guilty for cancelling the tour dates, 'cos *no one* could work. Although obviously I didn't wish that on anyone, 'cos people's livelihoods were being destroyed.

To pass the time between recording sessions with Andrew, I got back into shooting air rifles in a big way. I've always had air rifles, me. But the ones in America . . .

they're *nothing* like your average .177 BSA. (If you ain't familiar, BSA stands for the Birmingham Small Arms Company, although I'm told it's now owned by an American company.) I saw this guy on YouTube take down a two-thousand-pound bison in Texas with one. They'd never let you buy a rifle that powerful in England. And if you ever tried to bring one into the country, you'd end up in prison.

Shooting has always been very therapeutic for me, ever since I lived at Bullrush Cottage. There's a picture out there somewhere of me standing in the field behind the house, looking stoned out of my mind, holding a cocked rifle with an ammo belt slung over my shoulder. English gun laws were a lot less strict in the seventies if you owned a bit of land. I'd shoot anything in those days. I sent quite a few chickens off to meet their maker, which I ain't proud of. And I blew the head off this seven-foot-tall stuffed grizzly bear my old manager gave me. I'd also buy department store mannequins, tie 'em to a tree in the garden and execute 'em at dawn. I was drunk most of the time. I was a danger to myself and to society, honestly. One time, I tried jumping over a fence with a loaded shotgun in my hand, and I almost blew my leg off. Another time, when I was on acid, I pulled a gun on Bill. The chamber was empty – I think – but he had no way of knowing that. Then I went stumbling off into the fields and had a long conversation with a horse.

The fact me and Bill survived the seventies honestly never ceases to amaze me.

I only do target practice now. I don't kill living things any more. In fact, I've become an avid animal lover. I've done some bad shit in my life to all kinds of creatures, but when you get older, you realise everything's got a right to live. I rescue animals now, including a bulldog who was set on fire by his previous owner. His name's Walter, and he's doing great. I can't tell you how happy it makes me to give an animal a good life.

During that first summer of the pandemic, I built myself a whole shooting range in my back garden. I even made my own targets, cutting out these big circles, putting the dots in the middle, mounting 'em on cardboard, putting 'em on stands. I'd spend all day out there. It drove my neighbour fucking crazy. He'd be sitting out by his pool or having a nice lunch on his patio and these big-bore air pellets would be zinging over his head. The poor bloke must have felt like he was in a war zone. Mind you, the rest of LA was so bored during the lockdowns, people were setting off fireworks at all hours. At least I wasn't firing rockets at him.

Before we knew it, six months had gone by since the lockdown began. It was coming up on October now, when the European dates of *No More Tours II* were supposed to start. But with social distancing still in force, and the Covid vaccines still not ready, there was absolutely no way anyone was gonna be playing live. Not that I was in any state to travel anyway.

We didn't want to cancel the shows, like we had the North American leg. But rescheduling 'em also seemed pointless, 'cos no one knew how or when the world would finally get back to normal. In the end, we just said the tour would start up again in January 2022. That was more than a year away. Surely, I thought, the lockdowns couldn't go on *that* long. People were already getting restless and doing crazy shit to let off steam. It felt like there'd be a revolution if they didn't let everyone get back to their regular lives. Meanwhile, with sixteen months to recover – if I kept up with the physical therapy – it seemed impossible I wouldn't be ready to hit the road by then. But of course, after all the shit we'd been through, I'd be lying if I said there wasn't some doubt in my mind.

All those months spent hobbling around in my back garden gave me a lot of time to think. And what I couldn't get out of my head was what my old friend Lemmy Kilmister used to say: 'I'd rather go out with a bang than get old.'

'Do you really mean that, Lemmy?' I asked him once.

'Fuck yeah, I mean it,' he said. 'What the point of being ninety-five if you can't *live*?'

I understood what he was getting at. But I didn't agree. I was happy to grow old as long as I had Sharon, and as long as my family wanted me around.

But now, thanks to my injury and my Parkinson's, and all the nerve pain I was having – not to mention all the cancelled shows – there were moments I wondered whether Lemmy had the right idea. I mean, what's the point of being alive if you can't enjoy it? For a long time after that first surgery, I wasn't living, I was just getting through the days. The only thing I had to think about was, when's my next pill coming up? In my darkest moments, I did wish I'd gone out with a bang rather than ending up semi-paralysed and stuck at home. If it wasn't for Sharon and my family, I honestly don't know how I could have kept going. I'd have given up.

Even though I was in a better place by now, I'd still get knocked down by depression sometimes. The thing

is, you don't realise how lucky you've been 'til you lose
the things you used to take for granted. Like being able
to use your right arm. Or just going for a stroll around
the block on your own.

Thinking about Lemmy never failed to cheer me up,
though.

I first met him when he was in Hawkwind. He played
bass and sang. A lot of people ain't that familiar with
Hawkwind, 'cos they never really broke through to the
mainstream, but they had some seriously hardcore fans.
They were big into phaser effects and all that space-rock
psychedelic stuff. But thanks to Lemmy, there was also
a bit of pre-punk in there. Sabbath shared a rehearsal
space with 'em for a while down in the Wye Valley at
Rockfield Studios. This would have been around 1973,
a couple of years before Queen went to Rockfield to
record 'Bohemian Rhapsody', which really put the place
on the map.

The thing with Rockfield is, 'cos it's on a farm in deep-
est South Wales, miles away from anywhere, you get to
know people pretty well when you're staying there. Me
and Lemmy would spend hours outside in the rain with
the livestock, smoking fags and shooting the shit while
Lemmy swigged jet fuel or whatever the fuck it was he
had in his hip flask. Even then, his voice was so rough
he sounded like he'd been gargling with ball bearings
and lighter fluid. And that was on a *good* day. He was an
original, was Lemmy. The grease-stained black T-shirt
and biker jacket. The bushy mutton-chop sideburns and
moustache. The bullet belts and cowboy boots. I don't
think I ever saw him wear anything else.

A couple of years later, Lemmy got busted at the

Canadian border for drugs – they thought his speed was cocaine, apparently – then he left or got fired from Hawkwind. That was when he formed Motörhead. Apparently, he'd wanted to call the band 'Bastard', but his management wouldn't let him, 'cos it meant they'd never get on *Top of the Pops*. Not that Lemmy was exactly *Top of the Pops* material. He got the name Motörhead from a song he'd written for Hawkwind. It meant speed freak, apparently, but Lemmy assumed the BBC types at *Top of the Pops* wouldn't know that.

He was right, they had no idea.

The greatest times I had with Lemmy were when Motörhead opened for us on my first solo tour in 1980. Everything was on the line, 'cos I'd just left Sabbath. We were playing anywhere they'd have us. Poole Arts Centre. Nottingham Boat Club. The West Runton Pavilion, wherever the fuck that was. And we blew the doors off everywhere we went, 'cos we had something to prove, and we had Randy Rhoads, who was an un-known at the time. He wouldn't stay that way for very long, of course.

Motörhead were on fire, too, 'cos they'd just done 'Ace of Spades'. That was their 'Paranoid', as far as I was con-cerned. It even got 'em on *Top of the Pops*, so it's a good job Lemmy hadn't called the band Bastard. I mean, 'Ace of Spades' is just one of the great metal anthems of all time. When that came out, I was like, okay, they've made it. They're gonna be around for ever now.

They lived like pirates, Motörhead. There were just three of 'em. Lemmy on bass and vocals. 'Fast' Eddie Clarke on lead guitar. Phil 'Philthy Animal' Taylor on drums. Their tour rider was a case of Jack Daniel's, a case of vodka and a boatload of Coke and orange juice. The rider cost more than their booking fee. Like, *a lot* more. The first thing I came to realise about those guys was, they just didn't sleep. When they finished a gig, they'd come off stage soaked with sweat, no showers, no towels, nothing, and they'd just get on their bus, open up the case of Jack and go. Then they'd drive however many hours to the other end of the country, get off and just carry on. I asked Lemmy once, 'When was the last time you went to bed, man?' And he was like, 'I dunno, ten days ago?'

It was nuts. I couldn't do it. Lemmy was the one guy I just could not keep up with. I didn't even wanna try, man. It was a catastrophic level of partying.

Actually ... there was one other guy I couldn't keep up with. André the Giant. But that was different. If you've ever seen *The Princess Bride*, he's the guy who played the seven foot four character, Fezzik. I met André when I did an appearance with the British Bulldogs wrestling team at WrestleMania, a few years after *Blizzard of Ozz*. André had a condition known as acromegaly, I believe, when you basically don't stop growing. He wasn't just tall, he was also heavy – like, five hundred pounds or something. The guy would drink *whole jugs* of vodka and cranberry – and while he was sitting there, waiting for 'em to be made, he'd get through a six-pack of beer. The guy was physically incapable of getting drunk. There's a story out there that he once drank sixteen bottles of plum wine during a four-hour bus ride, then he got off and did three wrestling matches. Having been out with him a couple of times, I don't doubt it. Sadly he didn't live very long. He died of heart failure at forty-six.

With Lemmy, on the other hand, his secret weapon was speed. Speed *and* methamphetamine, which is bad stuff, man. It'll make all your teeth fall out. I asked him once, 'Why d'you do all this speed and meth all the time?'

''Cos I like it,' he said.

'It'll kill you, y'know.'

'Life will kill you,' he shrugged, lighting up another fag. Lemmy was always lighting up another fag. It was probably the first thing he did after being born. 'I mean, okay,' he admitted, 'maybe the drugs will kill me a bit *earlier*. But what's the point of ten extra years if I'm bored shitless?'

As for why he chose speed, Lemmy said if you were gonna get high, you might as well do it with a drug that also helped you keep working. Of course, no one but Lemmy could do *anything* while taking that shit.

I tried some of it once. I was in a club, totally fucked up on booze, somewhere in London. Noddy Holder from Slade was jamming on stage. I'd known Noddy for years. He'd been Robert Plant's roadie in the early days, and Geezer knew him well. It was just one of those nights you didn't want to end. And I'm bouncing around this club at two o'clock in the morning after God knows how many hours of drinking, but the exhaustion's starting to set in. Then out of the darkness comes this dagger with some powder on the end. It's Lemmy. 'You'll probably want a bit of this,' he goes.

Fuck it, I thought, how bad can it be?

Never again. It was like snorting fucking rust filings. I felt like I'd be having nosebleeds for the rest of my life. And I didn't sleep for days. How the fuck he could put that shit up his nose every night and keep working, I've no idea.

People underestimated Lemmy, though. Because he looked like a biker, people thought he was some kind of yobbo, the kind of guy who'd get into bar brawls or steal your wallet for drug money. But he was this peaceful, educated, highly intelligent man. On that first tour we did with him, he had this little plaid suitcase, and all he had in there was a pair of knickers, a pair of socks and a pile of books on every subject you could imagine. He loved reading, Lemmy. He was like a walking *Encyclopædia Britannica*.

We got on so well with Motörhead on the British and European legs of the *Blizzard of Ozz* tour, they also joined us for the American shows. When we got to LA, we all went to stay at Don Arden's house, a big Spanish-style mansion at the top of Benedict Canyon. Howard Hughes had once owned it, apparently. Cary Grant lived in the house next door. And it had all these bungalows around the grounds for guests to stay in, like a resort. We couldn't get Lemmy out of the library. He'd just stay up all night doing speed and reading books. Don was like, 'Who the fuck is that caveman in my library? Get him out of my house!' Sharon had to explain to him that he was the lead singer of the support band.

Meanwhile, whenever Lemmy had a hangover – which was rare for him, 'cos his tolerance was off the charts – he'd say he'd had a 'heavy night on the chemistry set'.

At Don's house, I saw him emerging from his room after one of those nights. He looked like he'd been dug up after five hundred years under a slab. He stank. His eyes were redder than a bulldog's. And the first thing he said to me was, 'Fucking hell, Ozzy, if I look half as bad as you, I'm going back to bed.'

I almost called an ambulance for us both.

Many years after that *Blizzard of Ozz* tour, I bumped into Lemmy in Japan. We must have both been on tour there. It was towards the end of the eighties by then, and I was starting to write the *No More Tears* album.

'How's it going, Ozzy?' he asked.

'Not well,' I said.

'How come?'

'It's the lyrics for the new album,' I groaned.

'What d'you mean?'

'I'll know what I want a song to be about,' I told him, 'but I can never get past the first line.'

'Well, if you want . . . I'll help,' he said.

I couldn't say yes fast enough. The thing with Lemmy was, he'd read so many books, words came naturally to him. He had a gift for it, honestly. And I knew he'd written for other artists, including 'Can't Catch Me' for Lita Ford. That was on the same album as the duet I did with her, 'Close My Eyes Forever'.

On the plane back to LA after that first conversation, some guy came up to me in first class and gave me a book about a German general. I didn't have the heart to tell him I was never gonna read it. Not 'cos I wasn't interested. I love history, me. Especially anything war related. I must have watched every Second World War documentary that's ever been made. It's just my dyslexia and ADHD make reading a form of torture. Then I thought to myself, you know who'll like this? *Lemmy*.

A few days later, I went over to Lemmy's place to

give him one of the demos for the songs that needed words. He had this bachelor pad in West Hollywood just around the corner from his local, the Rainbow on the Sunset Strip. He was like the mayor of that place. He had his own seat at the bar with plaque on it that said 'Lemmy's Chair'. He'd spend hours there drinking his Jack and Cokes and playing the video poker machine in the corner. Then when it closed at two o'clock in the morning, he'd stagger back down the hill and around the corner to his place.

His apartment was something else, man. It was like one step above a squat, and one step below student accommodation. He never opened the curtains. There were ashtrays and empties all over the place. And he had Nazi shit everywhere. Hitler Youth daggers. Iron Cross flags. SS uniforms. It was like the set of *The Young Ones* crossed with the Imperial War Museum.

He wasn't a Nazi, obviously. 'I only collect the stuff, I don't collect the ideas,' he used to say. He was just fascinated by that period of history. I'm the same way, and I'm married to a Jewish woman, so I hardly share the opinions of Adolf Hitler. You've gotta remember, we grew up right after the war, so it was still a very recent memory. In Aston when I was a kid, entire streets were still in ruins after the Birmingham Blitz. In the fields, there were still concrete pillboxes everywhere, so the Home Guard could defend the country if Hitler invaded. And everyone had a friend whose dad had seen action somewhere or other. The bottom line is, if you're interested in dark subjects, the Nazis and the terrible things they did are the darkest of 'em all. That didn't mean Lemmy was going around doing *Sieg Heils* and goosestepping.

The first demo I gave him was for 'Mama, I'm Coming Home'. I'd had the melody in my head for years. Then me and Zakk had sat down at the piano and worked out the whole song. But I didn't have a clue what the words should be. 'Take a listen to this,' I said, 'and see if anything comes to you.'

Then I remembered the book I'd been given on the plane. 'Oh, and do you want this?' I said, showing him the cover. 'It's about some German bloke.'

'Okay,' said Lemmy, lighting up his seven-hundredth fag of the day, 'leave the demo with me, and yeah, I'll take the book, cheers. When do you need the lyrics?'

'As quickly as you can,' I said.

'Okay. Come back in two hours.'

'You're joking.'

'What . . . you need 'em faster?'

'What? No! Fucking hell, Lemmy. How are you gonna write lyrics in just two hours?'

'It's not *War and Peace*, Ozzy. It's a song. Give me two hours.'

'All right . . . if you say so,' I said. I didn't think he was serious. I was fully expecting to come back and find he'd written half a verse then fucked off to the Rainbow.

So I left him to it, and came back four or five hours later, just to be on the safe side.

As I walked in the door, he goes, 'Where the fuck have you been?' Then he hands me this sheet of lined paper with his lyrics carefully written out in longhand, with a couple of fag burns at the top. 'Here you go.'

I looked at what he'd written, and my mouth fell open:

Times have changed and times are strange,
Here I come but I ain't the same,
Mama, I'm coming home . . .

As anyone who's close to me knows, 'Mama' is one of my pet names for Sharon. And Lemmy had somehow managed to capture the beautiful, fucked-up madness of our relationship and our life on the road – which I'd just tested to breaking point by getting fucked up on booze and pills and attacking her one night – with these words. I got chills as I was reading it. It was like he'd been able to peer into my soul. Later on, whenever I sang the song on stage, I'd have the same reaction.

I had tears running down my face by the time I got to the end.

'Lemmy . . . I . . . I just don't know what to say,' I said.

'You don't like 'em?' He shrugged. 'That's okay, I wrote two other versions.' Then he handed me two other sets of handwritten lyrics for the same song. I just stood there, looking at 'em, in this state of total disbelief.

'Oh,' he said, 'and that book you gave me?'

'Yeah?'

'It's crap.'

'What?? You can't possibly have—'

'Here you go,' he said, shaking the fag ash off it and handing it back to me.

He'd already finished it.

Lemmy ended up writing four songs on *No More Tears*: 'Mama, I'm Coming Home', 'I Don't Want to Change the World', 'Desire' and 'Hellraiser'. Later on, he said he'd earned more in publishing royalties from those four songs than he did from his entire Motörhead career. I have mixed feelings about that. On the one hand, I was very glad he got to earn some dough. On the other, if it's true, Motörhead deserve a lot more recognition.

One of the many things I liked about working with Lemmy was that he was totally honest with his opinions. You'd play him something, and if he didn't like it, he'd go, 'That's shit!' He'd tell you straight. There was no sugar-coating with Lemmy. And he had the best sense of humour. I mean, one of his own songs was called 'Killed by Death'. As far as great titles go, that's right up there with *Death at a Funeral*, the Frank Oz movie.

After *No More Tears*, we worked together a few more times. Other than 'Mama, I'm Coming Home', the song of ours I really love – also written with Zakk's help – is 'See You on the Other Side'. It's on the *Ozzmosis* album. The title's a reference to a standing joke we had whenever we were getting fucked up – along the lines of, 'Which one of us will live to see tomorrow morning?' Mind you, a lot of people back then thought we'd live for ever. You'd hear stand-up comedians saying things like, 'What kind of world are we gonna leave for Lemmy, Ozzy and Keith Richards?'

In the end, I've gotta say, it wasn't a total surprise that I outlived Lemmy. There came a point where I slowed down. He never did. He kept the pedal to the metal, even when he could see the brick wall up ahead. His last gig was in Berlin, just a couple of weeks before he died in LA.

The last time I saw him was on a plane going to Rio. It must have been April 2015. We were doing the Ozzy & Friends tour in South America. Motörhead were part of it. Geezer and Slash were there. Lemmy was sitting up at the front, so we didn't have much of a conversation or anything. He'd dropped so much fucking weight, man. I remember him walking down the jetty thing when we got off, and his legs . . . he had his cowboy boots on, and his legs were like sticks inside.

'Yeah, I'm probably gonna die,' he said to me at one point during that trip. 'But I never thought I'd make it this far, so I did good, as far as I'm concerned.'

He was sixty-nine at the time, turning seventy on Christmas Eve.

It was cancer that got him. He was riddled with it. I saw the same thing happen to my father after a lifetime of breathing in all kinds of toxic shit at the GEC factory where he worked. But as Lemmy himself said, the fact he lasted as long as he did, when he lived his entire life like he was twenty years old, was quite an achievement. When we got back to LA, I heard from friends that his health was declining. I was texting him all the time. 'If you need anything, call me.' He'd text right back, 'Thanks for caring.'

A week before his seventieth birthday, just after he got back from Berlin, they held a concert for him at the Whisky a Go Go. Slash was there. Billy Idol. Lars Ulrich from Metallica flew in. After that, Lemmy was pretty much bedridden. Apparently, the Rainbow unplugged the video poker machine from the bar and took it over to his flat. Meanwhile, he'd cut down on the fags. He'd switched from Jack and Coke to vodka and orange juice. But he was still doing the old speed.

And he made it to seventy, God bless him. But four days later, he was gone.

I phoned him up on the day he died. I kept wanting to

talk to someone who was with him, but whoever was there just kept putting Lemmy on the line. He couldn't talk at that point. All he could do was groan down the line at me. I kept asking, 'Is Lemmy okay? Can someone give me an update?' But all I got were these groans in return. It was fucking awful. I really, truly hope he wasn't in too much pain. I had to hang up in the end. I thought to myself, I'd rather remember him as I want to remember him. It was so frustrating and sad. Then a few hours later, the news came through: we'd lost him. But he made his mark, man. The patio at the Rainbow is called Lemmy's Lounge now. There's apparently a statue of him there. And 'Ace of Spades' will never, *ever* get old. Meanwhile, he had his ashes put in bullet casings and sent out to all his friends.

God bless you, Lemmy. You were a warrior and a legend.

I'll see you on the other side.

Aside from Lemmy, I've had the privilege of hanging out with a few of the other great hellraisers in rock 'n' roll history. But what people don't realise is, in the early days of Sabbath, I was the sensible one, relatively speaking.

Take the one and only occasion I spent time with Keith Moon from The Who. I'd been invited to some charity concert in Coventry that Tony had helped organise. Moon was there 'cos Tony had made friends with him when they both played *The Rolling Stones Rock and Roll Circus* in 1968. That was during the five minutes when Tony was in Jethro Tull.

Now, my favourite thing to wear in those days was the tasselled suede shirt I'd brought home from America. I thought it was the bee's knees, that shirt. I'd wear it with

a matching suede tobacco pouch clipped to my belt, and
the necklace with a tiny coke spoon on the end. I couldn't
have been much older than twenty-three at the time. I
thought I was this sophisticated, worldly rock star. But
really I was still just a wide-eyed kid.

Moon was already pretty arseholed when we got there,
even though it was early in the day. What you've gotta
remember is, not only was he a couple of years older than
me, but he was also on a different level entirely. The Who
had been going for five years by then, and *Who's Next*
had just come out, with 'Won't Get Fooled Again' on
it. They were at their peak. On top of that, Moon was
known for being one of the craziest fuckers on the face of
the earth. Two or three years earlier, at his birthday party,
he'd driven a Lincoln Continental – then the equivalent
of a Rolls-Royce – into a Holiday Inn swimming pool.
Just for a laugh.

Moon hadn't come to the charity thing alone. He'd
brought his mate Viv Stanshall from the Bonzo Dog
Doo-Dah Band. Another stage-five nutter. This would
have been just before Stanshall did that track on Mike
Oldfield's *Tubular Bells* where he just walks around a
country house, shitfaced.

All I remember is being in the canteen of whatever this
venue was, with all these kids running around – maybe
that's what the event was for, a kids' charity – and Moon
and Stanshall were sitting on the floor, completely arseholed, falling about laughing, ripping the piss out of
anyone who walked by. I felt so intimidated by them.
They were these huge rock stars and I was still the new
kid on the block, y'know?

And of course the second I walked in there, my shirt

caught Moon's attention. He kept coming up to me and going, 'Hey man,' in this fake hippie accent. 'You look so cool in that shirt, man, you really do, man.'

Over and over again. He just wouldn't get off my case. Neither would Stanshall. Meanwhile, I was totally sober, 'cos in those days, I wasn't in the habit of getting loaded at a kids' charity event at eleven o'clock in the morning.

Eventually I managed to lose 'em, but then during the rehearsal for the gig later on, I was standing on the side of the stage and Moon spotted me. Fuck, I thought. But now, on top of doing the whole 'hey man' thing, he'd run up to me and just put his hand in my pouch. The first time, I kind of smiled and brushed him off. But he kept doing it, and doing it – finding it funnier and funnier – until eventually it really started to piss me off.

'Hey man—'

'WILL YOU JUST FUCK OFF!'

I almost decked the guy.

They were a pair of clowns, Moon and Stanshall, looking back. And I suppose they were giving me a taste of my own future medicine, 'cos it wouldn't be long before I caught up with them and became a clown myself.

They'd do all kinds of outrageous shit, I've since learned. Like dressing up in Nazi uniforms before going out on the town. Meanwhile, Moon once tried to put his waterbed in a lift, so it would explode when it got to the lobby. And of course he loved food fights and throwing TVs out of hotel windows. Also blowing up toilets with M-80 firecrackers, something I also came to enjoy . . . which I'll get to in a minute. But I wasn't in on the joke that day. And thank God for that. I mean, imagine if

Moon the Loon, Stanshall and *me* had become drinking buddies. We'd have been the dynamic trio. None of us would have lived to see 1973.

Moon was an electrifying drummer, of course. I mean, 'My Generation', fucking hell. No one was playing drums like that in 1965. He was like this wild animal, but so precise at the same time. Not that I was ever a *crazy* fan of The Who. But Pete Townshend always had a good vibe. I actually got to meet him once, at Sabbath's Rock & Roll Hall of Fame induction. We were crying with laughter, we were having such a good time.

Moon tragically didn't make it to the end of the seventies because of his accidental overdose. But in some ways, it's amazing The Who even survived the sixties. Very few bands were as famous as they were during that decade and kept it going for as long as they did. And the sixties cost a lot of people their minds. I never knew Syd Barrett from Pink Floyd – who famously went crazy, which apparently inspired their *Wish You Were Here* album – but I'll never forget the time I ran into Peter Green from John Mayall & the Bluesbreakers (and later Fleetwood Mac) at an awards show in London. What year this was, I honestly can't tell you. But I hadn't seen Green out in public for years – no one had – 'cos he'd quit the music game and become a grave digger. He wanted nothing more to do with music, apparently, so I dunno why he was even at this event. And he walks in wearing a handkerchief on his head with four knots on top.

It was just very odd. I heard from someone in the business he was still getting pretty big royalty cheques, but he kept sending 'em back to the record company, saying, 'I don't want these, fuck off.' Even a cheque for forty grand. He was like, 'You've really gotta stop sending me this shit.'

It must have been very sad for the guy's friends and family, not to mention his bandmates.

He was still there, but he was gone.

Within a couple of years of that charity thing, I was drinking far more often, and far more heavily. Any kind of event, no matter what the time of day, was an excuse to get lollied. And although I didn't see Moon or Stanshall again, I did run into John Entwistle, The Who's bass player.

I was in London, I remember. At the time I was very friendly with the comedian Billy Connolly. I'd got to know him while we were on the road, 'cos often we'd stay at the same places. This was when he was still drinking and doing powder. He gave all that shit up in the early eighties when met his wife Pam. On this occasion, though, he was still at it, and he was having a big book launch party. If I had to guess, it would have been for a collection of those comic strips he did at the time, called *The Big Yin*.

Now, in those days, I'd often while away an afternoon in London doing blow and drinking beer in our manager's office. Which is exactly what I'd just done. So by the time I got to this book launch – which started at five o'clock on a weekday – I was absolutely shitfaced. The event was on the basement level of some bar or restaurant, I remember, and I was staggering down the stairs just as Entwistle was coming up.

He stopped me as we passed. 'Do I know you from somewhere?' he asked.

'Maybe,' I said. 'I'm the singer of a band called Black Sabbath.'

He just went, 'Oh, yes,' and carried on. That was it, my one encounter with Entwistle. Next thing I knew, I was in this hot and loud basement packed full of journalists and celebrities. And suddenly I'm starting to feel absolutely knackered and next-level loaded at the same time. And I'm standing beside this huge board thing – like a frieze, maybe even displaying pages of the book, I don't know – and I'm so tired, I start to lean against it. I thought it was part of the building, not something that could fall over. And of course I go crashing right through this thing, hit the floor with a wallop, and this huge display collapses on top of me, and I'm lying there covered in bits of foam and cardboard and whatever, while the metal posts that were holding it up are rolling around the floor.

All I remember is looking up and seeing this crowd forming around me, everyone still chatting away and eating nibbles and holding their champagne glasses. Then out of the crowd comes the face of one of the most famous men on earth, the footballer Bobby Moore, who'd captained the England team back when they beat Germany in the World Cup.

'Oh, hello there,' he goes.

Then he fucks off again as I'm groaning and trying to get back to my feet.

That was the first time my drinking really started to cause me problems in public.

There was no looking back after that. I was off to the races. Although in the seventies, it wasn't so much the drinking itself that was the problem. It was the *things I did* when I was drinking. And it was during our tours of America that it all started to get out of hand.

What none of us in Sabbath could get over was how easy it was to buy cherry bombs in America, or M–80s as they were called over there. Except like everything else in America, M–80s were far, far more powerful than any kind of firework they'd ever let you buy in England. I mean, the American military would use 'em as practice bombs, they packed that much of a punch. And you could buy these things just about *anywhere*. Meanwhile, the only limit on how many you could buy in one go was how much cash you had, and how many they had in stock. The likes of Keith Moon were buying five hundred at a time. If you tried that today, they'd think you were a domestic terrorist. Except you can't buy M–80s today, 'cos they're illegal now, which in all honesty they should have been all along. I mean, yeah, they *can* be safe if you use them carefully. But no one was using 'em carefully. People used 'em to fuck around.

The first trick I learned with an M–80 was to extend the fuse wire and hook it up to something else, so the explosion would go off on a delay. For example, you could poke a hole halfway down the side of a cigarette, stick the end of the M–80 fuse wire into it, then light the cigarette and leave it in an ashtray. And of course the cigarette would eventually burn down to the fuse, which would then set off the explosive. The fucking clatter it made was unbelievable. It really does sound like a bomb going off. People would be sitting there on the sofa, smoking dope and being all seventies and mellow, talking about love and the vibration of the universe or whatever, then suddenly the whole room would shake as this mini stick of dynamite detonated under the table.

I'd laugh so hard, man. But looking back . . . what the fuck was I thinking?

I probably gave a few people PTSD.

Not to mention the damage to their eardrums.

And of course I was handling all this flash powder while I was out of my skull.

Smoke bombs were another great way to prank people. In those days, nothing was more amusing than throwing a smoke bomb into the shower while a roadie was in there singing to himself and washing his hair. At first, they'd think it was just the steam. Then suddenly they'd realise they couldn't see anything, and they'd try and get out of the shower, but they'd be walking into walls, inhaling all this smoke, totally freaking out.

We kept doing it to this one poor guy. Every single time he took a shower. And it just got funnier and funnier. He got exposed to so much smoke, all his rings turned black. That was when we realised we should probably stop.

Again . . . I don't know what we were thinking. We could have killed the fucker.

And let's not forget bottle rockets. Those things were deadly. They were like this cheap firework you'd stick in an empty pop bottle and light it. Then . . . VRRRROOOOOSSSSSSHHHH!!! It would shoot up into the sky. Then a few seconds later – BANG! I mean, you can only imagine the fun we had with those. Mainly by turning 'em sideways and firing 'em down hotel corridors. Between the bottle rockets, the M-80s and the smoke bombs, everywhere we stayed ended up looking like downtown Beirut.

Of course, not everyone saw the funny side.

I remember one time in this hotel, I had a bottle rocket in my hand and I was about to fire it down the corridor towards Bill's room when I heard—

'FREEZE, MOTHERFUCKER!'

When I turned my head, I saw a cop standing there with his gun raised . . . but it was too late: the fuse was lit and the thing went off. VRRRROOOOOSSSSSSHHHH!!! All I could do was apologise. 'Oh, I'm very sorry, offi—'

BANG!

With that, Bill bolted out of his room, screaming, running smack into a wall 'cos he couldn't see through the smoke. Then all the fire alarms went off.

I spent that night in jail.

The closest call I had, though, was in Honolulu, Hawaii.

I'd bought a whole bag of M-80s, and I had them at my feet in this rental car as a roadie was driving me around. We weren't going anywhere in particular, we were just bored and killing time before a gig, seeing the sights, smoking a bit of the local weed, drinking a few of the beers I had in a crate on the back seat. Meanwhile, to entertain myself, I was lighting the M-80s and throwing 'em out of the car window. Not the cleverest idea. But I thought it was hilarious to make the cars behind us honk and swerve as these little bombs went off in the middle of the road.

'Ozzy, stop doing that!' the roadie kept saying. 'You'll cause an accident!'

'No, I won't,' I said. BANG! 'No one's driving fast enough.' BANG! 'Heh-heh-heh.'

'Seriously, Ozzy. Just fucking stop.'

'Oh, okay then.' BANG! BANG!

'Ozzy!!'

'Heh-heh-heh.'

BANG!

I was getting tired by this point. So I was like, okay, last one. But just after I'd lit the fuse and chucked the M-80 out of the window, the roadie hits the brakes and stops the car. 'What the FUCK you are doing?!!' I said, twisting around to watch the M-80 hit the side of the kerb, bounce off it and roll under this incredibly long chromed-out old American sedan behind us, which had also stopped. Worse than that, inside the sedan I could see four heavy-set, scowling Hawaiian dudes with long hair, no shirts and what looked like prison tattoos. They were all smoking cigarettes and shooting the shit, totally unaware of what was about to happen.

'DRIVE!!!' I screamed. 'JUST FUCKING DRIVE!!!'

'It's a red light!' said the roadie. 'I told you to stop throwing those things!'

'JUMP IT!! *Jump the light before the cherry bomb goes*—'

BANG!

'Fuuuck!!!' I was sweating bullets now. Meanwhile, in the rear-view mirror, I could see smoke billowing out from under the sedan. The whole car just disappeared in this white cloud for a few seconds. Then all four doors opened and the Hawaiians got out. They looked fucking *pissed*.

'*Get down!*' I hissed to the roadie. '*Get down in your seat!*'

In the wing mirror, I watched as the Hawaiian guys started peering under their car and checking out their exhaust pipe, wondering what the fuck had caused such a loud explosion, and where all the smoke was coming from.

A few seconds passed. For a moment, I thought we were gonna get away with it. The Hawaiians were just shrugging at each other as the smoke started to blow away on the breeze. But then this young blonde American woman comes running out of a strip mall by the side of the road, waving her arms around to get their attention. And she starts pointing at me, going, 'It was HIM! He did it! HE THREW A BOMB UNDER YOUR CAR!!'

Now all four Hawaiian dudes notice me staring at 'em in the reflection of the mirror. Then they nod at each other and start walking slowly towards our car.

I had no idea if they had guns or knives or what, and I had no intention of finding out.

'DRIVE! DRIVE! DRIVE!' I started screaming at the roadie, who was just sitting there frozen in panic, gripping the wheel, looking dead ahead.

'IT'S A RED. FUCKING. LIGHT.'

'JUMP IT! JUMP THE LIGHT! JUMP THE FUCKING LIGHT!'

'WE'LL FUCKING DIE!'

He wasn't wrong. ZZZZZOOOM. ZZZZZOOOM. There were cars, trucks, buses, motorbikes, you name it, barrelling through this intersection on both sides. It was a busy road. But I spotted a couple of gaps.

'WE'RE GONNA DIE ANYWAY!! JUMP THE FUCKING LIGHT! GO, GO, GO!'

The Hawaiian guys had split up now, ready to jump us from either side.

'HEY YOU, MOTHERFUCKER,' I heard. 'WHAT THE FUCK YOU THROW AT OUR—'

VVVRRRRAAAAAAAAAAGHHHH! Finally the roadie stomped his foot to the floor, closed his eyes and screamed at the same time. And by some incredible stroke of blind, dumb luck, the car squealed out into the intersection on a black trail of rubber at the exact same moment the light turned green.

I almost cried.

When I looked back, the Hawaiians were standing there in the middle of the road, choking on our exhaust fumes, as the cars behind 'em honked to get past.

I decided to take it a bit easier on the M-80s after that.

If there was a moment when it finally sunk in just how easy it was to kill yourself by living the way I did, it was after Bon Scott and John Bonham died within months of each other in 1980. Not that it stopped me drinking or doing coke every five seconds. But it made me more careful.

I never actually went drinking with Bon, which was probably just as well. But Sabbath used to tour with AC/DC, so I got to know him pretty well while we were out on the road. Some lead singers in those days could be a pain in the fucking arse, to be completely honest with you, but Bon was the opposite of that. He was just this nice, funny, very down-to-earth guy. And what a great singer. To me, as much as Brian Johnson did a great job of taking over from him, he'll always be the voice of AC/DC.

It was in Australia that we first met up with 'em. This would have been 1974, when they were opening for us during an event called British Rock 'N Roll Month. Uriah Heep and Status Quo were also part of it.

I didn't know what to make of AC/DC at first. When I first saw Angus Young put on his short trousers and schoolboy cap and walk out on stage with his guitar around his neck and a knapsack on his back, I've gotta admit, I thought, *what a weird thing*. He reminded me of Jimmy Clitheroe, a comedian from when I was growing up. Clitheroe's whole thing was dressing like a schoolboy even though he was a grown man. He had some kind of genetic disorder, apparently, so he really *was* the size of an eleven-year-old boy. Angus is on the shorter side too, of course, but nothing like that.

The second Angus started to play, though, it all made sense. What he does with a guitar is so clever, man. It seems simple, but it's not. He knows how to get the meat out of those six strings. He just pile-drives that fucking thing. And when he gets out there and works himself up, fucking hell, no wonder the guy never got any taller. At the end of a show he doesn't have a drop of sweat left in him. It's like he runs a marathon, night after night. I love the guy – as a person and as a performer. He's great.

The one unfortunate thing that happened with AC/DC came a few years later when they were opening for us in Switzerland on the *Technical Ecstasy* tour. Geezer had just got himself a flick knife, and he thought it was great to flick it all the time. I said to him, 'Geezer, you want to be careful about that. Do it in front of the wrong person, at the wrong time, and they might get pissed off.' But it had become a habit by then, so Geezer kept doing it. And sure enough, me and Geezer and Angus's older brother Malcolm – who played rhythm guitar in AC/DC but was also sort of the unofficial leader – were having a few beers in my room one night, Geezer starts flicking his knife and Malcolm gets pissed off.

It happened in an instant. One minute we were sitting

there having a chat, the next they were at each other's throats. All I remember is that they had a bit of a scuffle, and I had to break them up. I mean, like I said to Geezer at the time, AC/DC might be an Aussie band, but the Young family are from Glasgow, and they're Scots people deep down. They're fighters. Malcolm might have been only five-foot tall like Angus, but he could scrap with the best of 'em, and he wouldn't back down. You didn't want to fuck with him.

I don't know where Bon was when all this went down – or the rest of Sabbath for that matter – but AC/DC had to leave the tour after that. Who made that decision, I don't know. But Malcolm never forgot it. I mean, he did at the end unfortunately . . . he forgot everything. Many years after that tour, he moved into a place near mine in Buckinghamshire and he would come over every so often. But as time went on, I started to get the feeling the lights were on but no one was in. It turned out he had dementia. It was sad, man. I was so concerned, I asked Angus about it – I was just like, 'How's Malcolm doing?' and he got really pissed off. He didn't realise Malcolm lived right next to me, so he thought that news had got out or something. They're a very tight, very protective family.

As for Bon, the last time saw him was in his dressing room at Bingley Hall in Stafford. This would have been 8 November 1979. I'd been fired from Sabbath and was only just starting to get my solo career together. They were touring to promote *Highway to Hell* – the album that took 'em to the next level – with Def Leppard opening for them.

So I'm in there, shooting the shit with Bon, and I

remember someone calling out, 'You're on in five minutes!' And Bon had this big glass of what I thought was Coca-Cola in front of him. Not a small glass. A big tall glass. And he picked it up, glugged it all down in one and shuddered.

'Aren't you gonna need to piss after drinking that much Coke?' I said to him.

'Jack and Coke,' he said. 'Not Coke.'

It was unbelievable. I mean, that's *lot* of Jack Daniel's to start flowing through your veins just as you're about to walk out on stage. It's a lot of alcohol to drink in one gulp, full stop. Even I would have taken it a bit easier.

But I didn't think much more of it. I was too busy making my way down to the side of the stage so I could listen to Angus tear into the opening riff of 'Highway to Hell' at the kind of volume that could make your ears bleed.

Duh-n-nuh!

Duh-n-nuh!

Duh-n-nuh, duh-n-nuh-*DUH!!*

DUH-DUH.

Talk about an anthem, man.

After it came out, I remember thinking to myself, Bon's got the world at his feet.

I was a lot closer with John Bonham than I ever was with Bon. In fact, I knew all the guys in Zeppelin from way back. It was Geezer who first introduced me to Robert Plant, at the time when Plant was wondering if he should join Zeppelin – or the New Yardbirds, as they were then – or stick with his own band. His own band was called *Obbs-Tweedle*, if you can believe it.

Then one night at Henry's Blues House – the club

owned by our first manager, Jim Simpson – I saw Plant jamming with Bonham. This would have been early 1968. Talk about chills, man. Even then, Bonham's right foot had so much speed and power it sounded like he was firing artillery shells out of a machine gun. A year later, the rest of the world would get to hear it for themselves on 'Good Times Bad Times'. What he could do with a single bass drum was bordering on physically impossible.

And Plant's voice was something else. The range, the wailing he could do, the sheer volume of it. I mean, you could hear the beginnings of 'Dazed and Confused' on that night. He looked the part, too, with his golden curly hair and those tight trousers he wore that probably gave him an extra octave. He and Bonham were taking the blues in this totally new, much heavier direction – and it was one of the most exciting things I'd ever heard.

And that was *before* you added Jimmy Page on guitar and John Paul Jones on bass.

Anyway ... as the years went by and Zeppelin and Sabbath both took off, I realised Bonham lived within an hour of me, and we started to go drinking together.

He didn't just have a house, John. He bought an entire farm. Like a real one, with horses and chickens and a prize-winning Hereford bull called Bruno. Old Hyde Farm, the place was called. It was near Cutnall Green in Worcestershire. It was a hundred acres or something, at the top of a hill, so you got these amazing views over the countryside. It was such a peaceful, beautiful place. I loved going there. John was never happier than when he was driving around on his tractor, wearing his farmer's hat. John's dad Jacko was also there a lot. He was a builder, and he was always hard at work renovating the old farm buildings. One of the reasons John drank so much, I heard later, was that he got so homesick for the farm and his family when he was touring on the other side of the world.

To get to the main house, there was this long, winding driveway with a white picket fence alongside it. And at the other end of the driveway, where it met the road, there was a pub. John didn't own the pub, but he might as well have. They'd let him in there any time of the day or night.

The thing with John was, he was a great guy – sober. But add the jolly juice and he was absolutely fucking nuts. He'd just drink himself to bits. He was also big into Quaaludes, which were called mandrakes in England. He had a whole plastic bag full of 'em. People took 'em to relax in those days.

John's assistant was called Matthew, I remember, and we'd get him to drive us to the clubs in Birmingham in my XJ12. One night, John got so annihilated, when he came out of the club he thought it was *his* car and tried to drive away without me. All I can remember is knocking on the window going, 'John, this is my fucking car!' and him just going, 'Fuck off, I'm going home!' and locking the doors from the inside.

At one point, I thought I was gonna have to get a cab back to Stafford.

Or sleep in a hedge.

'JOHN, THIS IS MY FUCKING CAR!' I kept screaming at him.

Finally, something clicked in his head.

'Well, you should probably get in then, shouldn't you?'
he said, unlocking the doors.

I was close enough friends with John that I once
trusted him with my entire stash of coke.

I was about to leave the country to go on holiday with
the wife and kids – we were going to this very expensive
resort in the Canary Islands, I remember, all the way down
off the north-western coast of Africa – and I didn't want the
drugs at home where the housekeeper or one of the roadies
who were always coming and going might find them. So
before I left, I put this massive plastic bag of coke in the
boot of the XJ12 and drove over to Old Hyde Farm. I found
John in one of the workshops, next to the barn he'd turned
into a garage for his collection of antique motors.

'Will you look after this for me?' I said, holding up
the bag.

'What the fuck's in there?' he said.

'Waffle dust,' I told him. We called it waffle dust back
then 'cos it made you talk so much.

'Holy shit, Ozzy. That's a *lot* of waffle dust.'

'I know. Can I put it in your safe cupboard? I've gotta
leave the country for a while.'

'All right,' he said, 'you know where it is. I'll make sure
no one touches it.'

'Cheers, John,' I said. 'I owe you one.'

I remember feeling a bit weird about it as I drove back
home to Stafford on the M6. But that was nothing compared to how I felt once I got to the airport with my then
wife and the kids. Suddenly I was like, *that fucker's gonna
do my coke, there'll be nothing left when I get back.* It was ten or
fifteen grand's worth of the stuff in today's money. More
to the point, it was extremely hard to get in England at

that time. *Why the fuck had I ever thought John Bonham was the best custodian for a pile of cocaine big enough to march the Bolivian army to the moon and back?* The second he gets a few pints in him, I thought, he's gonna be opening the bag and going to town on the stuff. He'll be throwing it around like confetti. Giving it to the sheep. Half of Cutnall Green is gonna be bouncing off the ceiling thanks to my coke.

I thought I'd calm down and forget about it once we got to the Canary Islands.

But no.

For some reason, I just got more and more upset about the whole situation.

I was thinking about it when I was on the water slide with kids.

I was thinking about it when I was knocking back daiquiris and bottles of Guinness by the pool.

I was thinking about it when I had a romantic dinner with the missus on the beach.

Eventually she asked me what was wrong. I couldn't think what to say. 'I'm just really worried about my ... the future of the world, y'know?' I said.

I ended up going home early, I was in such a bad way.

The second the plane touched down at Heathrow, I was running to the long-stay car park. Then I drove at 110 mph all the way back to Old Hyde Farm.

The entire journey, all I could think was, *it's gone, it's gone, it's all fucking gone.*

Two hours later, I was roaring up John's driveway. I didn't even switch off the engine or close the car door when I got to the barn. I just ran straight to the safe cupboard in the corner where I'd left the coke, nearly ripped the doors off their hinges, rummaged around, throwing out hammers and chisels and whatever the fuck he kept in there, then – there it is! – I saw the corner of the plastic bag. I pulled it out. *Haha!* I went. *I knew it!!*

Then—

Actually . . . *hang on a minute.*

The bag still seemed full.

I weighed it in my hand.

I took a look inside.

I weighed it again just to make sure.

Yup.

He hadn't touched it. Not a single bump.

I couldn't believe it.

John, my old friend, if you're reading this up there, I'm sorry I ever doubted you.

Three months after that night with Bon at Bingley Hall, I was at home in Stafford, getting ready to head to Ridge Farm Studios to start recording *Blizzard of Ozz*. I don't remember if Randy was already there, or if he was still trying to get his visa or whatever. The phone rings. It's Jean, my big sister.

'Did you know a singer's been found dead in his car in London?' she says.

My blood ran cold. 'Who?' I said. 'What's his name?'

'Bon Scott.' She was reading from the paper. 'With the band AC/DC. Do you know him?'

I didn't hear anything after Bon's name. I felt like I'd been punched in the face.

It freaked me the fuck out. I was like, 'But I just saw him!' I also couldn't understand how it had happened. I mean, yes, I'd been surprised by him drinking so much

Jack and Coke right before a show, but I didn't think he was *that* bad a drunk. They said he'd choked on his own vomit while he was sleeping. But in my world, at that time, that just didn't seem like something that would kill you. I used to puke in my sleep *all the time*. All over England, people were doing it every Friday and Saturday night, without fail, and they weren't all dying. So how had it happened to Bon?

I was in shock when I ended the call. And I felt so sad for him. I knew exactly how tired he must have been when it happened, how much pressure he must have felt, 'cos I'd been there myself when I was on the road.

They toured a lot, AC/DC. And when touring becomes a drag – when you're fed up with the constant checking in and checking out of hotels, all the hours on the bus, the bad food, the chemical toilets, the petty arguments, day after day, doing interviews, straining your voice – it can grind you into the ground. When it's great, it's great. But if you don't take breaks, you can get into real trouble. The AC/DC song 'It's a Long Way to the Top (If You Wanna Rock 'n' Roll)' sums it up better than I ever could.

Bon had spent fifteen years on the road – he'd started out in 1964, long before he joined AC/DC – working his arse off to make it. And with *Highway to Hell*, he'd finally got there, at the age of thirty-three, the time of life when a lot of singers are starting to wonder if it'll ever happen. He was about to become one of the biggest rock stars on the planet. He had so much to look forward to . . . so much to give. It was an absolute tragedy what happened.

Bon, we've missed you, man.

Then seven months later – another call.

This time, I was in Liverpool. On a payphone in the lobby of a hotel where I was staying, I believe. My wife was on the line, breaking the news that John had been found dead at Jimmy Page's house after a day and night of heavy drinking during rehearsals. It was apparently John Paul Jones who'd found him the following afternoon, with the band's tour manager. They'd tried to wake him up. Then they'd had to tell Robert and Jimmy.

It must have been a terrible scene. I can't even imagine.

John's death shook me up badly. He was only thirty-two, and he left behind his wife Pat and their two kids, Jason and Zoë. Meanwhile, it was the end of Zeppelin. At the end of the year, they put out a statement saying 'the loss of our dear friend and the deep respect we have for his family, together with the sense of undivided harmony felt by ourselves and our manager, have led us to decide that we could not continue as we were'.

He'd pushed it, John, he really had. He was a hard player. He'd just drink and drink and drink. Me, I'd drink, then I'd smoke a joint and pass out. John never stopped.

On the day he died, he'd drunk forty shots of vodka, apparently, starting at breakfast. They said the cause of death was the same thing as Bon, choking on his puke in his sleep. When I heard that, I started to realise just how easily it can happen if you make a habit of drinking 'til you drop.

But y'know, I thought I was a *clever* drunk. I thought I knew all the tricks to avoid that fate, even though I'd once fallen asleep in my Range Rover in the driveway of Bullrush Cottage, a very similar situation to the one that killed Bon. That was the night someone had to come out and put a sleeping bag over me. When I woke up, my eyes were frosted shut. I could have died of hypothermia, never mind choking on my own puke. When I met Sharon, on the other hand, she wouldn't stand for it. She'd break my balls every time.

'No one *ever* thinks it's gonna happen to them!' she'd scream at me. 'Do you think Bon thought that's how his night would end? Or John? Wake up, Ozzy!'

The message must have eventually got through, 'cos after losing Bon and John, I started to sleep on my side, after sleeping on my back my whole life before that. I still sleep on my side to this day, just in case I throw up.

As for going out with a bang when you're young, the problem is everything you miss. Lemmy proved himself wrong in a way, 'cos he had such a full life. I've had a full life. But Bon and John left this world with so much still ahead of 'em. I wish they could have stuck around.

Many years after they died, on a break between tours, I took a drive back down to Old Hyde Farm. I pulled over by the pub at the entrance to the driveway and just sat there, looking at the picket fence and all the rolling fields beyond it. The last time I'd been there, John's dad or one of the farm workers had just given the fence a fresh coat of white paint. But now it was all rotten and weathered and peeling.

The good times always end, I suppose, I remember thinking to myself.

And sometimes far too soon.

11

I've Had a Few

Covid caught up with us eventually.

Andrew was the first to get it. I've gotta say, until that point I'd never, *ever* wanted to use Zoom. I mean, meetings are bad enough. But a meeting on a computer seemed like one stage removed from having your teeth pulled out. But when Andrew said, 'Why don't I come over, I'll wear a mask?' I found myself saying, 'Oh, have you heard of this Zoom thing?'

Catching the virus was the absolute last thing I needed on top of all the other medical shit I was dealing with. Unlike a lot of people in my world – including my Kelly – I couldn't *wait* to get shot up with the vaccine. Kelly was like, 'No way am I ever taking that shit.' Personally, I'd have taken gasoline. I didn't care if it had been tested for five minutes or fifty years. I just never, *ever* wanted to end up in an ICU again. Especially not with a breathing tube shoved down my windpipe. Yeah, no thanks.

Then just before Christmas, Sharon got it. Now, she's four years younger than me, Sharon, and a lot healthier, but the virus knocked her down hard. She was hospitalised for two days. Then she went into quarantine over at Elton John's house in Beverly Hills. What's amazing is that I didn't get it.

'Maybe it's true what they say,' Sharon said to me on the phone one night, as she was coughing and sniffling. 'Maybe you really *are* indestructible.'

'Must be all the devil-worshipping,' I said.

But the worst of the pandemic for Sharon was to come.

The way I see it, people were losing their minds during that period. They'd been stressed out beyond belief by the whole world shutting down. Then they'd been cooped up at home for almost a year with their other halves and their kids. They were arguing about politics, vaccines, where the virus had come from. Some people had gone broke. Others were riding the Covid gravy train. And so many people had died, it was unbelievable.

It was just a fucked-up time, y'know? And as the world went crazy, it become a kind of sport to tear people down and destroy their careers if they had the 'wrong' opinion. For a while people were getting cancelled left, right and centre. And sure enough, 'cos Sharon was out there on *The Talk* every day, discussing what was in the news – *which was her job* – it happened to her. I don't wanna rehash the whole thing, but she basically defended her mate Piers Morgan, who she's known since they were both judges on *America's Got Talent* way back when. Piers had made some comment about not believing a word that came out of the mouth of Prince Harry's wife, Meghan Markle. The second he said that, of course, all the pitchforks came out, with everyone calling Piers a racist and every other name under the sun. And Sharon basically said her friend was entitled to his opinion, even if she didn't agree with him. She also said not believing Markle doesn't automatically make you a racist. That was it, as far as I know. *That's all she said.*

Honestly, Sharon was fucked the second the subject even came up. It was a complete carve-up, what happened. The person she is convinced set her up – and I ain't gonna name names, 'cos the last thing I want to do is stir all that shit up again – knew what they were doing, I think. And Sharon, when she feels like she's being cornered, she's gonna come out fighting.

Like I said before, the whole TV world is just so fucking awful, man. I kept telling Sharon before it happened, you've gotta watch out. The knives always come out when you're least expecting it. It was really terrible to see her go through that. She was devastated for a long while. You think you've got friends in TV. They ain't your friends.

It was hard, man. Really hard.

The thing is, Sharon was already fighting to keep her head above water before it happened. My injury and my Parkinson's, the cancelled shows, then the pandemic on top of it all – it had been a heavy burden on her. I mean, don't get me wrong, you'll never hear Sharon complaining. That ain't her style. She's a rock. Also, we've both been very lucky in life. A lot of people have it far harder. But she's still a human being.

Her job at *The Talk* was a huge part of her life. She was one of the original hosts. She'd been on it *eleven years*, an eternity in showbusiness. She poured her heart and soul into that show, she was a big character, she loved the work. Being in front of the cameras had always been Sharon's dream after spending so many years behind the scenes as a manager.

They ended up putting the show on pause for a couple of weeks while they did an 'investigation' – then two weeks later they pushed Sharon out. Just a few weeks earlier, when Sharon had been in hospital with Covid, the same people had gone on Instagram to say 'Mrs O, we love you'.

What a bunch of phoneys.

The worst part was Sharon being called a racist for supporting Piers. I can tell you without any doubt, my wife is not a racist. It's against everything she's ever stood for. Anyone who's spent more than five seconds with her knows that. The people she worked with on that show knew that. To be stuck with that label, it was just fucking wrong. Because you can never get a gig anywhere on TV once that's what people think of you. It's game over. They knew that when they took her down.

She was gutted for the first few weeks. It really broke her up. But the thing I admire about Sharon is, she gets to a point when she thinks, okay, I'm done.

Me, I'd still be writhing around to this day, re-living every second of the whole thing in my head, over and over, wanting to get my revenge.

But that ain't how Sharon works. Once she's cried all her tears and gets over something, she just lets it go and never talks about it again. In fact, she's still friendly with a lot of the girls who used to work on the set. She's an incredible woman, my wife. As for *The Talk*, poetic justice was served in the end. It got fucking cancelled.

Meanwhile, once she got the knife out from between her shoulder blades, Sharon came roaring right back.

A lot of marriages ended during the pandemic, or so I've heard. Ours only got stronger.

I honestly believe you only get one true love in your life. Sharon's mine. She's my heart and soul. She saved me. There's no doubt in my mind I wouldn't be alive without her. I wouldn't know how to survive without her.

I was attracted to Sharon from the moment I saw her. But it was during the summer of 1980, after we finished recording *Blizzard of Ozz*, that I fell for her hard. I was living with Randy in London at the time, while we got ready for the tour. Our first gig was gonna be in early September at a nightclub next to the Norbreck Castle Hotel on the Blackpool promenade. Sharon had wanted us to do it under a fake band name – 'The Law' – to try and get some buzz going. She was always one step ahead of the game with the press, was Sharon.

Randy's flat was in the Shepherd's Bush area, I believe, near the roundabout. Sharon would come over and the two of us would get pass-out drunk. That's when I realised she was as nuts as I was. I mean, when we went out people thought we were brother and sister, we were so alike.

One time, we hit the pubs in a big way, got absolutely arseholed and barely made it through the front door when we got back to Randy's. We just collapsed, right there on the floor. When Randy got up the next morning, he thought we were both dead. It really freaked him out, the poor guy.

Another time, I made Sharon a beef stew, and I may

or may not have accidentally put some black hash in it. When Sharon realised she was starting to trip out, she went absolutely mental with me. I remember her picking up the phone in the flat – one of those big old rotary-dial things – and throwing it at me as hard as she could. I ducked just in time, it hit the wall, bounced off and smacked her in the jaw. It was like something from a Laurel and Hardy film. She was furious and holding her jaw and laughing at the same time. Then she picked up one of Randy's guitars and smashed it against the wall like she was Pete Townshend. She was left holding just the neck. I don't remember Randy's reaction, or if he was even there at the time. He couldn't have been very happy.

It was a crazy time, looking back. I was in this weird limbo, not knowing if my solo career would take off or not, caught between the woman I was still married to at the time and the woman I was falling in love with.

At some point in the middle of all this, there was a surreal moment when Randy's mum Delores – everyone knew her as Dee – came to visit. Randy absolutely loved his mum. He'd written an acoustic piece for her, 'Dee', that we put on *Blizzard*. It's the most beautiful thing. I can't listen to it without tearing up. Anyway, Dee had flown over from LA to see how he was doing. She also wanted to meet me. The first I knew about it was when I woke up on the sofa one afternoon after a heavy night, and there was Randy standing in the living room with this older woman.

'Hey Ozz,' he goes, 'meet Mom!'

It took me a while to realise where I was. I was stinking and sweating and farting, totally hungover. Then Bob Daisley and Lee Kerslake, who were playing bass and drums on the tour, walk into the room. Also hungover. So I get up to say hello, and it suddenly becomes very clear that Randy's mum has no idea who any of us are.

'So, Randall, when do I get to meet Aussie Osbourne?' she goes. 'And your new band?'

It made sense, I suppose. Randy was Mr Cool, and there we were, these three fat, boozy old fucks. We looked like the local working men's club darts team. No wonder Randy's mum thought we were the road crew.

A few weeks after that, we went to Shepperton Studios out near Heathrow airport to start rehearsals. I wouldn't normally remember that kind of thing. But it was at Shepperton that things finally started to happen with Sharon. We were all staying at the hotel opposite, and one night I used my special pick-up line on her. 'Can I come back to your room and watch your telly?'

My room *also* had a telly, of course. Which Sharon knew. So when she didn't say, 'Fuck off, watch your own telly,' I got the feeling maybe she liked me as much as I liked her. But I was nervous, y'know? I still wasn't sure.

Next thing I knew, she was taking a bath, and I was climbing into the tub with her.

'So are we gonna bonk now?' I asked her once I was in.

'Oh, how very romantic—'

That's when I finally went in for the kiss. Or maybe she did, I don't remember. Either way, from that moment on, we couldn't keep our hands off each other.

And we couldn't stop laughing. We would just crack each other up *all the time*.

For a while, I tried to keep things going with Sharon and my wife at the same time – for the sake of the kids, or that's what I kept telling myself. But that never works.

The truth is, you can't get married so young, then go on the road for nearly a decade – while developing a coke and alcohol problem – and hold it together. My wife and I were living totally different lives. Meanwhile, Sharon was the first woman I'd ever met who didn't care that I was crazy, 'cos she was crazy herself. We were like the loonies who'd taken over the asylum. We were in love and in lust and having the time of our lives. We were soulmates. It was obvious to anyone.

I just had so much fun with Sharon. Later on, I remember being in New York with her and the welder-turned-roadie-turned-personal assistant Dave Tangye. We'd hang out at this old-time bar on the east side of Midtown called P.J. Clarke's. It's still there, apparently. One night, at closing time, it was just the three of us left at the bar, along with a couple who'd just got married that same day, and a hooker. And it turned out the couple had enough coke on 'em on to sink a battleship, so we all went rampaging around Manhattan 'til the sun came up again.

Those were some good times, man.

But Sharon soon realised she couldn't keep up with my level of drinking.

I don't know how long it was after we started seeing each other, but one day she just turned to me and said, 'I don't want to feel like this any more. *One* of us has to be sober.' I thought to myself, yeah right, she'll be back on it tomorrow. But other than a glass of wine or a cocktail once in a blue moon, she's never touched the stuff again. I don't know how she did it, I really don't. When you're not an addict, I suppose, you don't need to hit rock bottom. You can see the damage you're doing and stop.

If only I could be that way . . .

What didn't change was how much time we spent with each other. We were inseparable, and got married on 4 July 1982, just a few months after we lost Randy. It felt like something beautiful we could do at a time of so much sadness. Sharon chose the date so I'd never forget our anniversary. But it didn't stop me forgetting the wedding. I was pissed out of my mind, which I regret to this day.

Looking back now, it was when I tied the knot with Sharon that I truly became Ozzy.

My first wife had refused point-blank to ever call me Ozzy. To her, I was always John. Ozzy was just my nickname from school, a short version of Osbourne. I mean, okay, the guys in Sabbath called me Ozzy. I was Ozzy at the Hand & Cleaver, the pub next to Bullrush Cottage. I was Ozzy to my old mates from Aston. But that was about it. I was John to my wife's family and friends. I was John to my mum and dad. I was John to my brothers and sisters, my aunts and uncles, and to all my other relatives. In fact, my sister Jean still calls me John to this day, which is weird, 'cos when see it on her texts, I don't *feel* like a John. I'm at the point now where if someone shouts out 'John!' on the street it doesn't even register.

Before I met Sharon, Ozzy was like a separate identity. He was the person I became on stage, the sweaty long-haired rocker with no shirt, tattoos all over, a crazy laugh and an evil grin. Meanwhile, John was the guy who lived in a quaint English village, who drove a Range Rover and wore wellies in the garden. Who had a normal wife, and two kids at nice schools. Who put his name on the contracts and knew to stay clean before a show.

But the second the lights came up and *Carmina Burana*

started playing, John turned into Ozzy the human wrecking ball – and I'd stay as Ozzy all night and most of the next day while I destroyed myself with drugs and booze. Then it was a day in a room with the blinds down to recover, then back to being John . . . before the whole thing started all over again.

Eventually, of course, I had to give up the booze and the drugs. But for whatever reason, once I divorced my first wife and married Sharon, John never came back.

I asked Sharon about it once, why she never called me by my birth name.

'I like you as Ozzy,' was all she said.

Now I'm Ozzy all the time.

I don't believe in regrets, generally speaking. When I left Birchfield Road Secondary Modern with nothing more than a piece of paper that said 'John Osbourne attended this school between such-and-such dates', I could never have imagined the kind of life I'd end up living. I went from a council house with no indoor toilet, to owning more diamonds and cars and houses than in my wildest dreams. How could I have regrets when that's how things turned out? I must be one of the luckiest guys alive.

Saying that, when I had all that time on my hands after my injury, then during the pandemic, there were moments I found myself looking back at the times when I could have been a better husband, a better father, a better son, a better bandmate. We've all done things we ain't proud of in life, and I've done my fair share. The way I look at it, that's how you learn, by making mistakes. But some mistakes are bigger than others.

And if there's one person who deserves an apology from me, it's Sharon.

The fact my wife has stuck with me is amazing, 'cos I've been a pretty bad guy over the years. If there's one regret I have, one thing I wish I could go back and redo, it would be the night in September 1989 when we went out to the Chinese restaurant near our old house in Little Chalfont, Buckinghamshire. We were celebrating our Aimee's sixth birthday. Not that I remember much about the evening. I'd just come back from the Moscow Music Peace Festival with Mötley Crüe and the Scorpions, and I was drinking neat Russian vodka with crushed-up pain pills on the side. I'd been out of my shitter for five days straight. It was too much. I'd gone too far. I was out of control.

Me and Sharon had been arguing for a while over little things. Just the usual shit about feeling overworked, 'cos those were the days when I took touring for granted. But the little niggles had been building and building, like they always do ... before they explode into something much bigger.

That's basically what happened. But 'cos I was so loaded, it almost turned deadly.

I feel sick and cold just thinking about it. I don't believe in a devil with a tail and little red horns, but I'm pretty sure he was with me that night.

The first I knew about any of it was when I woke up on the floor of a jail cell at Amersham police station with the worst hangover of my life. There were bars in front of me, a bucket next to me. The walls were sprayed with shit. I'll never forget the stink of that place. Some of it was probably coming from me. Then a copper walks in

with a sneer on his face and tells me I've been booked
for attempted murder. My first thought was, fuck, I must
have driven drunk. 'No,' he said, 'you tried to kill your
wife.'

It was like a bad dream. When he read me the charges,
I couldn't believe it.

Maybe I really *am* insane, I remember thinking.

Apparently, after leaving the Chinese restaurant, I'd
taken Sharon and the kids back to Beel House, where
we lived at the time. It was a proper old mansion that I'd
bought in the early eighties. The Duke of Buckingham
had once lived there, and later on, the actor Dirk
Bogarde. It was on thirteen acres with a tennis court and
swimming pool, the whole bit.

While Sharon put Kelly and Jack to bed I must have
kept drinking and doing more pills. Then, according
to what Sharon told the cops – 'cos I have almost no
memory of it – I walked into the living room, completely
calm, while Sharon was on the sofa reading a book. And
I said to her something like, 'We've had a little talk and
it's clear you have to die.' Only I wasn't clowning around
like I usually was. Whatever was in those pills I'd been
crushing up, it was some bad, *bad* shit. I was psychotic.

Then I lunged at her, putting my hands around her
throat.

According to Sharon, we ended up on the floor, with
me on top of her, trying to strangle her. She was panick-
ing, scratching at my face, until eventually she wriggled
free and hit the panic button on our burglar alarm system.
She said if she'd had a gun, she would have shot me in
self-defence. I don't doubt it for a second. I'm a lot bigger
and stronger than her, and I was off my face, dead-eyed,

just gone. She must have been terrified. A few minutes later, half of Thames Valley Police showed up.

I tried to make light of it to the cops while I was locked up in the cell, which wasn't too clever given the gravity of the situation. 'The things people do for publicity, eh?' I joked to one of 'em. But Amersham wasn't LA. No one was buying my rock star bullshit in that place. They'd have loved nothing more than to send me off to HMP Belmarsh for the next thirty years.

The first thing the cops did was go back to Sharon and tell her what I'd said. She was beyond pissed off. There was no communication with her for the two days I was locked up in that place, nothing. I thought for sure I'd lost her, that she'd never want to see my face again. Meanwhile, her father tried to call me – no doubt to spread a bit of poison – but he couldn't get through. No one could. I was in a jail cell, not a hotel suite.

After an appearance at Beaconsfield Magistrates' Court, which was an absolute shitshow thanks to the mob of reporters and photographers that showed up, I was granted bail on the condition I booked myself into rehab and stayed the fuck away from Beel House, Sharon and the kids.

I ended up in a place called Huntercombe Manor, not far from the court, where I spent six of the longest months of my life. The craving I had for alcohol in that place was the worst I'd ever experienced. I was shivering and puking, shitting myself, the whole deal.

It took Sharon five months before she made contact with me again and came to visit. That's when she told me she'd dropped the charges. She said she didn't believe the sober-world version of me was capable of murder.

But she never wanted to see Ozzy from the drunk world ever again.

A year later, I was standing in Lemmy's flat in West Hollywood, tears running down my face, as I read his lyrics to 'Mama, I'm Coming Home'.

Sharon, I'm sorry.

And thank you for giving me another chance when almost anyone else would have walked away.

That wasn't the only occasion I thought I'd lost Sharon, I ain't proud to say.

The other time was after the last Black Sabbath tour, when my addiction started telling me it would be a great idea to start seeing a load of women on the side.

Sharon had every right to dump me when she found out what was going on. I'd become addicted to sex, basically. It was no different than when I was addicted to booze, pills, cigars, ice cream or Yorkshire fucking tea.

When you say you're addicted to sex, of course, people don't believe you. They're like, yeah right, that's just an excuse for fucking around. But what you've gotta understand is, you *hate* yourself afterwards. It's no different than drinking four bottles of cognac until you're passed out on the floor in a puddle of your own piss. It's got nothing to do with love or romantic feelings. It's an obsession, it's filling a void inside you, and you can't stop, even though you know it could wreck your life and hurt the people you love the most. I wish I could have been stronger.

What I've realised is, when you start seeing another woman on the regular, you're like a kid in a sweet shop. You take the sweets, you eat half the bag, then you're like ... *oh shit, I feel sick now*. But you eat the rest of the sweets anyway, 'cos they're there, and that's what you do. Then at some point you get trapped and you can't stop seeing 'em, 'cos you think they'll go to the press or whatever. Which is pretty much what happened. Sharon was like, 'What the fuck did you expect, Ozzy? If you're seeing enough women, one of 'em's gonna want more. And that's the one who's gonna bring the whole thing crashing down on everyone's heads.'

So I put my hand up – I was a bad guy. I fucked around for a while. I broke my wife's heart, and I'm lucky she forgave me. I just hope all the people I hurt know how sorry I am – including the kids, who were badly affected.

And that's all I wanna say about any of that, 'cos bringing it up just causes more pain.

People are always asking both me and Sharon, how the fuck are you still together? How have you survived all the heavy-duty shit you've been through when so many other marriages fall apart over far less? I mean, you hear of celebrities breaking up 'cos they don't like each other's taste in shoes. Some of 'em divorce each other over text. Some don't make it past a few days.

Here's the thing. Whenever you see one of those couples who make a big show of everything being all lovey-dovey and perfect, I'm like, pull the other one. No one can keep that up. That ain't real life. Sooner or later, the mask's gonna slip, and then what? And if you walk away 'cos you can't take the bad with the good, who's to say the next time will be any easier?

People are people. Life's messy. And the longer you

live, the messier it gets. And guess what? Marriage might be hard, but going through a divorce ain't exactly a walk in the park, as I know from my own experience.

The only other thing I'll say about marriage is that it took me a long time to realise love ain't just about good sex. And that you can love your wife without having to agree with every single thing they say or do.

But when a marriage is working, and when you have a family that's full of love – like ours is – it's the greatest thing in the world. Just the other day, I got a text from Jack, and all he said was, 'I love you, Dad.' In the old days, I would have been, *uh-oh . . . what does he want now?* But I don't think that way any more. I just felt really good for the rest of the day.

I mean, what more could you want?

Sometimes your fuck-ups in life don't even occur to you until long after they've happened.

Someone asked me recently, for example, 'What's the best gift you were ever given?' I couldn't think of anything. Like I said, I'm a lucky guy, I don't want for much. Then a few days later, it hit me. Suddenly I was back in Birmingham in 1967, taking the bus with my old man to George Clay's music shop, down by the Rum Runner nightclub. After I'd walked around the place in a daze, I picked out a fifty-watt Vox PA system. Then my dad got out his pen and his chequebook, and put down a deposit on a two hundred and fifty quid hire-purchase agreement.

For a guy who lived in a terraced council house, had six kids and worked in a tool factory, it was an astronomical sum. Probably the equivalent of two or three grand in today's money. And he didn't even like the kind of music I wanted to play. He was into pub singalongs like 'Knees Up Mother Brown'. He'd tell me The Beatles 'don't have any tunes'.

Without that PA system, I'd never have left Aston. None of it – Sabbath, my solo career, *The Osbournes* – would have ever happened. It was only 'cos I had a PA that Geezer replied to my ad in the window of Ringway Music. And it was only 'cos I met Geezer that Sabbath came together.

But I never sat my dad down and said thank you.

I can't believe it.

The second I got that PA, I was off and running, not looking back once. Then when Sabbath got successful, I was like, okay, party's on. I honestly thought I'd get a couple of years out of being a rock star at most. Next thing I knew, fifty years had gone by, my old man was long gone, and there I was, wondering why the fuck I'd never told him how much I appreciated what he'd done for me. Because he could have so easily have said, son, you failed at school, you landed yourself in prison, why should I buy you anything? *Buy your own PA.* The guy even gave me a ten-bob note when Tony left Earth to join Jethro Tull, 'cos he could see how devastated I was. He was always looking out for me, my old man, and I wish I'd slowed down for a second to let him know how much it meant to me.

The other fuck-up I made in those early days was not taking the time to get familiar with the words used in contracts. Although to be fair, that wasn't just my fault. None of us in Sabbath had a clue. And the people advising us were often the same ones trying to rip us off. If I could go back in time and teach myself one legal term, it would be 'perpetuity'. Thanks to that one word, we lost control of Sabbath's publishing rights for ever.

They're the bread and butter of the music business, publishing rights. It's how you get paid for a song being played on the radio, streamed on Spotify, used in a movie or TV show, pressed on vinyl, or printed out as sheet music.

Sometimes you can get the rights back if you give 'em up in a bad deal when you're young ... *unless* the word 'perpetuity' was used. Instead our rights went to a company called Essex Music, which was run by a bloke called David Platz, who died in the nineties. They've passed on to his kids now, I believe.

I once asked our accountant how much money we lost 'cos of that one word. He took a deep breath. 'Look, are you *sure* you wanna know?' he said to me.

'Yeah.'

'Really? You're absolutely—'

'Just fucking tell me!'

'One hundred million pounds. Roughly.'

I had to go and sit down. Then again, like I said before, it's hard to regret that we didn't get everything we deserved. I honestly don't think all four of us would still be alive today if that had happened. We were kids who'd come from nothing. It takes time to learn how to handle that kind of dough. And to us, we had all the money in the world for a while. After our first record advance – my share of it was £105 – it was insane how quickly our lives changed. The first thing I bought was a bottle of cologne, 'cos I was paranoid about the way I smelled. You can't wash it off, the stink of poverty. It follows you around. When I was a kid, my parents had never even bought me *underwear*. They said it was a waste of money.

But suddenly I could afford as many pairs of underpants as I wanted. Another thing I could afford was cigarettes, and packs of *twenty*, not just ten. Even better, I could walk into a pub knowing I didn't have to borrow or scrounge to get a pint of beer. That was the ultimate luxury in my working man's world. And we just kept going up the scale. First it was pub lock-ins, staying after closing time and drinking ourselves silly. Then we were in Miami, swimming in a rooftop pool at midnight, eating Colonel Sanders's chicken in a bucket, thinking nothing of handing over a hundred dollars for a gram of cocaine. And when we got our first cheque for touring America, it was for ten times the amount of that first advance.

The only *real* regret I have when it comes to Sabbath is that Bill was left out of the *13* album and tour. Our last gig was in Birmingham, and it should have been this incredible, emotional homecoming for all of us. But there was kind of a heavy feeling on stage, 'cos Bill wasn't there. We didn't talk about it much, but we all felt it. I could tell. It was sad, man. We'd all started off together. We'd all grovelled through the shit together. We'd all got successful together. We'd all travelled the world together. We'd all got fucked over together. There are no two ways about it, Bill should have been there, and he should have been on the album.

Without him, it wasn't Black Sabbath. It was just a close approximation.

I suppose all of this is leading up to what happened to Randy and Rachel. Not a day goes by when a part of me doesn't wonder, *why them? Why not me?*

Since I don't like to talk about it, I'll start at the end, when me and Sharon were trying to keep a band and a tour on the road when we were badly fucked up by it all. One of the weirdest things after leaving Sabbath was becoming a boss, being responsible for everything. I tried to leave as much of that as possible to Sharon. But at the end of the day, I was the guy whose name was on the tickets and the tour posters, and I had to make the decisions about who was in, who was out. And it was at a time when I was in shock and grieving, and trying to cope with it all by staying drunk all the time.

After the accident, we took a two-week break from the *Diary of a Madman* tour. That was it – *two weeks*. There was no tour insurance in those days, so you *never* cancelled a tour. You'd get taken to the cleaners, and you'd probably never get booked again. Besides, we all thought it was what Randy would have wanted, for the show to go on. But we were in no fit state, really.

There were two funerals during those two weeks, and they couldn't have been more different.

Rachel's was like a gospel thing. It was down in South LA somewhere. She was a big church person, Rachel. She hadn't even really wanted to be on tour with us, blowing out our hair every night, sewing our stage clothes, doing our make-up. She was fifty-eight, I believe, and not in the best health. She missed LA. Missed her church friends. She took the gig to raise money to buy her church a new roof or a computer or something.

Me and Sharon and the band were probably the only white people at the service. Everyone was crying and singing and praising God. 'Jesus love you, Rachel!' It was a beautiful, joyous thing. But obviously devastating at the same time. I'd never experienced anything like it.

Then a day or two later, we were at Randy's funeral

at a Lutheran church in Burbank. Very reserved, very traditional.

I was one of the pall-bearers, along with Tommy Aldridge, and our bass player Rudy Sarzo, who'd been in Quiet Riot with Randy and even taught with him at his mother's music school for a while. We all had on the black suits and black ties. In the church, all you could see – and smell – were white flowers. Gardenias, I'm told. And there were pictures of Randy placed around the altar. It was beyond heartbreaking. Terrible. Just terrible. Especially to see his mum Delores there, trying to hold it together. The worst nightmare of any mother, any parent, is outliving your kid. And Randy thought the world of her, y'know? There was so much crying. And I felt so guilty. He'd been in my band. I'd taken him away from his mum, taken him to England, then on tour. And I was the one who'd been courting disaster the whole time while he'd been the sensible one.

When the service was over there was a motorcade to San Bernardino, out in the desert. Mountain View Cemetery, the place was called. Randy's grandparents were buried there. That's where he was laid to rest. Every year I send flowers to his graveside.

Then suddenly we were in an LA rehearsal hall, trying to find a new guitarist. We were just walking around in a daze, feeling sick and empty. You'd feel okay for a second then suddenly the memories would come back and you'd be shaking and crying. No one could sleep. No one was saying much. It was hard to accept that what had happened was even real.

The only way I could handle the waves of emotion was by drowning 'em with booze.

The guitarist we found – or someone at Jet Records found – was Bernie Tormé. He was an Irish guy who'd played with Ian Gillan from Deep Purple. It must have been incredibly hard for Bernie, stepping off a plane from London and walking into that kind of heavy scene. He even had to use some of Randy's equipment, 'cos he'd come over at such short notice. And he had to learn all of those solos note for note, in no time at all – I think it was our keyboard player Don Airey who sat with him as he did it – all while Sharon gave him a complete make-over. He had a kind of bohemian sixties look, and it didn't fit with the Gothic Victorian vibe of *Diary of a Madman* at all. He was such a lovely, gentle soul, Bernie, with the biggest heart. He helped us out at a time when very few established players wanted to take on that gig. Musically, he had a looser, more bluesy style than Randy. But he got us through six or seven shows.

The only gig I remember with Bernie was Madison Square Garden. We all knew it was the one venue Randy had always wanted to play, so it was hard. Really hard. Every time I looked over, I expected Randy to be standing there. And of course the whole crowd was trying to carry us along. Everyone had signs saying 'We love you, Randy' and 'You can't kill rock 'n' roll'. It was so much to take in. I saw a picture of the gig once and you can see how numb we all look. It was a battle just not to break down.

The weird thing is, Zakk was in the audience that day. He was only sixteen. Still living with his parents in Jackson, New Jersey. He idolised Bernie 'cos of that show.

I watched an interview with Bernie once, when he

was talking about what I was like during that period, the things I was saying. The guy had been stone cold sober, so it must have happened the way he said it did. But I couldn't remember a single thing. I couldn't watch the interview. I had to switch it off. I felt like I was reliving that terrible time all over again.

I actually met up with Bernie right at the start of *No More Tours II*. It was the first time I'd seen him since those gigs after Randy died. We were both at the Sweden Rock Festival. Someone came in and said, 'You'll never guess who's outside.' I didn't even recognise him, it had been that long. Zakk was with me, and he did a selfie with him. We all hugged. It was nice to see him, but the pain came right back. Probably for him too. A year later, I was very sad to hear he'd died from double pneumonia.

Bernie, God bless you, thank you for saving our arses during that awful time.

After Bernie, Brad Gillis took over until the end of the tour. Though Bernie was such a gentleman, he stayed while Brad learned the songs. He even waited in the wings for the first few shows, in case he needed to step in.

Brad was a very different player, but he did well as anyone could in that situation. He was more into the flashy, whammy-bar stuff that Eddie Van Halen had made popular. But he also had his own vibe going on. When the tour was done, he wanted to go off and do his own thing. I can't say I blame him, given how messed up I was. He ended up forming Night Ranger. They had a big hit with that song 'Sister Christian' a couple of years later.

The one thing Brad got roped into doing along with the rest of us was the live album *Speak of the Devil*, or *Talk of the Devil* as it was called in the UK.

I hate that fucking record.

It was a contractual thing we had to do for Sharon's father. We owed him a live album, basically, so the idea was – this was when Randy was still alive – we'd put together a collection of the Sabbath songs we played on the tour. But when Randy died, there was no way we could put out a live album so soon after the accident. Randy never really loved Sabbath anyway. 'Iron Man' just wasn't his kind of thing. He'd say to me, 'It's so simple, a kid could play it.' We'd argue about it. 'Not everything has to have ten thousand notes,' I'd say to him. 'Look at "You Really Got Me". A kid could play that, too.' But I was never gonna convince him.

In the end, we put the live tapes of Randy in the vault and took the new band – with Brad on guitar – to the ballroom of the Ritz Hotel in New York and recorded the songs live that way. Sabbath thought we'd done it to fuck 'em over, 'cos it came out right before *their* live album. But it had nothing to do with that. We needed to get out of Don's contract, 'cos we wanted to get on with *Bark at the Moon*. That was it.

We honoured Randy's live playing five years later with the *Tribute* album, mostly recorded during the *Blizzard of Ozz* tour. 'Randy would be very proud of this,' Randy's mum wrote to his fans in the liner notes, before thanking them for all the love and support they'd given her. 'He accomplished so very much in his short life. Only the Lord above knows how much more he could have given us. May God bless each of you.'

After Brad, we knew we had to find a permanent replacement for Randy – we couldn't keep changing guitarist every five minutes. But it was hard, 'cos all we wanted was Randy back. We must have auditioned hundreds of people.

Then Jake E. Lee showed up. That's when we were like, okay, we can stop looking now.

It wasn't just that Jake was a great player. He was the total package, y'know? The guy's half Welsh, half Japanese, which gave him a very different background and vibe to most of the other guys out there. He had this massive mane of jet-black hair, he didn't smile much and he held his guitar low and wide. A lot of metal guitarists at that time were getting a bit hammy, but not Jake. He was just fucking cool. As for the work he did on *Bark at the Moon* and *The Ultimate Sin*, it speaks for itself.

The biggest problem we had in the band once Jake was hired was our bass player. Mainly 'cos we had to hire someone very quickly after Rudy Sarzo left. Rudy had been very close with Randy, and the accident just devastated him. He couldn't do it any more. He said he needed a break. So we ended up getting a guy called Don Costa, who'd just left W.A.S.P.

Now, Don was a great player. The problem was he was nuts.

And I mean *really* nuts.

Like, he had a cheese grater screwed to the back of his bass, and during a gig he'd use it to grate the skin off his knuckles. And other parts of him. The pain must have been unreal. He had this big frizz of hair and he never wore a shirt, just a pair of white jeans that would be splattered with his blood by the end of the night. I was like, Don, *what the fuck is wrong with you?* Could you imagine? The bloke would literally grate himself like he was a block of Wensleydale. Meanwhile, he was the horniest guy I'd ever met. He'd fuck anything. He'd have fucked a bumble bee if he could get it to stop buzzing. Nothing was too outrageous for him. He used to be a stripper at one time, I believe, which made sense. He also collected girls' knickers. He reminded me of Rasputin, the mad monk.

I went to Texas with him once, and on a night off we went to see ZZ Top play. Halfway through the gig, there's a commotion in front of the stage. Pieces of the set are moving, but it's out of whack with the music. So security are called in, and there's Don, under the stage, trousers down, hammering away on top of this woman. While ZZ Top are playing right above him.

He was too much, Don, right from the beginning. His time with the band came to an end when he tried to make out with me at the back of the bus. It wasn't a joke. He was in my business, trying to stick his tongue down my throat. Why he did it, I don't know, other than he was fucking mad. I didn't appreciate it. My arsehole is exit only. So I smacked him in the nose.

I didn't see him again for at least twenty years.

Then one morning I was going to the log cabin in West Hollywood for an eight o'clock AA meeting, and there he was, hanging around in the car park. He called out to me when he saw me. I said to him, 'Are you in the programme?' He said, 'Oh no, I'm just coming in here to get a cup of coffee.'

I thought, okay, that's a bit strange. Then again, this was Don Costa we were talking about. Then it clicked. AA gives out free coffee at all its meetings. And Don wasn't just hanging out in the car park. It looked like he was *living* there. Before I could say anything, he said, 'I'm homeless now.'

I didn't know what to say. I felt bad for the guy. So I said, 'I'm sorry to hear that, Don,' and gave him all the cash I had on me, a few hundred bucks.

That was the last time I saw him.

The one thing I do regret from that period was how Jake E. Lee left the band.

The thing is, after Randy, and after the whole shit-show with Don, I just didn't mix with the band all that much. All the bitching and griping that went on behind the scenes, it started to seem like kids in a playground to me.

The problem with that was, having a rapport with someone's really important to me. Take Tommy Aldridge. He was always a drummer I respected and admired. He'd get on the stage, night after night, and always play a perfect set. He even did this drum solo where he played with his hands. It was phenomenal. I couldn't fault the guy at all when it came to his reliability. But he'd never hang out much after a show. He wasn't offensive. He didn't give me the cold shoulder or anything. I just got the sense he didn't really like me. And I thought, well, if you don't like me, it's best to move on. So he ended up going to Whitesnake. We were just working partners at the end of the day. He was like a hired gun.

It was the same with Jake. I just never really connected with him on a personal level. And at the time I had an English guy called Phil Soussan on bass, with Randy Castillo, who later joined Mötley Crüe, on drums. And Phil and Randy had some kind of beef with Jake. What it was, I don't know. I never had a beef with him. And one day Phil and Randy came to me and said Jake was saying all kinds of bad things about me. They were setting him up, y'know? And because I didn't have much of a rapport with Jake, I just believed the bullshit. It was sad, really, and I felt bad when I found out what really went down. I never really spoke to Jake after that. I knew he had a band called Badlands that was very well respected.

But y'know, everything happens for a reason. It was when Jake left that I had to go out looking for a new guitarist again. That's when someone gave me a demo tape made by the kid from New Jersey who'd been at that Madison Square Garden show. By now he was twenty years old.

I was blown away by what I heard, and I hired him right away.

This was 1987.

Almost forty years later, Zakk's still with me today.

I've avoided the subject for long enough now. So I suppose, for the very last time, I should talk about what happened on 19 March 1982.

It doesn't take much to send me back to that morning in Leesburg, Florida.

Before the internet, I could go weeks without that tape running in my head again. But nowadays it's impossible to avoid, especially around the anniversary of Randy and Rachel's deaths. I'll be googling something, watching TikTok videos or looking at YouTube, and some image will pop up. Then I'll be back in that field with the horses, not knowing where the fuck I am, what's happened, the nightmare starting all over again.

The photograph that always knocks the shit out of me is the one of my old brown and orange tour bus with the stainless-steel siding. Randy and Rachel are standing next to it, Randy in a straw hat, Rachel in some kind of captain's hat, her arms around Randy. I don't know if it was taken on the morning of the accident or not. If it was, I would have been passed out on my bunk inside. They'd have been just about to get on the plane.

The second I see that picture, I'm down the rabbit hole. The burned-out white mansion. The bombed-out garage with the wing of a small plane sticking out of it. The toxicology reports. Pages from the accident investigation. The Florida cop giving a press conference. Or that bullshit Channel Nine *Eyewitness News* report about Randy going on an 'early morning joyride after staying up over twenty-four hours', which pisses me off every time. It's hard, 'cos you can't stop yourself looking, but every time you see or hear some new piece of information, you're done, the tears are coming, your heart's racing, you've lost the rest of the day.

The night before the accident, we'd played the Knoxville Civic Coliseum in Tennessee. We never hung around after a show – that was Sharon's rule number one – so we got straight on the bus and started the ten-hour drive to what was then the Tangerine Bowl in Orlando, Florida.

The bus got hotter and hotter as we went further south. The AC was broken, apparently. I didn't know that at the time. I was on the gin that night, getting through bottle after bottle. I also didn't know our tour manager and the driver had been talking about stopping to get the AC fixed.

All I remember is hanging out in the bus's lounge area with Randy and the band. He was telling me he wanted to go to university, get a master's degree in classical guitar. I didn't understand. I said to him, 'Randy, if you keep doing what you're doing, you can buy your own fucking university.'

He just laughed, then went off to bed. The bunks were behind a door in the middle of the bus, each with their own little privacy curtain. I carried on drinking until I could see the sun coming up. Then I followed Randy back there. I was probably the last one with a bunk to hit the sack.

Sharon was already sleeping. So were Randy, Rachel, Tommy, and Rudy.

Meanwhile, the bus driver was up front, chewing gum, staring at the road ahead.

As I drifted off to sleep, I could feel the grooves in the road as we barrelled down the freeway.

Orlando was still a few hours away.

BANG.

I'm almost thrown out of my bunk by the impact.

What the . . .?

We've crashed, I'm thinking, as I'm blinking open my eyes.

Shit. This is the last fucking thing we—

I'm glancing out of my little porthole window. Where are we? Where's the freeway?

All I'm seeing is . . . grass. There's an overwhelming smell. Burning. Something's burning. Fuel. Not gasoline. Stronger than gasoline. I'm starting to choke on it . . .

Where are we? Why aren't we moving?

Where's the freeway?

Sharon and Rudy are awake, getting out of their bunks. They're confused, bleary-eyed. 'What just happened?' Rudy's asking. 'Where are we?'

Then screams.

Outside.

They're coming from outside.

Horrible, hopeless screams.

I'm getting to my feet.

My head's pounding from the fucking gin.

I'm jiggling the latch of the door to the lounge area. Shoulder charging it—

What the . . .?

There's a six-foot gash in the side of the lounge area, right where I was sitting just an hour or two earlier. Like someone sliced it open with a knife. The windows are blown out. There's glass everywhere. The driver's seat is empty.

I'm stepping off the bus.

Blinding sunlight.

I'm breathing the heavy, swampy Florida air.

I'm looking at . . . horses? A woman in riding gear is walking a horse like it's a normal thing to do in a field full of people on their knees, screaming and crying.

How did we skid this far off the freeway?

Where are the other cars?

What did we crash into?

What's everyone so upset about?

Why can't I hear sirens?

Where's the bus driver?

WHAT. THE FUCK. IS HAPPENING?

Now I'm seeing the wreckage. Twisted metal. A wheel. Broken plastic. Other things . . .

And I'm noticing the hangar and little drug-runner-type

airstrip in the distance. A banner that reads 'Flying Baron Estates'. A sign warning of alligators.

The smell of the fuel's starting to get to me. I'm having trouble breathing.

Don's running past holding the world's smallest fire extinguisher.

I'm turning to see the grand white mansion behind me. It's on fire. The roof is starting to collapse. There's a garage next to the house, totally flattened. Black smoke billowing up. Like someone dropped a bomb on it.

Don's dribbling foam in the direction of the fire. It would be comical if it weren't so fucked up.

I'm seeing other wreckage in the trees. The tip of what looks like a wing in the flames.

Don's on his knees now, like everyone else.

It still doesn't make any sense.

We were on a freeway. Where did a plane come from? Why are we in a field?

Sharon's trying to do a headcount. I don't know where Tommy or Rudy are. We're all going into shock, getting that dead, numb look in our eyes. Sharon's taking off a shoe. Beating our tour manager Jake Duncan over the head with it, trying to get some sense out of him. He can't get his words out.

'What happened?' Sharon's screaming. 'Where's Randy? Where's Rachel?'

He's just pointing at the fire.

I'm stumbling towards the mansion, still in my underpants, to make sure no one's inside.

Two months earlier, I was at a hotel bar in Chicago.

The bus driver had just pulled up a stool next to me. Andrew Aycock was his name. He'd wear those half-tinted aviator glasses like Hunter S. Thompson. He was telling me about how he used to work in the Middle East, flying these business guys around 'cos he was a pilot as well as a driver. He said his wife had run off with one of 'em, so now he was divorcing her. He said he couldn't stand her, although he didn't put it as nicely as that.

While he's telling me all this, Randy comes over. He asked me how long it would take to drive from New York to Georgia. There was a break coming up in the tour when we'd all be going off and doing our different things, and Sharon had booked us all on flights ten days later to Atlanta for the next show. Only Randy was thinking of renting a car instead.

'It's gotta be thirteen or fourteen hours in a car,' I said to him. 'Why would you do that?'

'I don't think I ever wanna get on a plane again,' he said.

He didn't have to explain. A lot of people were feeling the same way. There'd been a really terrible plane crash in Washington DC. What happened was, an Air Florida flight took off from Washington National Airport with ice on its wings, it couldn't get enough altitude and crashed into the 14th Street Bridge. What made it even more of a mind fuck was the fact there'd been a news chopper overhead at the time, and it had broadcast the rescue operation live. Only six people survived. One of 'em drowned after he stayed in the river to help the others get out. The bridge is named after him now. Arland D. Williams, Jr.

Anyway . . . I didn't give those conversations in the bar another thought until the day of the Knoxville gig, when a strange woman suddenly appeared on the bus. I said to Jake, our tour manager, 'Who the fuck's that?'

'Oh, it's the driver's wife,' he said. 'Wanda, I think her name is. She needs a ride.'

'Aren't they getting a divorce?'

'I think he's trying to make up with her.'

'He was calling her every name under the sun last time I spoke to him.'

'Maybe they were just going through a bad patch.'

'It was more than a bad patch if they were getting a divorce. But okay.'

That was when it all started.

After picking up his wife and realising the AC was on the blink, the driver told Jake he happened to live in a place called Leesburg, on the way to Orlando. Again, I had no idea about any of this at the time. I only heard about it later. And as it so happened, the company that owned the bus was also based in Leesburg. So the driver said, why don't we stop at the depot there and fix the AC? That's what Flying Baron Estates was, it was the headquarters of this bus company, which was apparently owned by a country act called The Calhoun Twins. And it wasn't just buses they owned. They also had helicopters and small planes, a whole operation. Which is why they had the little hangar and landing strip there. The big white mansion was where the Calhouns lived.

The bus must have got to Leesburg at about eight in the morning, only an hour or so after I hit the sack. Since Randy and Rachel had gone to bed early, they were already up. So were Jake and Don.

Now, what none of us knew was, when the driver was working in the Middle East, he'd been involved in a fatal helicopter crash. And although he was qualified to fly a small plane, his medical certificate had expired. Not that anyone thought he'd be flying a plane anyway. He was our bus driver.

Meanwhile, the Calhouns were out of town, and based on what they told the cops later, they'd never given the bus driver permission to borrow any of their planes. But that's exactly what he did. The second he got to the depot, he started offering everyone sight-seeing flights in this little single-engine Beechcraft Bonanza that was being stored there for some guy. Even though he'd been up all night driving and, as it later turned out, doing coke.

Don and Jake went up with him first. Apparently, he did one low pass over the bus, but nothing too crazy. Then he asked Randy and Rachel if they wanted a turn.

I'll never understand why they said yes. Randy was so scared of flying he'd seriously considered spending thirteen hours in a car instead of one hour on a plane. Rachel was in her late fifties and had a heart condition. They didn't even really get along with each other, 'cos Randy was messy and Rachel was always cleaning up after him. What I've heard is, Randy had a camera on him and fancied the idea of taking some aerial shots for his mum. And I guess the driver must have promised Rachel he wouldn't pull any stunts, or she wouldn't have gone.

What was going through the bus driver's mind in that plane, no one will ever know. But according to the cops, he did three treetop-level passes over the tour bus. All while his wife was standing there in the bus doorway, and while Don was taking photos from the ground with his own camera.

But when it came to the fourth pass, the guy went so low he would have crashed into the trees even if he'd been able to pull up in time. We're talking six to ten feet off the ground, which is insane. Don had to duck, I later heard. There's also been talk of Don seeing some kind of struggle in the cockpit, but there's so much bullshit out there, I dunno what to believe. Some people think Randy was trying to get the bus driver to pull up. Some people think Rachel might have had a medical emergency.

All anyone knows for sure is the wings of the plane were wiggling from side to side as it approached the tour bus, and one of 'em clipped it. That's what put the gash in the side. The wing sheared off, the plane cartwheeled into the trees, bounced off, then exploded as it fell nose first into the garage.

Based on what the investigators said later, it would have been over in an instant 'cos of the force of the impact. That's at least some comfort. Meanwhile, the fire meant the bodies had to be identified using jewellery and dental records.

I couldn't believe how long it took for the fire brigade to arrive.

When they did finally show up, the amount of water they had was a joke. They ran out almost before they started. The fire just burned itself out.

Then the cops came, and of course they were hostile from the get-go. Accusing Randy and Rachel of being on some drugged-up joyride. That's presumably where that *Eyewitness News* report came from. But of course when the toxicology reports came back, it showed the only drug in Randy's system was nicotine. As far as I know, there was no autopsy of Rachel, 'cos when Sharon was asked if they should do one, she couldn't face it. Meanwhile, they found coke in the bus driver's urine.

I don't remember much about what happened next. We booked ourselves into some shithole of a hotel, the Hilco Inn. We had to hide in our room 'cos the press were camped outside. Sharon eventually managed to call her father, who flew out. The cops weren't really that interested in getting to the bottom of what happened. They just wanted to get us the fuck out of their town. Sharon had to call Randy's mum. I can't even imagine. Then she had to call Rachel's best friend, Grace.

Sharon was in pieces after those calls. Just shattered. She had no more tears left to cry. And I don't even wanna think about what it must have been like to *get* one of those calls. No one should ever have to hear that kind of news.

Meanwhile, back home, everyone was freaking out. My mum saw a newspaper stand with 'Ozzy Plane Crash Horror' on it or something, and she thought I was the one who'd been killed. News from America wasn't that easy to get in those days. The guys in Sabbath thought the same thing. All of 'em reached out, as did the guys in AC/DC, who knew how much we would be hurting after their own tragedy with Bon two years earlier.

Those messages meant a lot to me.

A few days later, once Sharon's father had arrived, we had to go back to the crash site as part of the investigation. It was still a police area with all the tape around it. And as we were coming out of the hotel I saw this group of kids, and out of the corner of my eye, I noticed one of 'em wearing an Ozzy Osbourne tracksuit. We'd had 'em made specially for the band and the crew. I said to Sharon, 'We're not *selling* those are we?' She said no. So I stopped, and went and confronted this kid, and it turned out he'd nicked it from the tour bus. I absolutely lost my shit, man.

Just pure fucking rage.

They had to drag me away.

It wasn't just that the kid had snuck under the police tape, broken into the tour bus and stolen our stuff. It was the whole situation. The fucking injustice of it. Randy and Rachel had been the two most sensible people on the entire tour. Meanwhile, I was the one who'd been acting like a madman for the last year while drinking myself into oblivion.

Whey had *they* died?

Why not *me*?

It should have been me.

It should have been me.

The older I get, the more I believe in fate.

When your number's up, it's just your time to go. Even when it's cruel. Even when it's unfair. Even when it's far too soon. It doesn't make it any easier when you lose the people you love. But it's a way of accepting it, I suppose.

What I do know without a shadow of doubt is that if I'd been awake when Randy and Rachel got on that plane, I wouldn't have just gone with them, I'd have been sitting on the wing. That haunts me to this day.

For the record, I don't have a theory about what caused the crash. It seems pretty weird the bus driver flew so low that he couldn't have recovered even if he'd wanted to – and that his wife, who he told me he couldn't stand a few weeks earlier, was there in the bus doorway. But whether he was trying to kill her, impress her, scare her, or do some kamikaze shit, who knows. It's also entirely possible he was just fucking around and showing off, and misjudged it, 'cos he'd been up all night doing coke.

All these years later, there's still nowhere to hide from those memories.

Every time I hear the song 'Flying High Again' off the *Diary of a Madman* album, I see Rachel's smiling face. Everywhere we went, she'd collect bottles of booze from our dressing room, put 'em in a special bag and hide it in her bunk for me. Whenever I ran out, she'd get a glint in her eye and go, 'I got liquor!' Then she'd tell me not to go too crazy with it, 'cos 'Mama's gonna worry'. It's a line from the song.

As for Randy, like I've said so many times before, he was the one true musician I've ever played with. The only guy who was at home teaching at his mum's music school as he was playing a classical recital as he was wearing his high-heeled boots and doing a metal solo in front of twenty thousand fans. I was eight years older than Randy, and unlike him I'd already been in a successful band. In theory, I should have been *his* mentor. But it was mostly the other way around. He'd even give our *support acts* music lessons when we were on the road.

When he got inducted into the Rock & Roll Hall of Fame four years ago – I wish I could have been there, but I couldn't travel 'cos of my injury – Tom Morello got up and said, 'You could study Randy's songs in a university-level musicology class and bang your head to them in a 7-Eleven parking lot.'

That sums it up perfectly for me.

I couldn't accept the loss of Randy for the longest time. It was part of the reason why I spent the rest of the decade almost drinking myself to death.

I couldn't handle the reality.

Part of me still can't.

12

Dr Fix It

Almost two and a half years after my spine surgery, I finally went and got a second opinion.

By now it was early summer, 2021. The Covid backlogs were starting to clear. Places were opening up again. The only catch was, the guy who Sharon wanted me to see was two thousand miles away at some specialist place just outside Minneapolis.

Flying anywhere was still an unbelievable pain in the arse. You basically had to zip yourself into a full hazmat suit before you set foot in an airport. But I had no choice. It was obvious I needed more surgery on top of whatever Dr No Socks had done. It wasn't just that the physical therapy wasn't working. I was getting *worse*. A few months earlier, I'd built up enough stamina to walk eight laps around the block with my cane. Now I could barely do one. Meanwhile, every time I moved my head, it still felt like I was being ripped apart. The way things were going,

I wouldn't just need a walker for the rest of my life. I'd be in a wheelchair. And I'd be wearing a neck brace 'til they put me in the ground.

Sharon kept telling me not to get my hopes up about the new docs. But I couldn't help it. I had this fantasy where they shot me up with a local anaesthetic, adjusted a couple of screws in my neck and I went hopping and skipping out of there and all the way to Madison Square Garden.

So off we went to Minnesota.

Whatever hospital it was, I was there for three days. One test after another after another. I was poked, prodded, scanned, squeezed, jabbed, X-rayed, run through an MRI machine, run through it again, hooked up to all kinds of monitoring devices. They took enough blood from me to fill a swimming pool. I was asked every question under the sun about my health and medical history. Meanwhile, they sat Sharon down and asked her . . . how much we wanted to donate to the hospital.

People in Britain don't realise how good they've got it with the NHS, they really don't. In America, they'll check your bank balance before they check your pulse. I suppose all that money is why they keep inventing world-beating new treatments. But it gets a bit much. Especially when you're also dealing with the health insurance system. After any kind of surgery, you're getting bills from everyone in the room. Plus a bill for the use of the room. Then another bill from the guy who sends you the bills. And of course everything's marked up by 10,000 per cent. Each screw they put in my spine probably cost a couple of grand. I mean, I'm very lucky, I can afford it. Some people wind up bankrupt.

Finally, when the tests were all done, we sat down with the head specialist guy.

'Well, after looking at your scans, going through your medical records and reviewing your symptoms, we recommend one more surgery,' he said.

Thank God, I thought. *They can fix me.* I could handle one more surgery. I mean, okay, I didn't like the idea of getting laid up again and doing yet another round of physical therapy. But if it got me back on my feet . . .

'Surgery to do *what?*' Sharon jumped in.

'Well . . . we'd be implanting metal rods into your husband's neck to hold it in place. That would alleviate the pain he's experiencing when he moves his head.'

'What about walking?' she said. 'He needs to go back on tour.'

The doc just sighed. 'Well, unfortunately, because of Mr Osbourne's Parkinson's . . .'

Here we go, I thought. 'But these rods,' I said, 'they'll fix my neck?' That would be something, at least. It was my neck that was causing me the most pain.

'They'll stabilise it, absolutely,' said the doc.

Better than nothing, I thought. Then I realised something. 'Hang on a minute,' I said. 'If my neck's held in place with rods, how will I move it?'

'Well, uh . . . it would be fixed.'

'What d'you mean, *fixed*?' said Sharon. She was getting that pissed-off sound in her voice.

'There'd be no autonomous movement of the cranium. It would be locked, so to speak.'

'You mean . . . I'd have a totally rigid head?' I said, struggling to believe what the guy was proposing. 'I'd just be staring in one direction the whole time?'

'There'd be no left or right mobility, correct,' he said. 'Other than using your torso.'

'What about up or down?' I asked.

'Again, uh . . . you'd need to use your torso. But you'd no longer be in so much pain.'

'Look, no offence,' I said, 'but I didn't come all the way here to join the cast of *Thunderbirds*. You'd be turning me into a fucking marionette!'

'Look, I know it's a lot to take in,' he said. 'But given your injury and your Parkinson's, there aren't many good options. Why don't you think about it?'

I'd already thought about it.

An hour later we were at the airport, hazmat gear on again, heading back to LA.

Once again, the thing that saved me from losing hope was working on a new album. Whenever I felt myself wallowing in self-pity – which was often, I ain't proud to say – I'd channel it into a song. If there's one track on *Patient Number 9* that really sums up where my head was at, it's 'God Only Knows'. It was inspired by that moment when I was crawling through the back door after my first surgery, realising the physical therapy wasn't working.

The problem was, of course, the *Ordinary Man* album had come so easily and been received so well, how were we gonna top it? I mean, no one ever says, okay, I've had a great run, it's about time I went out there and made a fucking dreadful record. But it happens *all the time*. 'The bigger you get,' as Sharon says, 'there's only one way to go – and that's down.'

That was one of the reasons why I always had so much respect for David Bowie.

I remember vividly when *The Rise and Fall of Ziggy Stardust and the Spiders from Mars* came out. It would have been 1972, the same year as *Vol. 4*. It was the biggest thing on the planet, an absolute monster of an album. Any other singer would have kept milking that thing for the rest of their career. Not Bowie. He killed Ziggy at its peak. Just walked away and started over. The balls it must have taken to do that, the belief in himself, it was incredible. And it worked for him. If he hadn't killed Ziggy, he'd have never done *Young Americans*, *Station to Station*, or the Berlin albums – never mind *Let's Dance*.

You could tell the stakes were higher with *Patient Number 9* because Sharon and Andrew were arguing a lot more. Sharon called him a 'stubborn little shit' at one point, which didn't go down too well. But Andrew could give as good as he got. And at least they could be *real* with other, y'know? Whenever you're working hard, doing something that's important to you, there's always gonna be a few blown gaskets.

The other tough part about following *Ordinary Man* was the fact we'd got Elton John for that album's lead single. We couldn't exactly call him back and say, 'Hi Elton, could you pop back to the studio again?'

Meanwhile, Andrew kept on throwing out all these other names. Eric Clapton this. Jeff Beck that. I was like, 'These guys are out of our league, man. They're *megastars*.' I mean, so was Elton, but he's one of Sharon's closest friends.

The crazy thing was, though, *they all said yes* – including Tony Iommi. That left us with a very different problem. 'How are the fuck are we ever gonna do another album?' I said to Andrew at one point. 'We've used everyone!'

Even now, I look at the credits on the album and can hardly believe the line-up we got. Aside from the holy trinity of Eric, Jeff and Tony on guitar, we had Duff McKagan and Chad Smith again, along with Andrew's songwriting collaborator Ali Tamposi. We also had Robert Trujillo from Metallica. Ryan Tedder from OneRepublic. Chris Chaney and Dave Navarro from Jane's Addiction. Josh Homme from Queens of the Stone Age. And the great Mike McCready from Pearl Jam. And of course Zakk was all over the album, playing on most of the tracks, both lead and rhythm. He even played the organ on 'Nothing Feels Right'. The only reason Zakk hadn't been on 'Ordinary Man' was 'cos it happened so quickly. If it had been a normal album, I'd have called him right away. But like I said before, Andrew, Duff and Chad had the music done in four days flat.

The two songs I did with Tony were among the highlights for me. 'No Escape from Now' took us all the way back to 'Planet Caravan' and 'Into the Void'. Tony's riff is just massive. But it's also got that slightly more modern, melodic vibe. Meanwhile, we went all out with 'Degradation Rules'. I'm not sure Tony even knew it was about some seedy bloke pleasuring himself, 'cos the lyrics hadn't been finished when he did the guitar part. But it was a nice surprise for him in interviews, *heh-heh-heh*. One of the lines I shout out on there – 'Red Tube rules!' – came from Taylor Hawkins from the Foo Fighters, God rest his soul.

Taylor didn't play on that song, but he did on 'Parasite', 'Mr. Darkness' and 'God Only Knows'. Sadly, they were some of the last things Taylor recorded before he died of a heart attack. He was in Bogotá, Colombia, for a Foo Fighters gig when it happened. He had such a young, playful spirit, Taylor. He was like a kid. And what a phenomenal drummer.

He was only fifty when he died.

Another great talent we lost far too soon.

I almost got *too* excited about Eric Clapton playing on the album. Back in the day, I was a huge fan of Cream. I still am. Every time I hear 'White Room', it takes me right back to the summer of 1968. I said to Andrew, 'It's been so long since we've heard the old bluesy, psychedelic Eric – why don't we write something like that for him?' Then I got an idea. 'Why don't we ask him if he'll use his wah-wah pedal?' Wah-wah's the effect that sounds like the guitar's talking, if you ain't familiar.

Andrew didn't need any persuading.

The thing with Eric is, he puts so much feeling into every note, all he has to do is play. And the crazy thing is, you can tell it's him *immediately*, even if his name ain't on the record. He's from that magic time before guitarists had to start coming up with all kinds of tricks to stand out.

The song he ended up playing on was called 'One of Those Days'.

Before he recorded his part, though, I started to get paranoid that Andrew would forget about the wah-wah. It's all over those early Cream records and a lot of other psychedelic stuff from that time – and of course Isaac Hayes used it on 'Theme from Shaft'.

'I'm on it,' Andrew kept reassuring me. 'I'm gonna talk to Eric.'

'I just *really* want the wah-wah,' I kept saying.

'I know! I want wah-wah, too.'

I couldn't stop thinking about it. I convinced myself

Andrew was gonna forget about it, or that Eric was gonna show up to the studio with an overdrive or chorus pedal instead. Every other day, I'd send him a text. 'Wah-wah?'

He'd text right back – 'YES! WAH-WAH!'

I even sent him a few emails about it in the middle of the night when I couldn't sleep.

From: Ozzy
To: Andrew
Subject: WAH-WAH . . .?!

It got a bit much in the end. Andrew had to say to me, 'Look, this is God we're talking about, Slow Hand himself, one of the top three guitarists of all time. We can't push the wah-wah thing too much. We'll just have to see what kind of mood he's in on the day.' But I'd worked myself up about the wah-wah so much I wasn't gonna take any chances. So I looked up the address of the studio where he'd be recording the guitar part – Church Studios in Crouch End, London, I believe – and I FedExed him a wah-wah pedal, just in case he forgot to bring his own.

He used it, thank God. Whether it was mine or his, I don't know.

It's one of my favourite tracks on there. It sounds absolutely amazing.

It was funny working with Eric, 'cos for a long time – at the height of my coked-up paranoid period – I thought he hated me. It was 'cos of the time the two of us posed for a photograph with Grace Jones at the International Rock Awards. This must have been 1989. Grace was in her underwear with this black mesh stuff on top. She looked incredible. She was there to present an award with me.

Anyway, when we posed for the picture on the way in, I made my crazy 'Ozzy face' just as the flashbulb went off. And even though Eric was smiling, I got the feeling he was pissed off. Then when I didn't see the picture anywhere, I got it into my head that Eric had called his publicity people and had it pulled from circulation. People can do that. They just buy the rights to the picture themselves. For weeks and weeks, I kept looking for it in magazines, but it was nowhere to be seen. I felt like one of those generals in Stalin's Russia who'd been airbrushed out of history.

For years, I thought I'd made an enemy of one of the most famous guitarists on earth 'cos I'd pulled a stupid face at the wrong time. Any time I spotted him at an event, I'd duck out of the way. Then one day he was there at the log cabin in West Hollywood during an AA meeting. I was sitting right behind him. So of course, the moment the meeting's over, I just about run out of there so we don't have to have an awkward encounter. But he's back again the next day. This time, he follows me out to my car.

'Hey Ozzy!' I hear.

Oh fuck, I'm thinking, he's gonna rip me a new arse-hole for that photograph. So I turn around, ready to go, 'Look, Eric, I'm so, *so* sorry, I'd been drinking, that face is just a thing I do when I'm in front of the cameras, I really didn't mean to fuck up your picture,' but Eric just says hello, good to see you again, and we have a very nice chat, like nothing ever happened.

I started to think to myself, *hang on, maybe he was never pissed off with me, after all* . . .

Then a few days later I'm at some radio station in LA to do an interview, and there's the photograph of the two of us with Grace Jones – and me doing my crazy face – right there on the cover of an old magazine. Whether it was framed on the wall or just lying around on a coffee table, I don't remember. But I couldn't believe it when I found myself looking at it. Eric hadn't killed it, I just hadn't seen it. I've since found out it appeared in a few other magazines, too.

It was crazy. Thanks to all the cocaine I'd been doing, I'd spent the best part of a decade avoiding the guy who sang 'Cocaine', for no good reason at all.

After the guy in Minneapolis proposed turning me into a Thunderbird, I wanted to get a third opinion.

The problem was finding a surgeon who didn't wanna immediately reach for his power drill and screwdriver. And 'cos the combination of a spine injury and Parkinson's is relatively rare, it ain't like you've got a lot of choices.

Where Sharon found the name of Dr Robert Bray down in Marina del Rey, near Santa Monica, I've no idea. She might have just gone on the internet. He used to be at Cedars, apparently. But now he had his own practice.

Sharon liked the sound of him 'cos his whole philosophy is to be as minimally invasive as possible. He's also a neurological spine surgeon, not just an orthopaedic guy, which is what you need when you're dealing with Parkinson's. And Sharon said a lot of his patients were surfers, rock climbers, motocross riders, that kind of thing. I ain't saying being a rock star's in the same league as any of that, but just being *me* is kind of an extreme sport in its own right. So it felt like I'd be in good company.

I've gotta say, though, no matter how good Dr Bray *sounded*, after what had happened in Minneapolis, I didn't have high hopes for our first meeting.

It was early August 2021 when we went down there.

Within two minutes it was obvious Dr Bray was very different to everyone else we'd seen. Once he'd put me through the MRI machine and given me some X-rays – my spine had had more close-ups than Meryl Streep by this point – he sat me down and gave me some real talk about what was going on.

First of all, he said the plates Dr No Socks had installed were too tight. That meant whenever I moved my head, it didn't just *feel* like I was ripping apart my neck muscles . . . I really *was* ripping apart my neck muscles. I mean, fuck me. *No wonder I was in so much agony.* I almost teared up, 'cos I'd been worried it was all in my head, that the pain was just my addiction fucking around with me in some way. Dr Bray said that in his opinion, the plates were over-kill for what I needed. Then he showed me some blobs on an X-ray that he said were 'bone debris'. Basically, 'cos the plates were too tight, the screws that held 'em in place were starting to come loose. That was causing the bone around 'em to disintegrate, and the debris was getting trapped between my vertebrae.

'Have you been feeling any discomfort lower down your back?' he asked.

I almost broke down again. *'All the time,'* I said. 'I feel like I'm living inside one of them medieval torture devices! Except no one knows it's there but me . . .'

I can't tell you how much of a relief it was, finally knowing *why* I was in such a terrible state.

'So what do we do?' Sharon asked.

'Well, first of all, we need to remove the plates and screws,' he said. 'Then we can take it from there. SLOWLY. Without doing any more damage to your spine.'

'Doc, be honest with me,' I said, still trying to hold it together. 'Do you think you can fix it?'

'Honestly, Ozzy?' he said. 'Too early to say. But . . . that *is* what they call me.'

I was confused. 'What?' I said. 'What do they call you?'

'Dr Fix It,' he said with a big grin, pointing at something on the wall above my head.

I turned to look. That was when I noticed the framed magazine article. It was a photograph of Dr Bray in his blue scrubs, wearing his special magnifier glasses and surgical hat, with the headline 'DR FIX IT' underneath.

Suddenly it all came back to me. By complete accident, Sharon had found the exact same bloke Zakk had recommended the day after my fall.

The bloke we'd never bothered to call.

Until now . . .

I couldn't believe it. If my legs had worked, I would have kicked myself.

Meanwhile, Sharon was groaning as the same thing dawned on her.

When we finally caught each other's eye, we just burst out laughing. I mean, what else was there to do? The doc must have wondered what the fuck was wrong with us before we explained it all to him. I wanted to call Zakk right then and there to apologise for not listening.

But whatever, man.

Everything happens for a reason.

And as they say . . . better late than never.

Sharon got really serious about us moving to Las Vegas that summer. The pandemic was making everyone stir crazy. People were moving house left, right and centre.

Jack had even bought a farm way up north in Idaho, on the edge of Yellowstone National Park. I was like, Jack, what the fuck are you gonna do with a hundred and thirty-three acres? Become a shepherd? But he and his new girlfriend Aree – this was just before they got engaged – they wanted to make a go of it. Welders Ranch, Jack called it, after Welders House in Buckinghamshire. We went to visit one weekend. It's so peaceful up there, man. I could see why he likes it. I used to love lording it up in the countryside when I was his age. Most of all, it was just great to see Jack looking so happy and in love and excited.

For Sharon, moving to Vegas was all about getting me a residency. She was *desperate* to get me out of the house. But I've gotta be honest, I never really saw it happening. I wouldn't have lasted, doing the same gig, over and over again. I mean, my friend Billy Morrison, he did it for a while in Billy Idol's band, and he said it was okay. They found ways to switch things up, so it didn't feel like they were trapped in the plot of *Groundhog Day*. But I like to do a show and move on. I wouldn't mind a couple of weeks at the same venue, but a residency needs to be longer than that.

The other thing is ... I don't really *get* modern Vegas. It's boring. I mean, okay, you've got the Strip, which has all the lights and whatever. But in the old days, it was funkier, cooler. It used to have a kind of Wild West saloon vibe. The hotel rooms were all from the thirties. Now it's like a giant Disneyland for grown-ups. All the character has been sucked out of the place.

Mind you, in the early days of Sabbath, we were always very wary of Vegas. If you got caught with coke in Sin

City, you were fucked. The cops there were no-nonsense, not like in LA. They'd put you straight in jail for that shit. Or in some prison out in the desert if you were really unlucky. Everyone remembers Jim Morrison's mugshot from when he got busted there. And that wasn't even for drugs, or so I'm told. He was standing outside, pretending to smoke a joint – or so the press said at the time – and they booked him for vagrancy, of all things. And for being off his face on booze, obviously.

These days, marijuana's legal in Vegas, Jack tells me. I worry about that, I really do. It's so strong now. I mean, okay, not everyone's an addict like me, but once you get started on the weed, you tend to move on to other things.

Even worse are the guns everywhere. You can buy a fully automatic machine gun in Vegas, as long as it was built before a certain date. It's ridiculous. Mind you, the shooter at the Route 91 Harvest music festival just modified a normal semi-automatic rifle to do more or less the same thing. He fired off more than a thousand rounds, the news said. Sixty people were killed – and close to nine hundred were injured. It was just absolutely atrocious. To me, music's one of the few things that can still bring people together, so for that to happen at a concert . . . there just aren't any words. The violence with guns in America – especially the school shootings – is just out of control, man. I get so tired of hearing about all these killings. It really gets me down.

On the same subject, I was shocked to hear when Jake E. Lee got shot near his house in Vegas not that long ago. He was out walking his dog in the early hours, or so the news said, and some random guy emptied a clip on him. He got hit multiple times, but by some miracle he survived, thank God. Jake's an incredibly talented guy, and like I said earlier, I regret the way he left the band during that fucked-up period. Jake, God bless you. I wish you a full recovery from your injuries.

The only other thing I'll say about the Vegas residency is that people forget Black Sabbath's first major gig was a residency at the Star-Club in Hamburg, Germany. It was the same place The Beatles had their famous run in 1962, when Stuart Sutcliffe and Pete Best were still in the band. Sutcliffe was the guy who left The Beatles to be an artist, then died of a brain haemorrhage six months before 'Love Me Do' came out. Only by the time we got to the Star-Club – seven years later, at the beginning of August, 1969 – the place had been run into the ground. We were one of the last bands there. It closed a few months later. It's totally gone now. The whole building burned down.

What a crazy summer that was, man. The moon landing. Woodstock. The Manson Family murders in LA. The Vietnam War still raging on the other side of the world. We were still called Earth, and still doing blues covers, but we'd already decided to rename ourselves Black Sabbath. I remember breaking the news about the new name in a postcard to my mum. I look like a kid in the band pictures we had taken. Tony, Geezer and Bill had the dodgy moustaches and leather jackets, and I'm all fresh-faced, wearing a raggedy old jumper and sandals.

There are a few tapes of those shows knocking around out there somewhere. We'd play things like 'Early One Morning' by Little Richard. It's weird, 'cos we sound like Black Sabbath doing a Little Richard cover. We also did these long jams that were the beginnings of songs like 'N.I.B.' and 'War Pigs'.

Meanwhile, Hamburg in those days was what a *real*

Sin City looks like. Dodgy porno shops. Peep shows. The smell of the sweat and the smoke. And that gated cobbled backstreet where the hookers would pose behind steamed-up shop windows under red lights.

I'm glad we did it, but it was also one of things where you're like, never again. We'd start playing at noon and end at two in the morning. Sometimes we'd play seven sets a day between the visiting bands. We were absolutely fucking knackered. I'm pretty sure we ended up playing more gigs there than The Beatles did. We'd take anything we could to stay awake. Booze. Speed. A shitload of dope. Then, at the end of every night, we'd crash out in some flea-infested hotel around the corner.

There's no better way to get tighter as a band, though. You learn how to read each other. How many drinks you can have before you forget how to keep time. How to get the crowd going when they're bored. Whenever the punters were getting restless, Tony would shout over to me, 'Ozzy! Go and organise a raffle!' But the best thing about the residency was earning a regular wage, which until then we'd only ever dreamed about.

If there's one song on *Patient Number 9* that takes me back to our Star-Club days, it's 'Darkside Blues'. For most of the early pandemic, I'd be walking around the house singing this one Muddy Waters-type line, over and over, until eventually Jack was like, 'Dad, how many more times are you gonna sing that? Can't you turn it into a song already?' So I did. I even play harmonica on it. If anyone wants to know what Sabbath would have sounded like if we'd stayed as Earth and made a blues album . . . that's as close as you're ever gonna get.

*

I was almost *excited* to get my first corrective surgery in September. Anything to reduce the pain, get me walking again. So off I went down to Dr Bray's medical building in Marina del Rey, hoping for a new start. It was night and day compared with my first operation. There was no extended stay in the ICU. No catheter. No hallucinations of Elvis. I don't remember how long I was under for, but it was nothing like the five hours I spent with Dr No Socks. Dr Bray just went in there, removed the screws, removed the plates, sucked out the bone debris, made whatever adjustments he needed to make, and closed me back up again. Easy.

But there was no good news at the end of it.

Although my neck was now in much better shape – and would improve with physical therapy – there was still a lot more work to do to fix the vertebrae below my skull. Also, my old quad bike accident was starting to fuck me up in ways that weren't related to my fall two years earlier. Further down my back, said Dr Bray, I had two vertebrae where the quad bike hit me that had now basically disintegrated.

The bottom line was, I was gonna need at least *two more* corrective surgeries. And they weren't gonna happen quickly. Everyone had delayed their treatments during the pandemic, so it was almost impossible to book an operating room for anything that wasn't life or death. Realistically, I was looking at a couple of years before all the work was done.

It was a heavy blow to take, especially when I was still all banged up from the surgery.

But . . . at least it was a plan.

What I didn't know, of course – and I'm glad I didn't – was

that each surgery would wipe out all the physical therapy gains from the previous one. Meaning I'd be starting over again each time. And of course I wasn't getting any younger, and my Parkinson's was progressing, which would make it even harder to bounce back. The one thing I *did* know for sure was that I wouldn't be playing any gigs any time soon. Not that it mattered. The world was a long way from getting back to normal. Covid restrictions were still in place for large crowds. And flying overseas was a big risk, 'cos if you got the virus there, you were stuck. So in November we postponed the European tour by one more year.

The shows were now set for May 2023.

There wouldn't be any more postponements, I'd already decided. If we couldn't make the gigs happen then, it was time to bow out. But I still had hope.

Not a *lot* of hope, to be honest with you. And it was fading by the day. But if there was still even a tiny chance I could do the gigs, I wasn't gonna give up.

The only thing I had to look forward to over Christmas was *The Beatles: Get Back*, the documentary by the *Lord of the Rings* guy Peter Jackson. As a fan, I couldn't wait to see all the unfiltered, behind-the-scenes footage of John, Paul, Ringo and George making the *Let It Be* album. After all my ups and downs with Sabbath over the years, I was expecting to find it reassuring to know The Beatles had to deal with the same shit. Especially when Yoko Ono started sitting in on their recording sessions.

All I can say is . . . what a disappointment. It just didn't seem like the real thing to me. You're not *seriously* telling me that in the sixty hours of footage the director had, they were all happy and friendly? If we'd had someone in

Sabbath say, 'Okay, my girlfriend's gonna be here from now on,' there'd have been blood on the studio floor. I thought it was gonna be one of those fly-on-the-wall things. But the fly on the wall must have been deaf and blind, 'cos it didn't see or hear anything interesting at all.

My mood didn't get much better as 2022 arrived.

It was gonna be a big year for me, in many ways. The fortieth anniversary of the bat thing. Of Randy and Rachel's deaths. Not that I wanted to be stuck at home, thinking about the past. Fuck that. I've never been one to look back, me. I've always been about the next big thing. But there were times when the only big thing in front of me seemed to be a headstone with my name on it. It pissed me off. I wanted to fight it. But there's only so much fighting you can do when your body's failing.

Then out of nowhere came a phone call.

I don't know who it was exactly who reached out to Sharon, but they worked for Prince Charles, as he was then. He'd become king just a few months later.

They wanted to talk about the upcoming Commonwealth Games, which Prince Charles would be opening. He's also the patron of the whole games organisation, I've since learned. Now, I didn't know it at the time, 'cos I'd been so out of it with my injury and recovery, but the 2022 games were being held in Birmingham. The main venue would be Alexander Stadium, which is in Perry Barr, right next to where my old school used to be. They were even expanding the stadium's seating for the occasion, so it would fit thirty thousand people, double the usual capacity.

Sharon was buzzing when she got off the phone. It was gonna be the biggest games in the history of the

Commonwealth, she said. They were spending eight hundred million quid on it. Seventy-two countries were taking part. Five thousand athletes. Meanwhile, a million tickets had already been sold for the main stadium and the other venues around the city. It was a *huge* deal, she said. Up there with the Olympics.

But I was confused. 'So why are they calling *us*?' I asked. 'I ain't gonna be doing the hundred metres any time soon. I suppose I could cut a ribbon . . .'

'Actually . . .' said Sharon. Then she stopped. She suddenly looked upset. Like she had bad news and good news at the same time. She had to take a breath and wipe away a tear. I was starting to get freaked out.

'What?' I said. 'What's wrong? What *happened*?'

'They wanted to know . . .' she continued, pulling herself together, 'if you'd be interested . . . in performing at the games. With Black Sabbath.'

'Like . . . at the opening or something?'

'No.'

'So . . . *what*? A side event?'

'At the closing ceremony.' Sharon was fully in tears now. 'The final act. As the fireworks go off. In your home town, Ozzy. Literally a few streets away from where you went to school. They're asking if you'd do "Paranoid".'

'Fuck . . . me.' Now I was tearing up too. And grinning so hard my face hurt.

'The eighth of August is the date,' said Sharon. 'BUT, Ozzy—'

I didn't hear anything else she said. I was away with the fairies, thinking about Aston . . . thinking about how I'd break the news to Tony, Geezer and Bill . . . thinking about Prince Charles. I've met Prince Charles loads of times. Every time I see him, we have a right old laugh. He's a great guy. After my quad bike accident, he sent me a bottle of Scotch, which was very nice of him. The only problem was, Sharon confiscated it before I could get my hands on it. It went to the 'loft of no return' where Sharon hides all the things she wants to keep but doesn't want me to see.

When I was growing up, if I'd have told anyone the future king of England would be sending me booze in the post, they'd have put me in a room with rubber walls.

When I was born, it was Charles's grandfather who was king, George VI. I was too young to remember his reign. But my very first memory, funnily enough, is of the Coronation of Queen Elizabeth. I must have been four.

The only reason I remember it is 'cos my dad dressed up like his hero Al Jolson, including putting that awful black make-up all over his face. Just writing that down sounds absolutely horrendous, but this was 1953. It was the kind of Victorian music hall shit they'd grown up with – although even by then, people were starting to realise how fucked up it was.

As a four-year-old, all I knew was that I wanted nothing to do with it. I cried and screamed and wouldn't let my sisters get one speck of that stuff on my face.

The thing I was most excited about after getting the call from the games was just going home. It had been eight or nine years since I'd been back to England, never mind Birmingham. But my home town had been on my mind since my fall, especially during all the months when I was laid up.

In the old days, when I was living in Staffordshire, then

Buckinghamshire, I'd jump in the car and drive back to Aston whenever I had any kind of major freak out. Even if it was four o'clock in the morning. I'd park my Range Rover on Lodge Road and sit there for thirty minutes, thinking back to the days when I was young and hungry. And I mean *literally* hungry. We had a saying in our house – first up, best fed. School dinners were an absolute lifesaver for me. A lot of the other kids wouldn't touch the food they served. I'd be having triple servings of lukewarm mashed potatoes and lumps of rock-hard mystery meat.

It's still there, amazingly, 14 Lodge Road. Last time I went back, I realised just how *tiny* that house was. You could see where I'd carved 'IRON VOID' into a brick by the front step. I must have been fifteen when I did that. I thought it would be a cool name for a band. You could also still see the nails they put in the wall to hang the bunting for the Coronation.

It's funny how the most random things take you back. The smell of candyfloss, for example. One sniff of that and I'm at the old Aston Onion Fair, which they used to hold every year at the Serpentine Grounds, before they built a seven-lane motorway on top of it. I'm told the fair got its name from when they really did sell onions there. People would come from as far as France to set up stalls. Then it became a proper Victorian carnival. Famous boxers had big fights there. They had travelling exhibitions of lions and tigers, and sideshow attractions – like the world's ugliest woman, or the horse with two heads. But by the time I was a kid, it had turned into more of a funfair. They had shooting games. Ring tossing. But it was the dodgems and waltzers I loved the most.

Then suddenly it was just gone, all of it bulldozed to make

way for the Aston Expressway. Although they did put a curve in the road to save the Ansells brewery. And they put a pipeline over the top to carry vinegar between different parts of the HP Sauce factory. They shouldn't have bothered, mind you – both Ansells and HP are long gone now.

The smell of old houses also brings a lot of memories back. When I was a kid, there were still a lot of old Victorian mansions in Aston that had been hit during the Birmingham Blitz. They were bomb sites, basically. But they weren't bomb sites as far as me and my mate Patrick Murphy were concerned. They were playgrounds.

We'd smash the windows, start fires, knock holes in the walls, take up the floorboards.

The thing that sticks in my mind is that all the windows were painted black. They did that for the blackouts instead of hanging curtains. You never wanted any light to get out, 'cos it would give the German pilots something to aim at. Our imaginations ran wild in those houses. But I shudder to think how dangerous they must have been, not to mention all the toxic shit we must have been breathing.

It's crazy to think what it must have been like to live in the Midlands during the nearly three years of the Blitz. Fire and death rained on you every night. Not knowing if you'd wake up the next morning. Or which of your neighbours' bodies you'd be pulling out of the rubble. And still going to work at the factory every day, churning out more Spitfires, tanks and guns. Whenever it seems like things are getting out of hand in this world, I think about that, and it helps keep things in perspective.

'Yes!' I said to Sharon. 'Call 'em back and say yes! The closing ceremony? Of the Commonwealth Games? That's amazing! Will it be on the telly? Can we do "Iron Man", too? I need to call Tony. I can't wait to get back there—'

'OZZY! *Ozzy* . . .'

I didn't understand why Sharon looked so down. I thought she'd be excited.

'What's wrong?' I said. 'I can do it, can't I? I'll just have to sit down when I sing . . .'

'It's Dr Bray,' she said.

'What about him?'

'I already talked to him. He needs to do another surgery. In the middle of June. That's as fast as he can get you into the operating room. It's a big one. The surgery that will decide your quality of life from here on.'

'But the show's in *August*.'

'You'd only have seven weeks. Seven weeks to make a full recovery.'

'That's enough . . . right?'

'Ozzy – it's major spinal surgery. He's going to be fixing vertebrae all the way to your middle back. You're going to be bedridden for a long time. You'll be starting physical therapy from scratch. We don't know if you'll end up in the ICU again. How bad the swelling will be. How long it'll take before you can even *do* physical therapy. There are so many unknowns, Ozzy. You know that. You've lived it for the last three and a half fucking years. We all have. And you'd be telling Prince Charles and everyone at the games, yes, you can do it, even though you know deep down there's a very good chance you won't be ready. And it's not just the performance, Ozzy. It's the eleven-hour flight. The jet lag. The long drive. The hotel . . .'

She had to stop, she was getting too emotional again.

I was feeling pretty emotional myself.

Sharon was right.

I felt like I was sinking to the bottom of an ocean of shit.

I was gonna have to turn down what would have been one of the greatest gigs of my life.

13

Good as It Gets

I'd hit rock bottom a few times in my life, but always from booze and drugs.

In June of 2022, I hit rock bottom from spinal surgery and Parkinson's.

It started in April when I finally got Covid. Fortunately, I'd been shot up with about a gallon of vaccines by then, 'cos like I said before, my Parkinson's makes me a high-risk case. Sharon freaked out when I lost my sense of smell and started to sniffle, fearing the worst. But I was fine. I didn't get pneumonia. It just felt like a really bad cold that dragged on a bit.

But as always with me now, there was a domino effect.

Because I was in bed for so long, I started getting blood clots. If you've got a queasy stomach, you might wanna jump ahead. Basically, a haematology guy had to cut a hole in my groin, find a thick vein and stick a catheter in there. Then he inserted a folded-up filter thing into the catheter and pushed it up into the vein. Once it was in, it opened up like an umbrella. It's like I've got a little tea strainer next to my left bollock, basically. It lets your blood flow but catches the clots before they travel to your heart. When the clots are caught, meanwhile, they just break down naturally. Or the doc goes in there and removes 'em manually.

But of course the whole thing was a shitshow, 'cos halfway through the procedure, a rogue clot ended up in my stomach. So all these nurses were running around, pumping me full of anticoagulants – blood thinners – as about ten different klaxons went off. The side effects were absolutely horrific. Pissing blood. Bleeding gums. Nosebleeds. Bruising.

But at least when it was all over I could relax.

Yeah, fucking right.

The second I'd recovered, I was getting wheeled into an operating room for my second corrective surgery with Dr Bray. This was the BIG ONE. Half of my backbone was gonna be under construction. They were gonna need traffic cones, hard hats and pneumatic drills. I was nervous this time. Part of me expected to wake up in the ICU. Or not wake up at all. Even if it went well, I knew it was gonna be a long, hard road back. And I was tired, man. I was seventy-three. I was officially too old for this shit.

To say I was a wreck when I came out would be putting it mildly.

I felt like I'd been shat up a wall. Nothing worked. Not my arm. Not my legs. My neck was better without the screws, but it was still fucked.

Everything was fucked.

I lost hope again.

The thing is, when every two steps forward is followed

by eight steps back, there comes a point when you don't even wanna take the two steps any more. That's the problem with getting multiple surgeries. You lose the will, you really do. Because as I was starting to find out, every time you get laid up, all the stamina you've built up is gone within a week. Which means you have to climb all the way back to the top of the mountain again . . . knowing you're just gonna get knocked straight back down to the bottom when the *next* surgery comes up. It starts to feel pointless. You think, fuck it. You semi give in to it. You stop wanting to make the effort. Not that I ever got to the point where I wanted to end it all. I mean, knowing my luck, I'd fuck it up if I ever tried. Instead of topping myself I'd just end up setting myself on fire or something, and end up in an even worse state than I was before.

As I was lying there, I realised it had been my *sixth* surgery in four years. The hand surgery for the staph infection. The collarbone surgery. The first spinal surgery with Dr No Socks. The first corrective spine surgery with Dr Bray. The umbrella surgery for the blood clots. And now this, the second corrective spine surgery. I'd been up and down the recovery ladder so many times, man. I just didn't want to do it any more.

When I got home, my legs swelled up so much, physical therapy wasn't even an option.

I just stayed in bed, feeling like shit.

On Instagram, meanwhile, I tried to put a brave face on things, saying I was 'recuperating comfortably' and 'feeling the love and support from all my fans'. And of course I thanked everyone for their well wishes.

But the truth was, I'd never felt worse.

Fittingly, it was the same week 'Patient Number 9'

was released – a song about being trapped in a mental asylum and wanting to get out. Which was exactly how I felt. It was the lead single from the album – which we'd announced would be released in September – with Jeff Beck on guitar.

Hearing the song on the radio lifted my spirits for a moment, at least. It was good to know I could still work, still put out records. And it was a huge honour to have Jeff Beck play on there. His solo is next-fucking-level. It was a huge shock when we lost him six months later from meningitis. What a loss. He was the ultimate guitarist's guitarist, really. For someone who'd been in The Yardbirds, and had a band with Rod Stewart and Ronnie Wood, he kept a pretty low profile, but he was up there with Clapton, Page, Hendrix ... no question. Meanwhile, the music video we put out was directed by the comic book creator Todd McFarlane and the animator M. Wartella. They did a phenomenal job with it. They even animated one of my hand-drawn demons. It was great seeing it come to life.

I just wished I could get rid of the ones living inside my head.

Our fortieth wedding anniversary came around a couple of weeks after the surgery.

I was in no state to play Romeo. Sharon and I weren't gonna be putting on our old Lionel Richie records and swinging from the bedposts, that was for sure.

It was crazy to think we'd known each other fifty-two years. First as acquaintances. Then as friends. Then as manager and client. Then as lovers. Then as husband and wife ... then parents ... now grandparents.

Although we couldn't celebrate, I was very happy that five years earlier, in 2017, we'd renewed our vows at the wedding chapel of the Wynn hotel in Las Vegas. We did it on Mother's Day, which was the perfect occasion, 'cos I'm so grateful to Sharon for giving us our three kids.

The best part of the renewal ceremony was that I was sober. So it was the *real* Ozzy who said 'I do', not drunk-world Ozzy. And I got to remember it the next day.

When we first got married, it was on the island of Maui, in Hawaii. I got absolutely arseholed. There were seven bottles of Hennessy just in the wedding cake. I was also as high as a kite, thanks to the local weed – 'Maui-wowy', they call it. Tommy Aldridge was my best man. My mum and big sister Jean flew out to be there. Sharon's dad was lurking somewhere.

There was no consummating the marriage. The only consummating that went on was between me and every bottle of booze they had at the hotel bar. I fell asleep in the corridor at five o'clock in the morning. The hotel manager had to call Sharon to come and get me, 'cos the maids couldn't get past me and they were complaining about the smell. I even missed my stag night 'cos I blacked out before it started. *Who does that?* The funny thing was, 'cos of my British passport, I had to get a blood test before they'd give us our marriage certificate.

'What exactly are you looking for?' Sharon asked the guy who came to take the sample. 'Traces of blood in his alcohol?'

When we got back to LA, we did a proper Jewish wedding. And once again, I was totally off my face. I have almost no recollection of it.

After we renewed our vows, Sharon said it was like

falling in love all over again. But I didn't need to fall in love again. No matter how fucked up I might have been during the first two ceremonies, Sharon's the only woman I've ever loved. Without her, I'm nothing. Don't get me wrong, I ain't saying everything's perfect now. Whenever I hear 'Oh, we never argue' I'm like, well, you must be brain dead. But what I understand now is that being married is like riding a wild horse. If you can hold on to the horse, it gets better and better. We still bicker – of course we do. But what happens now is, if we have a disagreement, I'll just say I'm sorry. I'll defuse it. I won't dig in like I used to. It's liberating, when you can put your ego back in its box and not let it waste so much of your time and energy.

Besides, we've got our kids and grandbabies to worry about now. We can't be fighting between ourselves. And we got one more grandkid a few days after our anniversary – Jack and Aree's baby Maple. She was my ninth. Sharon's fourth. Meanwhile, Kelly announced she was pregnant with her little Sid. Her man, also Sid, plays in the metal band Slipknot. He became friends with Kelly at an Ozzfest all the way back in 1999. Then years later they reconnected when she walked into his record shop on Melrose Avenue. What blows my mind is that he's from Des Moines, Iowa. That's the same town where I ... well, you know what I did. What a strange coincidence.

It's almost as strange as when I asked Sid what he played in Slipknot, and he said, 'I'm the DJ.' I was like, 'What the fuck does a DJ do in a metal band?' Then Kelly pointed out I'd once sung 'Iron Man' with Busta Rhymes.

I was like, good point well made.

*

Six weeks after the surgery, I was finally starting to feel more human again.

In fact, I was desperate to get out of the house.

That's when Sharon suggested we take a trip down to San Diego, a couple of hours south of LA. It was the week of Comic-Con, which I'd always been curious about, but had never been to before.

Comic-Con's been going on for as long I've been a singer, I've since learned. It started out as a little get-together of comic book and science fiction fans in the basement of a hotel. Now it's this huge four-day thing that fills the entire San Diego Convention Center. More than a hundred thousand people from all over the world go there every year. There's all kinds of shit on sale there, they have special screenings and panels, comic book signings, appearances by guys like Chris Pratt from *Guardians of the Galaxy* and Patrick Stewart from *Star Trek*, people dressed up as every Marvel Comics and video game character you can imagine, it's crazy.

Sharon said Todd McFarlane was gonna be there, signing a comic book he'd made for one of the limited editions of the *Patient Number 9* album.

'Why don't you do the signing with him?' she said. 'It's close to home. You'd be sitting down. It's the perfect way to ease back into things.'

Honestly, I'd have gone to the opening of a fucking envelope just for the change of scenery.

Next thing I knew, I was on one of those electric golf cart things, whizzing through the convention centre after checking out the twenty-five-foot-high inflatable Ozzy someone had put outside. It was like another world. All these grown men and women walking around in capes and helmets and neon wigs, holding foam swords. I loved it. The booth we were at was absolutely mobbed. The queue went all the way out of the building. People had been waiting for hours. It was nuts. By the end of it, Sharon said our signing had been the biggest one of the whole convention.

No sooner had we got home than the phone rang.

It was the Commonwealth Games again. Someone in their office was a big sci-fi fan and they'd been keeping an eye on the news coming out of Comic-Con. And of course they'd seen me, alive and well, signing posters, looking much better than they'd expected. Mind you, I'm not sure how much of a compliment that was. It sounded like they'd been expecting me to look a cross between Herman Munster and one of them Iron Age blokes they keep digging out of peat bogs in fucking Denmark.

When Sharon told me they'd called, the first thing that went through my head was, shit, I must have really pissed them off, turning down the gig then showing up at a convention. But that wasn't the case at all.

'Okay, so there's absolutely no pressure, Ozzy, they were very clear about that,' said Sharon. 'But they wanted to let you know, in case there's *any* chance ...' She was grinning, 'cos she already knew what I was gonna say. 'If you still wanted to perform at the closing ceremony ...'

I couldn't believe it. I couldn't fucking believe it. What were the chances of them coming back and asking again? I was almost jumping up and down.

'I'm going!' I said.

'Are you *absolutely* sure you're—'

'I'm going! When is it again?'

'About that, Ozzy. It's ... fairly soon.'

'How soon??'

'In six days. Including today.'

It wasn't a choice, as far as I was concerned. If I'm ever asked to do *anything* for Birmingham, I do it. It's a rule I have. Although I haven't lived there for a while, Birmingham's part of my heart and soul. As soon as I clear customs at Heathrow and start driving up the M6, I become a Brummie again.

Of course, saying yes was the easy part. This was gonna be the first live gig I'd done since appearing with Post Malone, and that had been three years ago now. It would also be the first gig since the two corrective surgeries with Dr Bray, and since I'd had the tea strainer thing put in my groin.

The truth was, I couldn't really walk at all now. I was *very* shaky. So there was a lot of practical shit to think about. Sharon would be there to help me, of course, as would a nurse. And they'd need to crane-lift me onto the stage or something. Also, 'cos I couldn't stand up for very long, I need to lean on some kind of support while I sang. I was weird, thinking about it. I've always liked to feel part of the audience when I'm doing a gig. But I was in a new world now. This was how it was gonna be from now on.

Meanwhile ... there was no way we could get Sabbath together at such short notice. But Sharon had already called Tony, and he was up for it. She'd also called Tommy Clufetos, who'd said yes immediately, as had Adam Wakeman, who'd volunteered to play bass instead of his usual keyboards.

I can't even put into words how exciting it all was.

I was shitting myself too.

All I could think was, can this really work? Can I pull it off? Can I do this?

Not that it really mattered.

As long as I was still breathing, nothing was gonna stop me trying.

There was no private jet waiting at Van Nuys airport to whisk us back to London. When you ain't working – or at least touring – the old bank account starts to get a bit light. So it was a regular commercial flight out of LAX for me and Sharon.

In the good old days, of course, commercial meant Concorde. It's crazy we've gone back in time when it comes to planes. Who would have thought flying today would be *slower* than it was in the seventies and eighties?

Concorde was such a scene, man. I miss it.

Mind you, it was a lot more basic than people realise. When you sat at the back, you could smell the jet fuel. That thing was a flying bomb, really. And it was *small* inside. Like being in a test tube. But it was quick and it was fun.

I used to think of Concorde as like a sports car in the sky – although it had no engine noise 'cos you were moving so fast. You just outran the sound, it was incredible. You'd feel a couple of little bumps when you broke through the sound barrier, and that was it, BOOM, you were gone. And if you went up front, the captain would let you look in the cockpit, and you could see the curvature of the earth, with the darkness of space above.

What an experience, man.

And of course it was the absolute *best* way to travel if you were a raging alcoholic. The thing about the Concorde lounge at Heathrow was, you could clear American customs while you were still in London, which meant you could get there at the last minute and still have time for a couple of double vodkas at the bar. Then you'd take off at nine thirty in the morning, fly for three hours at the speed of an F-16 fighter jet while eating grouse for breakfast on a full set of Wedgwood china, followed by a cheese plate, a bottle of port and a couple of twenty-year-old single malts, then you were staggering down the jetway at Kennedy airport. And 'cos you'd crossed the Atlantic faster than the time difference, you were arseholed before you'd technically started drinking.

Trust me . . . it *never* got old.

The biggest problem with Concorde was there were only four toilets for just over a hundred very well-lubricated people. And no one would ever go until the very last second before landing – otherwise you might miss out on the pre-landing beverage of some eighteenth-century Madeira they were serving in a hand-blown crystal decanter or something – so there was always a queue. I stood there once and just pissed my pants. I'd had an entire bottle of some vintage French Armagnac on top of about three gallons of Belgian lager. I just couldn't wait. I was like, ah, fuck it. It's amazing BA didn't ban me. I suppose I was too good a customer. I mean, there was a time when I was using Concorde like it was a London cab.

Not everyone was comfortable with the Buckingham Palace levels of service you got on Concorde, mind you. Bill Ward was one of 'em. He'd bring two plastic carrier bags full of whatever provisions he needed for the flight.

I'd be like, 'Bill, why the fuck are you eating a day-old pork pie and drinking Kwik Save cider? What's wrong with you? They're serving champagne from Napoleon's private collection in a minute!'

'Oh, I don't wanna put them to any trouble,' he'd mumble.

The calibre of people you'd fly with on Concorde was also incredible. Titans of industry. Royalty. Politicians. One time, I was in the Concorde lounge and in strolls Paul McCartney. I'd just seen him play a few weeks earlier at the Forum in LA. I was like a starstruck little kid. It was the time when Hamish Stuart from Average White Band was touring with him, and I said to Hamish – 'cos I knew him – 'Tell Paul, I just saw you guys play in LA and you were fucking phenomenal.' Then I hid. Paul was sitting right at the front when we took off. I didn't dare go up there.

I'd already stopped flying Concorde when it crashed. There was no logical reason why I stopped. It was just pure superstition. I was watching something on the news and the announcer said it had been flying for twenty-something years without a single fatal accident, and I just thought, okay, that's tempting fate, that is. I mean, once that thing was going down the runway, it was so fast, there was no aborting. I felt so sorry for the people on the plane that went down just outside of Paris. They knew it was on fire. It must have been horrendous. They had no chance. And of course when one went down, they grounded all of them. That said something to me. It was an antique by then. And there were so few of 'em in service, it must have been costing a fortune to keep 'em flying.

But it was sad, the supersonic age coming to an end.

I doubt I'll be around long enough to see the next one . . . if it ever comes.

*

It's crazy how much flying's changed over the years. In the early days of my career, there was no walking through body scanners. No one even used to search you up. You could have all kinds of shit on you when you got on a plane, as long as you weren't stupid enough to try and take it through customs.

After Leslie West from Mountain introduced Black Sabbath to cocaine – we were opening for him at the time, so it would have been 1971, probably in Seattle or Denver – we eventually got to the point where we were flying everywhere with our dealer. That's how relaxed we were about carrying drugs around. He was basically a member of the band.

I vividly remember when I met the guy, 'cos I was coming back from some gig in Australia and our plane overshot the runway when it stopped in Hawaii. I got such a bad fright I had the hardest time getting back on board to continue on to LA. But I did. Then once we landed, I took a limo to Beverly Hills and checked myself into the Beverly Wilshire hotel – the one that would later become famous for the *Pretty Woman* movie – only to find Glenn Hughes from Deep Purple in the bar. He'd *just* joined Deep Purple, so this must have been a couple of years after the Mountain gig. We got talking, and I started telling him what a great time I'd had on blow, and he gave me the phone number of a guy who could hook me up.

So I called the guy, one thing led to another, and it was the beginning of a long and beautiful friendship. The guy never left our side. He was like our own personal blow butler. Even when I went back to England after the tour, he'd be sending me the stuff in the post. I'm pretty sure that's how I got the coke I hid in John Bonham's barn while I was on holiday. That's probably why I was so protective of it – 'cos you couldn't buy it in England, the only way to get some was if someone sent it to you from America.

Even in the days when security was lax, mind you, doing coke while you were in the airport was never the cleverest idea. But if you were on a long internal flight with a layover, you *needed* a quick bump between legs to keep you from crashing. I remember one time being at an airport in Texas, I forget which one, and I was coming down so badly I didn't know what to do with myself. I had chills and body aches. Fatigue. That jumpy, paranoid feeling.

So off I go to the bog to sort myself out. I find a stall. Lock the door. Sit down on the seat. Take out a little book of matches and start fashioning a coke spoon out of it. Then I scoop a bit of coke out of my 'snuff box' – *ahhhh, yes, this'll do the trick* – but just as I'm about to take a nice big sniff, I notice a pair of very shiny boots walking into the stall next to me.

I freeze.

Could that be a—

Probably not, I thought.

But let me just check . . .

I put away the coke spoon. Bend down as far as I can without making it too obvious. And sure enough, under the partition – fuck! – I glimpse the hem of a dark blue pair of cop trousers. Then I almost jump out of my skin as the rest of his trousers, including his belt and keys and gun holster and handcuffs, all clatter to the ground as he sits down to do his thing.

I couldn't believe it.

I really needed that bump, man. I was shivering. I had sweat running down my face. But I could hardly go *SSSHHHRRKK!!* in an almost totally silent stall with Captain Crapper sitting four feet away from me. I was just gonna have to give up and come back later. But then another part of me was, like, no, fuck it, I'm here, it's been a long day, *I deserve this coke.*

That's when I heard the familiar sound of pages turning. *The cop was reading a fucking book.*

In the end, I decided to just wait him out. He must have got through half of *Moby Dick* by the time I finally heard the plop. Then suddenly I was sitting bolt upright, spoon at the ready, when – PHHHWWOOOOOOSSSSHH!! – he flushed the bog and I vacuumed up the rest of my coke at the same time, so he couldn't hear me go *SNNNFFF-GAH!!*

We both left our stalls at the same time.

I felt like I was about a foot off the ground with a double rainbow shooting out of my arse.

'Oh, hello officer,' I said, giving him a nice big friendly smile, knowing that even if he patted me down the evidence was now safely up my left nostril.

He just looked me up and down with a sneer. Cops didn't like long-haired rockers in those days. They thought we were all drug addicts. Which, to be fair . . .

Then I got the fuck out of there.

Not long after that, I was flying back to London from the California Jam festival. Glenn Hughes was sitting near me in first class, along with some other guys from Deep Purple.

I must have had four grams of blow down my sock when I got on that plane, man. Those really were . . . *very* different times. And of course the second we're in the air, the sock comes off, the blow comes out and we're all having a grand old time. Then at some point the head stewardess comes up to me. 'Can I have a word with you, please?' she says. '*At the back.*'

I'm like, oh fuck, here we go. My eyeballs are throbbing. My heart's racing. I can't stop blabbering on about all the things that keep popping into my head. And she leads me all the way to the back of this 747. A few other stewardesses are all huddled there. And I'm expecting them to bust me, tell me there'll be cops waiting to arrest me when we land.

'*We know what it is you're taking,*' she says as my blood runs cold. I thought I was fucked, I really did.

'What d'you mean?' I said, trying really hard not to sniff. 'I'm not taking anyth—'

'Can *we* have some?' she goes.

It was one of the best flights of my life. We were so high, we just about beat the plane to Heathrow. But then of course we had to queue up for immigration, and the comedown was the worst I'd ever had. I was so obviously in a state of catastrophic cocaine withdrawal, Glenn Hughes took me aside before we got to customs, and he said, look, Ozzy, I've got two bumps left in my extra-special reserve, I was saving it for myself, but there's *no way* you can walk through customs looking like that, you'll be spending the next month on a table with a rubber glove up your arse. So he gave me the last of his supply, and I floated through the 'nothing to declare' door while all these grim-faced customs guys looked on.

That was the trick – you *always* got rid of whatever shit you had on you *before* you got to customs. That was especially important for me, 'cos I'd been busted for drugs in England early on, so I had a special code on my passport, flagging me for an extra search. On the way back to LA, I remember, this immigration officer flicked through my passport, saw the code and asked me what I'd been done for. 'Possession of drugs,' I had to tell him.

'Let me tell you something, son,' he said. 'Don't you even *think* of bringing any of that stuff into *this* country. We'll lock you up and throw away the key.'

All I could think was, *what are you talking about?* Bringing cocaine to LA in 1975 would have been like bringing coal to Newcastle in 1913.

'No, officer,' I said, 'of course not, officer, I wouldn't dream of doing that, officer.'

THUMP. He stamped my passport extra hard.

'Have a nice day.'

It was an incredible feeling, landing in England for the first time in eight or nine years, knowing that I was gonna be representing my country and my home town.

The old stage fright was coming back with a vengeance, though. Especially 'cos the closing ceremony of the games was gonna be broadcast live on BBC One.

Even without the cameras there, when it's a special event like that it's very different to being on tour. You only get one shot. If you make a mistake, that's it. Add the cameras, and it takes the fear to a whole new level. Nine times out of ten when there's cameras there, I fuck it up. Meanwhile, there's absolutely *nothing* worse than watching yourself back later on. When I see myself performing, I can remember exactly where my head was at every single moment. And if I yodel a line – meaning my voice cracks and I warble – I cringe so hard, man. It's like when I listen to myself talking in interviews. I can't stand it. I have to switch it off.

I wasn't all that worried about the jet lag, though. I have a tried and tested way for dealing with that – the second I land, I switch to the local time, no matter how hard it is for the first twenty-four hours. If I catch it straight away, I'm fine. It's when you try and stay on your own time that you up end falling asleep at random times of the day.

What I couldn't get over was the weather. When I was growing up, the one thing you could guarantee in August was fucking rain. But it was all cloudless blue skies and sunshine, with the kind of heat you'd normally get in the South of France. It was so hot we had to use a hotel as a dressing room, 'cos there was no AC at the stadium. I remember saying to Sharon, 'We've *got* to get AC at Welders House, or we'll never be able to stay there in the summer.' In my mind, I was like, global warming must be making England hotter, this must be normal now. But ever since then, every time I've asked someone from England how their summer was, the answer's always been the same: '*We didn't have one.*'

My family was there to meet me before the show. It was great to see 'em. But it was also very strange, 'cos my brother Tony had died in 2014, and my sister Iris two years after that. My sister Jean had also lost her husband Norman – he was like the older brother I'd never had – just before the start of *No More Tours II*. So it was just me and Jean, my other sister Gillian and my remaining brother Paul. It was the most peculiar feeling, because it had always been the six of us at family get-togethers over the years, and now there we were, down to four. Meanwhile, most of my old friends from Aston were no longer around.

The drive to Alexander Stadium was also weird. I used to know Perry Barr like the back of my hand. Same with Birchfield and Newtown, my other old stamping grounds. But so many streets and buildings have been re-built since the seventies, I couldn't get my bearings. None of the streets I was seeing had been there in my day. I was hoping some of the old memories would come back . . . but it was all so different, I could have been anywhere. I was also nervous, I suppose, which made it hard to focus on anything for very long.

The funny thing is, I didn't get to see much of the stadium itself, even though we did a run-through and sound check a few hours before the show. The backstage area was basically *under* the main stage. It was a whole world down there. There were jugglers and gymnasts and dancers stretching out. All totally enclosed, so they were invisible to the audience.

The first thing we did was go and talk to the stage manager.

All I had to do, he said, was stand on a mechanical plat-form that would rise up through an opening on the stage floor. That's how I'd make my entrance. It would *look* like I was standing up – and I would be, technically – but I'd have a curved seat back to lean on, attached to a pole. And no one would see it 'cos I'd be wearing this long, flowing black coat. Underneath the coat would also be a special harness, just to make sure.

I wasn't gonna be doing any stage-dives, that was for sure.

Sharon was still terrified I was gonna fall over as half the world watched. I kept telling her, 'I'll be fine! I'll be fine!'

It took the longest time for Tony to arrive. He's moved away from Birmingham now, so he had a long drive. By the time he got there it was all very rushed, very business-like. Not unfriendly or anything. We had a job to do – and Tony was probably as nervous as I was. And of course there were cameras everywhere, recording our every word.

It was hard to believe I was back in action again. I felt like Douglas Bader, the famous pilot who lost his legs in a plane crash but was allowed to come out of retirement to fly in the Battle of Britain. Bader was incredibly strong, apparently, so he could lift himself up into the cockpit using just his arms.

He got shot down and captured eventually. But even the Germans were like, holy fuck, this guy's been flying a plane with no legs, he deserves some respect . . .

The hours between the run-through and the show were some of the longest of my life.

Just absolute torture, man.

I went and sat in a corner, focusing on my breathing, trying to keep myself steady.

'Remember,' said Tony, just before we went on, 'we'll do the opening of "Iron Man", no verse, just the riff – then "Paranoid", okay?'

'Okay.'

'Break a leg, Ozzy.'

'You too, Tony.'

Other than the run-through and sound check, there'd

been no rehearsal. It hadn't even come up when we'd been planning the whole thing. I mean, we'd played those two songs just about every night for the best part of fifty years.

If we didn't know 'em by now, we never would.

Total darkness. Turning slowly to red.
Smoke.
THUD. THUD. THUD. THUD ...
A deafening roar goes up as the crowd recognises the song.
Chanting.
Clapping.
Cheering.
An ocean of pinprick lights from thirty thousand phones.
THUD. THUD. THUD. THUD ...
Every thump of Tommy's right foot on his bass drum feels like an incoming mortar.
Here it comes ...
DDNNNNNEEEEEEOOOOOOOWWWWW-WWW ...
That first note of 'Iron Man' gets me every time, man. You feel it in your bowels. Your teeth. Your bones. It's like the gates of hell grinding open. Like the groan of the Heinkel bombers as they dipped below the clouds to try take out the Castle Bromwich Spitfire factory, night after night. Like the thunder of the heavy machinery our fathers used to operate. And their fathers before them.
DDNNNNNEEEEEEOOOOOOOWWWWW-WWW ...
THUD. THUD. THUD. THUD ...
DDNNNNNEEEEEEOOOOOOOWWWWW-WWW ...

'I ... AM ... IRON ... MAN.' I'm on the platform, rising up into the glowing red mist. I don't just feel part of the crowd ... I AM the fucking crowd.

Video projections flicker on the fifty-foot-high speaker columns to either side of me.

DUUHG-NUUUUUGH, DUH-NUH-HUH ... D-N-D-N-D-N-DUH, DUH-NUH-NUH!!

Columns of fire erupt from the stage as Tony tears into the riff. I'm looking out over Perry Barr ... over Aston. Over the place I grew up, sixty, seventy years ago. Over a crowd that seems to stretch halfway to Wolverhampton. We're live on BBC One. Prince Charles is here. All I can think is, what an honour. What a life. What were the chances it would turn out like this?

'LET'S GO CRAZY!!' I'm screaming.

Explosions everywhere. Hundreds of rockets blasting up from every corner of the stadium into the night sky. They flare so brightly it feels like day.

And we're into 'Paranoid'.

Muscle memory at this point. I'm bouncing up and down. Grinning my face off. Raising my arms up. Clapping along with the crowd. I'm hitting the notes. No yodelling. Blinding flashes of red, orange, white and blue all around and above me. We're belting out the song like we're twenty-three years old. Then Tony's into the solo. The guy's as cool as the day I met him. Leather blazer. Shades on. Ripping through the notes, hands barely moving, making it seem like the easiest thing in the world, even though the tips of his fingers are still made out of Fairy Liquid bottle tops.

We're into the last verse. It's over almost before it's even begun. I'm buzzing, man. As high as a kite. And all without the help of a single drug or drop of booze.

'BIRMINGHAM FOREVER!' I'm screaming between

the booms and thuds of the rockets, as the skyline of the city where I was born glows and vibrates.

Then we're done.

One last burst of light.

Then darkness again.

DING.

The lift doors opened at the car park level.

This was maybe twenty, thirty minutes after the show.

'See you, then, Tony,' I said.

'See you, Ozzy.'

He went one way, I went the other. There wasn't much to say. We were both in a daze. What I didn't realise at the time – but Sharon pointed out to me later – was that I'd left my cane behind in the backstage area. I had so much adrenaline in my system, I was walking on my own, without thinking about it.

Later, as we were getting into the limo-van that was taking us to the airport, Sharon told me Brian May of Queen had posted on Instagram that he was in tears watching the performance. I'd shed a few tears myself as all those fireworks went off. Tony probably had too, but he was wearing his shades, so you couldn't tell. It was totally, utterly overwhelming. There are no words that could do any justice to what it felt like being up there. *I was home. I'd made it.* All the shit I'd been through in the last few years ... it just melted away. I just wished we'd done more songs. We were on such a roll up there, we could have done half a set.

As we drove out of the car park, Sharon kept telling me about the part of the stadium we couldn't see from the stage. The centrepiece of the whole thing, she said, was this giant mechanical bull, about thirty-three feet high, made out of what looked like scorched metal. It had been created by a movie special effects company, Artem, based in London.

She couldn't stop raving about this bull. 'You should have seen it, Ozzy, it could walk, it would rear upon its hind legs, even blow steam out of its nose!!'

The bull was made out of metal to represent Birmingham's heavy industry, she said. And the reason it was a bull was 'cos of the bull-baiting that used to happen on the green where the Bullring & Grand Central shopping centre is now. It was a horrible bloodsport, bull-baiting. The poor bulls were tied to a stake, then attacked by dogs until they were either killed or badly fucked up. Even if they survived the baiting, they were slaughtered afterwards. That's what the original British bulldogs were bred for – to go ten rounds with a bull. It's why they were so tough. I suppose it's all people had for entertainment in them days.

I was finding it hard to pay attention to what Sharon was saying, though, 'cos we exited the stadium a different way than we went in, and the second we made a left, I was like, *fucking hell, I know exactly where we are!*

We were just a block or two from my old school, Birchfield Road Secondary Modern.

Now I had my bearings, I asked the driver to take a few detours. Suddenly I was looking at the old Methodist Mission Hall where we used to rehearse, passing the Church Tavern just around the corner. It's one of the few old pubs still around. Most of 'em are gone, which makes sense 'cos Aston's a Muslim area now. Then we were at Villa Park. Then around the corner from there – just off Witton Road – we were at my old street, Lodge Road.

Meanwhile, the street where Tony used to live – Park Lane – has been wiped off the face of the earth, including his parents' old corner shop, Iommi's. It's all new buildings there now.

Meanwhile, the driver said the façade of the old GEC factory where my dad worked is still there – it's a listed building, apparently – but the factory itself is long gone. It's some kind of online shopping warehouse now. The last places we drove by were Lizzie's, where I used buy a cigarette and match, and the launderette, where my mum used to wash our clothes. There's a Chinese takeaway and a mobile phone shop there now.

Then we were off to Heathrow, to catch our flight back to LA. Meanwhile, back at the stadium, they were already starting to take out the extra seats and wheel away the mechanical bull, ready to take him apart and throw him on the scrapheap.

On the plane, me and Sharon agreed to move forward with something we'd been planning for a very long time. We wanted to give back to Birmingham in a meaningful way. Sharon had this dream of setting up a music school in a converted warehouse, in keeping with Sabbath's roots. They wouldn't just teach music there, but also theatre, set design, recording. There'd be guest lectures by well-known people. A permanent collection of my tour memorabilia. An interactive museum. A coffee shop.

'It sounds amazing,' I said to her, 'but that'll take ten years. I don't have ten years.'

'Give me three,' she said. 'And y'know what, Ozzy,' she went on, 'since you're officially performing again, why not do one last gig with Sabbath for the opening?'

I just laughed. At my age, with my injury and my

Parkinson's, it was hard enough to plan for next month, never mind 2025.

But I wasn't gonna object.

'Okay,' I said, 'you're on.'

For a moment after the games, I seemed like I could adjust to this new way of performing. When *Patient Number 9* officially launched in September – exactly one month after my trip to the Commonwealth Games – I did one more show, playing at halftime during the season opening game for the Los Angeles Rams. They'd won the Super Bowl the previous year, so there was a good vibe in the stadium. Zakk and Andrew were on guitar. Tommy on drums. Chris Chaney from Jane's Addiction on bass. We did two songs, 'Crazy Train' and the lead single, 'Patient Number 9'.

Meanwhile, I started doing this far-out thing called cybernics treatment, which was invented in Japan, apparently. You basically wear a bionic suit while you're doing physical therapy. They call it a Hybrid–Assistive Limb, or HAL. The idea is that your brain tells the suit to move, then when your body moves with the help of all these motors and gearwheels, that sends a message back to your brain. Over time, it helps 'regenerate your neural pathways' . . . whatever the fuck that means. It ain't a miracle cure, but I'll give anything a shot.

The trouble was, as the dates of the European tour drew closer and closer – the first date was gonna be in Helsinki, Finland – I realised the mountain was just too steep to climb. Especially when Dr Bray said he wouldn't be able to get my final surgery done before then. Time had finally run out. I had to face the reality. I was never gonna finish *No More Tours II*.

On 1 February 2023, I posted this on Instagram:

This is probably one of the hardest things I've ever had to share with my loyal fans. As you may all know, four years ago, this month, I had a major accident, where I damaged my spine. My one and only purpose during this time has been to get back on stage. My singing voice is fine. However, after three operations, stem cell treatments, endless physical therapy sessions, and most recently groundbreaking Cybernics (HAL) Treatment, my body is still physically weak.

I am honestly humbled by the way you've all patiently held onto your tickets for all this time, but in all good conscience, I have now come to the realisation that I'm not physically capable of doing my upcoming European/UK tour dates, as I know I couldn't deal with the travel required.

Believe me when I say that the thought of disappointing my fans really FUCKS ME UP, more than you will ever know. Never would I have imagined that my touring days would have ended this way. My team is currently coming up with ideas for where I will be able to perform without having to travel from city to city and country to country. I want to thank my family … my band … my crew … my longtime friends, Judas Priest, and of course, my fans for their endless dedication, loyalty, and support, and for giving me the life that I never ever dreamed I would have.

I love you all.

*

'Are you ready, Ozzy?' said Dr Bray. 'Last one, I promise.'

I was on a stretcher bed again. This was September 2023, more than a year after the Commonwealth Games gig.

It was all so familiar now. The disposable gown. The compression socks. The smell of the antibacterial soap I was scrubbed down with the night before. The wristband with 'John Michael Osbourne, born 12/03/1948' written on it in black marker. The vial of Jackson juice hanging by my head – 'milk of amnesia', one of the nurses called it.

Then off they wheeled me to the OR . . . for my seventh surgery in five years.

Who'd have thought?

Not me, man. Not me. But this time felt different. I wasn't nervous, for a start. At this point, going under the knife was like going for a fucking haircut. And since we'd officially killed *No More Tours II*, I didn't have to worry about the recovery time, 'cos no one was holding on to a ticket, waiting for me to get better.

Even my doctors had given up on me ever walking again. 'After this,' said Dr Bray, 'it'll be as good as it's ever gonna get. Any more operations would just cause more pain and suffering . . . and I think you've had enough of that.'

In a weird way I was happy when he said it was the end of it all. It's the hope that kills you, y'know? Sometimes it's the greatest thing in the world to be told there's no light at the end of the tunnel. I mean, as heartbreaking as it's all been, I've got nothing to complain about. I'm alive – or at least I am as I write these words. I've got my Sharon. I've got my family. I've still got my marbles, or whatever marbles I ever had. And the crazy thing is, my voice is fine. No one's gonna stop me singing. I'll be singing until my final breath.

There was at least *some* good news before the surgery.

It started with a call from someone at Birmingham City Council. They told Sharon there was a petition to save the bull from the Commonwealth Games. She had to remind me what it was, 'cos I'd never set eyes on the thing. I didn't even get a proper look at the stadium. I spent the whole night either on the stage or under it.

I was happy to hear the bull might not get thrown on the scrapheap, but other than that, I never gave it another thought.

Then a few days later, Sharon says to me, 'You know that petition? It worked!'

'Okay,' I said. 'So what does that mean?'

She said it meant the bull would be taken back to the workshop of the special-effects company that made it, where they'd modify it to make it a permanent installation. Then they'd take it back to Birmingham, wheel it to the middle of the concourse of New Street station and fix it in place. It wouldn't be able to move any more, but its eyes would still light up. It would be one of the biggest pieces of public art in the country.

Next thing I knew, Sharon was running back in the room, a huge grin on her face, saying, 'And they're gonna have a vote to give the bull a name!!'

I was like, 'Okay, that's very interesting ... but why is that so exciting? That can call it whatever they want. They'll probably call it something stupid like Bully McBullface, like they always do.'

'No, no, Ozzy, you don't understand,' she said. 'They've already drawn up a shortlist of three names, based on suggestions from the public.'

'Okay?'

'The first is Brummie.'

'Makes sense.'

'The second is Bostin. Which means "brilliant" in—'

'I'm a fucking Brummie, Sharon, I know what it means. But no one else will . . .'

'And the third is . . .' She just stood there, grinning at me.

'What?'

'Ozzy!'

'What?? What have I done?'

'No, Ozzy!!!'

'I'm right here, what?'

'THE NAME "OZZY" IS ON THE SHORTLIST!'

Finally, I realised what she was saying.

I was happy, of course. But there was no fucking way they were gonna name some massive landmark after me. I mean, there were more than a million Brummies. There's only one Ozzy. So obviously Brummie was gonna win.

But then a day or two later, the votes were counted . . . and fuck me . . . Ozzy came in first.

'It wasn't even close,' said Sharon. 'You won in a landslide.'

The phones at the house blew up the second the result was announced. It was unbelievable. But honestly, it wasn't until Ozzy the bull was finally put in place and revealed to the public that it hit me. I couldn't go to the ceremony, sadly, 'cos of how hard it is for me to travel these days. But Sharon flew over, and she went to see it with my big sister Jean. She goes to every little thing, Jean, she'll always show up for me, no matter what. She even went to see a Black Sabbath ballet. I thought she was taking the piss when she first told me about that. But it was a real thing. The Birmingham Royal Ballet did it. They're even touring with it now, taking it to the Kennedy Center in Washington DC.

Sharon and Jean called me from New Street station once the unveiling was over. Not that they had much to say, 'cos they were both sobbing too much. 'You don't understand, Ozzy,' Sharon kept telling me, 'it's massive. It takes up half the station! And people love it. It's going to be here for generations to come.'

When I got off the call, I was kind of in shock for a while. Then when I saw the news footage of it later, I was like, fucking hell, I had no idea. Sharon had kept trying to tell me just how big it was. I thought she meant it was just a bit bigger than a regular bull. But it's the size of a three-storey fucking building.

That they named the bull after me, that I won that contest, that I got to play the closing ceremony of the Commonwealth Games with Tony, that Sabbath is now this big thing in Birmingham – it's unbelievable to me. At the age of seventy-six, to be a part of what makes Birmingham Birmingham, the bench, the bridge, the ballet – even the Birmingham Walk of Fame before all that – I dunno what to say. I was kind of freaked out by it all after Sharon and Jean called me, honestly. I was just going around the house beaming, not knowing what to do with myself.

All I could think was, I've got so much in common with that bull. Made in Birmingham. Full of metal. Can't walk any more. Still drawing a crowd, even though my main gig's over. Meanwhile, my head's down, eyes glowing, plenty of fight left in me. Oh, and the funny thing is, according to Sharon, after the bull was installed, they found a screw loose in his head.

When I heard that, I was like, okay, now it's official.

I really am that bull.

And the bull's *definitely* Ozzy.

Outro

Summer 2025

Well . . . I made it.

Back to England.

Back to Birmingham.

Back to the beginning, as my final gig was called.

For a while, I was convinced my last trip home would be in a pine fucking box.

I mean, I've got to be honest with you, when Sharon first mentioned the idea of the Back to the Beginning gig to me, around the time of the Commonwealth Games, I didn't think there was much chance of me making it to 2025. I was also like, no one will wanna do this, and no one's gonna watch. But she's unstoppable, my wife. When she decides to do something, she's gonna do it, end of story. She was absolutely determined to give me one last goodbye to the fans – with Sabbath re-forming for the occasion and sets by a whole host of other bands – all while donating the proceeds to Birmingham Children's

Hospital, Cure Parkinson's and Acorns Children's Hospice. I still can't believe she pulled it off.

Things only got worse with my spine, if you can believe it, after my last surgery with Dr Bray. We were supposed to leave LA for England in early December 2024, giving me a good seven months to prepare for my big send-off at Villa Park. The plan was I'd move back into Welders House while Sharon took the kids and grandkids to see Father Christmas in Lapland. Meanwhile, I'd be getting my arse kicked by a physical therapist every day, so I'd build up the stamina to get through two back-to-back sets, first with my own band, then another with Sabbath.

But two days before we were supposed to get on the plane, I was suddenly in absolute agony again. It was my back this time. What had gone wrong, I had no idea, but I was in so much pain I was almost in tears. So off I went back to Dr Bray, who put me through an X-ray machine, then sat me down and told me the deal. The vertebra he'd fixed back in 2023 was fine, he said. But the one underneath was completely fucked, to use the technical term. I was literally falling apart. Whether it was age, a result of my old quad bike accident, or the fact I just haven't been very kind to my body over the years, I don't know. But there was no way I was in a fit state to travel.

While Dr Bray came up with a plan, Sharon went off to Lapland and I stayed in hospital. And that's when I got pneumonia. Which is bad enough for a normal person, never mind someone with Parkinson's.

So of course Sharon had to cut short her trip and come back to LA. Everyone braced themselves for the worst, but I recovered enough to get out of hospital just before

Christmas. And just as I was thinking, fucking hell, that was a close one, suddenly I couldn't breathe. It was terrifying, that feeling of not getting enough air, like you're drowning on dry land.

The pneumonia had come back. Only this time it had kicked off my emphysema, causing one of my lungs to go down. My whole system was crashing. I'd only just left hospital a day or two earlier. Then suddenly I was back, in worse shape than before. What a Christmas that was.

How or why I kept getting pneumonia, I really don't know. It seems to be something you just pick up in hospitals. I'm also a bit of a couch rat, and when I'm lying down, food goes down the wrong way and that can start an infection, and 'cos my immune system's fucked, I go from totally okay to death's door in about five seconds.

After my second time with pneumonia, Dr Bray said there was nothing he could do about my back. He just flat-out refused to operate. He said I was too weak, that the recovery could kill me. But I didn't want to hear it. Neither did Sharon. So we went and got a second opinion, then a third, until eventually a team at Cedars said they'd give it a shot.

My blood clots complicated things. For my last surgery, I'd had that little tea strainer thing installed next to my left bollock to catch the clots before they got to my heart. But the strainer has to be replaced every so often. And when they took it out, they couldn't get it back in, and between each try I was left with only blood thinners for protection.

It took three procedures before they could finally get it back in place.

It was the middle of January when I got the surgery. They put me under. Opened up my back. Then they filled the cracks in my dodgy vertebra with this human cement stuff. I mean, I've got so many plates and bolts inside me already, why not pour a slab of concrete in there too?

When I woke up, I felt like someone had picked me up and slammed me against a rock. The pain was just beyond. It didn't help that all I could take for it was Tylenol, otherwise I'd have been floating away to Happy Land and never coming back. It was so bad, I got that paranoid feeling again that Sharon was hiding something from me. I was like, 'Just tell me the truth, I can handle it. I'm dying, aren't I?'

'Ozzy, I'm telling you everything,' she kept saying. 'You're *not* dying.'

That's when I got sepsis. Caused by the bone cement, Sharon told me. At that point, no one was pretending everything was okay. It really was touch and go. I mean, at my age, with Parkinson's and blood clots and all the other shit that's going on, I had about as much chance of surviving a major sepsis infection as I did of winning the next season of *Love Island*. And of course when they put me on antibiotics for it, that churned up my guts so badly I couldn't get any food down, so I was getting weaker by the day. Sharon didn't tell me at the time, but the whole family basically thought I was a goner. They sat at the bottom of the stairs and sobbed their hearts out. As for me, I was like, okay, I've had a good run, it's game over now.

But it wasn't game over. After two months of antibiotics – on a twice-a-day IV drip – I somehow bounced back. I honestly couldn't believe it. The sepsis hadn't killed me. I was gonna live to do my last show.

I celebrated by getting pneumonia again.

*

Those were desperate days, man.

All I wanted was to make it to that final show. And to walk again, I suppose. I just couldn't get my head around the fact I'd be spending the rest of my life in a wheelchair or clinging to a Zimmer frame.

But the problem with being desperate is people try to take advantage of you – especially when it comes to dodgy docs selling miracle cures.

I ain't proud to say we got taken in by a couple of total quacks. First was a guy in Canada who said if we paid him $170,000 he'd put me through a new kind of CAT scan, which could show everything that was wrong with me. So Sharon wired him the money and we went over to his clinic. But the machine was just a regular fucking X-ray machine. Then he gave me this box of 'special medicine' that was just a bunch of herbs and whatever, the same stuff you can buy on Amazon.

What a con.

At least we got our money back after Sharon went stage-five crazy on him.

Then we got suckered again, paying $100,000 to another miracle healer who had something called a PAP-IMI machine, which can supposedly cure anything with electromagnetic waves. I spent six days on that thing, three hours a day, only to find out later that it hasn't been proven to be safe and is illegal in the US.

After all that, I was like, fuck it, I'll stick to Tylenol.

It was the end of May when we finally left for England. I was feeling a lot better, but I had no idea if I'd be well enough to do the show. Not that there was much I could do about it. It was up to the gods to decide.

There were five of us travelling. Me, my nurse, Sharon, Aimee and our private security guard. And of course it was a total shitshow, like most things are in our family. Ironically enough, we'd booked one of those private suites at LAX, which are like a separate members-only terminal, where you can go through security in peace, get some drinks and food and whatever, then have a car take you out to the plane. It's supposed to make things easier. Yeah fucking right.

The main problem was that we didn't know when or if we'd be coming back. And Sharon had got it into her head that 'cos people knew we'd be in England for the show, they'd try and rob our house while we were away. I mean, we'd been robbed before – more than twenty years ago now – when we were living in England. I'd caught one of the fuckers in the act, got him in a headlock as he tried to get out through an open window, but I didn't have the strength to pull him back in. So I dropped him thirty feet onto the lawn below. Then off he limped with his mate and two million quid's worth of our jewellery in a bag. They were never caught. But I doubt the guy ever walked in a straight line again.

Anyway, 'cos of that experience, Sharon thought we should bring all our most valuable possessions on the plane. Literally everything we had in the safe was in my carry-on bag. All kinds of watches, chains, diamond rings, you name it. Plus twenty-five grand in US dollars.

But of course the people who run security at the suites are just regular TSA government workers. And they just about shit themselves when they looked at their X-ray machine and saw the Osbourne crown jewels going through. So the conveyor belt thing was stopped, everything had to come out and they started going through every piece of jewellery, counting all our cash, making sure it was all allowed.

Meanwhile, Sharon realised someone had fucked up our booking, so we weren't all sitting together. Which was a bigger deal than it sounds, 'cos I couldn't exactly ask some random bloke sitting next to me to lift me out of my seat and walk me to the bog every five minutes during the flight. So of course Sharon went off at the ticket ladies, screaming like a banshee, and they were just looking back at her like she was insane. But eventually she managed to get it all sorted out – just in time for the TSA guys to declare they were gonna confiscate fifteen of our twenty-five grand, because the limit is ten grand per person.

'But there's *five* of us!' Sharon said to the guy.

'Yeah, but it was all in one person's bag.'

'THEN SPLIT IT UP BETWEEN US!'

The cherry on top was when they made me get out of my wheelchair and 'walk' through the body scanner. I almost went through that thing arse over tit. But 'cos I had something in my pocket, they had to pat me down anyway. Next thing I knew, I had some 500lb guy's hand between my arse cheeks while he was whispering in my ear – 'I'm at your buttocks now, sir, and headed to your inner thigh' – all while Sharon started screaming again, and the rest of the TSA guys did another count of the banknotes, 'cos they'd lost track the first time.

Well . . . this is going smoothly, I thought.

I managed three days at Welders before I was in hospital again. This time, though, it wasn't an emergency. It was just part of switching over from the American health-care system to the English one. It was Robbie Williams who sorted me out, funnily enough. He's a good mate of Sharon's. When he heard I was coming back, he said, 'Ozzy should meet up with my guy.' So Robbie's doc came over to the house, a very nice man, and looked over my whole medical history. He said the best way to come up with a plan was for me to go over to his clinic and get a whole bunch of tests. So, next thing I knew, I was checked into the Wellington Hospital in St John's Wood, north London.

I was there eight days in the end. Everything seemed under control other than my blood pressure. It can go from 83 to 300 in an hour, which is fucking crazy. Just standing up too quickly can cause me to black out. It's called 'orthostatic hypotension' or something. It's common in people with Parkinson's, apparently, 'cos all the things your nervous system is supposed to do on autopilot get out of whack.

By this point, it was only a few weeks before the show. Sharon was terrified it was gonna get out that I was in hospital, even though it was just for tests, 'cos people would think it meant the show was off. Initially we thought my trip to the Wellington would just be a quick in-and-out. But as the days dragged on, we began to seriously regret checking me in as John Osbourne. I mean, it didn't exactly take Inspector Morse to work out that was me. Every day, Sharon was *begging* the staff to keep quiet and stop any leaks getting out. Then on day five or six we get a phone call from the front desk. 'We've got a message for John Osbourne,' said the receptionist. 'His brother's here to see him.'

It was panic stations at that point. I mean, okay, yes, I've got a brother, Paul ... but he had no idea where I was. So this was a fan or a reporter trying to sneak in. Almost certainly a reporter. Which meant the news was already out. When I saw the fire in Sharon's eyes, I almost felt sorry for the guy. I was like, holy fuck, this bloke has got absolutely *no idea* what's about to come down on his head.

Instead of going down there herself, Sharon sent our security team. Ex-military, all of 'em. One of the guys is seven feet tall. They all have arms like Popeye. So they collar this guy, scream in his face, demand to know who he is, what he's up to, search him up and down, scare the living daylights out of him – and in the end all they find on him is a Tesco fruit platter and a get well soon card. And when they check out his driving licence, it turns out his name's Bob Osbourne or something. He really *had* come to see his brother. Who really *was* called John.

I mean, what were the chances of two John Osbournes being at the same hospital?

If you're reading this, Bob, I'm terribly sorry.

Give my best to John.

Once the tests were done, I had my stage fright to deal with.

I couldn't decide what was worse, the idea of *not* being able to do the gig, or the stress of having to follow Guns N' Roses, Metallica, Steven Tyler, Ronnie Wood and Sammy Hagar after breaking my neck and not touring for six years. Meanwhile, the show just kept getting bigger and bigger. Sharon was doing an incredible job. As was Tom Morello, who was acting as musical director, decid-ing who was gonna play what, and in what order. As all these huge names kept getting announced I was like, holy fuck, it's gonna be up there with the Freddie Mercury tribute concert. Or like metal's answer to Live Aid.

It didn't help that during my eight days in hospital, I had nothing to do but worry.

After all the shit that had gone down at the start of the year, I kept thinking, *what am I gonna get next?* I always seem to pick something up in hospitals. They're full of germs, those places. One more bout of pneumonia, I thought, and it's goodbye Ozzy, never mind the gig.

Don't get me wrong – when I had a clear head I thought, it's gonna be fine. But when I was lying in bed at night I'd be like, *I can't go, I can't do this.* I kept saying to Sharon, we'd better get a video made, 'cos there'll be an empty stage. She just looked at me like I was mad. She knows me better than I do. When I get all doomy, she just lets me rant.

She knew I was just scared.

For a while, I tried tuning my hearing aids into my iPhone so I could listen to music, to stop my head doing a number on me. But that didn't work. One day I'd say to Sharon, 'I can't do two sets, I'll just do Sabbath.' Then the next day I'd be like, 'Fuck Sabbath, I'll just do mine.' I'd go back and forth. I tortured myself.

Eventually Sharon said, 'Look, there'll be no back-up plan. No video. No pre-recorded anything. If you can't sing on the night, just talk to the crowd and thank them. All you need to do is get up there and be Ozzy.'

Rehearsals with Sabbath started about three weeks before the show. We went down to this studio owned by one of the guys in the Prodigy, somewhere out

in the countryside. No one knows where it is, so it's
very quiet.

It was great to see the guys again. It's fucking incredible we're all still here — how many bands can say that
after fifty-seven years? — but of course we've all got our
own shit going on. I can't walk. Bill's got a bad heart.
Tony's got this thing with his shoulder. The healthiest of
us is Geezer — maybe it's 'cos he's a vegetarian. It took us
a while to blow the cobwebs off, start playing like our
old selves again. But we got there eventually. And we
were having fun, joking around like we were still kids
in Aston.

What made it even better was our old road crew being
there. It was like this big family reunion. And of course
they're all getting on a bit too. We've all got pot bellies
now. We're all shrinking by the fucking day. The sad
thing was, one of our longest-serving roadies, Bobby
Thompson, a Scottish guy, isn't around any more. When
he died, the invitation to his funeral was in the form of a
backstage pass with his picture on it. What really touched
me was that a lot of guys came to the rehearsal with that
same pass around their necks. It was really special, man.

With my own band — Zakk on guitar, Adam Wakeman
on keyboards, Tommy Clufetos on drums and Mike Inez
from Alice in Chains on bass — we only rehearsed for a
day. It sounded fucking great.

Then it was time to relocate to Villa Park. And of
course that's when the heavens opened and it started to
piss it down with rain. It had been weirdly lovely English
summer weather until then. I was thinking, oh God, here
we go. A few days of this and I'll be coughing up a lung.
But the gods must have been smiling on me, 'cos the next

day it was nice and warm again – and it stayed that way until the day of the show.

The gates opened at 11 a.m. on Saturday 5 July, a couple of hours before the first band went on. Meanwhile, I stayed at the hotel with my vocal coach, trying to keep my head in the right place. I can never watch the bands before me. Maybe that's a bad thing, but if I get distracted, I'll forget what I've got to do. And of course the whole show was being recorded, so I knew I could watch it all back later.

It was 6 p.m. when I got to the gig. The feeling was just incredible. When I was in the dressing room, people were coming in and out constantly. All of my old road crew work for Metallica now so it was so great to see 'em all, as well as Martha, my lovely wardrobe lady. Slash was there, I remember, and all of my kids. Everybody kept crying. But they were happy tears, y'know? I shed a few myself.

I kept thinking how crazy it was that the house where I grew up, 14 Lodge Road, was just a quarter of a mile away. Sharon told me there was a line of fans at my old front door, waiting to take a selfie in front of it. Even some of the bands had gone over there. The doorbell must have been going off like crazy. My dad would have been livid – he used to sleep during the day 'cos he did the night shift at the factory.

The stage for the gig was a revolving one – like at Live Aid – so getting into position was easy. Certainly a lot easier than the lift I had to take at the Commonwealth Games. But 'cos I've lost even more mobility since then, there was no way I could stand up like I did at the

Games – even with a support – so they sat me on this massive black throne.

It was a necessary evil, the throne. And they made the best of it, giving it a skull on each armrest and bat wings on the back. At one point there was talk of making it fly over the stage and shoot water at the crowd, but thank fuck that didn't happen, 'cos knowing my luck, it would have crashed.

As the stage began to turn, all I could think was, is my voice *really* up for this? Parkinson's messes up your vocal cords, and it only gets worse as times goes on. If I didn't get constant voice and speech therapy, I wouldn't be able to hold any kind of tune at all. I'm lucky Sharon's forced me to do it over the years, even when I didn't want to.

But as soon as the curtain went up, I forgot about my nerves.

Suddenly I was looking out over forty-two thousand faces, with another 5.8 million watching online, not that I gave the livestream much thought when I was up there. That was when the emotion really hit me. I'd never really taken it on board that so many people liked me – or even knew who I was.

It was overwhelming, man, it really was.

We got through 'I Don't Know', 'Mr. Crowley' and 'Suicide Solution' no problem at all. The show was all about going back to the beginning, so that's why we chose those early songs. Someone said doing 'Suicide Solution' must have felt like a vindication, after that whole thing in the eighties when they tried to put me on trial for the lyrics, accusing me of encouraging people to kill themselves. But that never occurred to me when I was up there. I just did the song. I was having a ball.

But I choked up badly when I started 'Mama, I'm Coming Home'. I mean, it's Sharon's song, y'know? One of her favourites. And of course Lemmy wrote it with the two of us in mind. That alone was enough to bring tears to my eyes. But the feeling I had was about more than that. It was my last hurrah. I'd made it to the stage after six traumatic years, after losing the ability to walk or do anything on my own. It was just the whole thing, all of it coming together.

I just couldn't hold in my emotions any more.

Out in the crowd, everyone was holding up the lights on their phones. Someone said in the papers it was like I was attending my own wake, which would be a very metal thing to do. But it didn't feel like a funeral. It felt like a celebration. There was just so much love in that stadium, man. I could feel it coming at me in waves. It was how I imagined the first Woodstock festival must have been. I mean, I had tears streaming down my face, but I felt so uplifted by it all. And of course the crowd noticed I was struggling, and they started singing back the words. I've been so lucky to have had so many wonderful fans. God bless you all.

By the end of the song, thank God, I'd managed to pull myself together.

Then it was one last ride on the Crazy Train and time for the Sabbath set.

The guys in Sabbath were as nervous as I was about me doing two sets in a row. They had no idea if I could pull it off. They were also nervous about the revolving stage. During the last Sabbath tour, we played on a re-volving stage in California, and every time it turned all our fucking amps fell over. Either that, or our cables got unplugged. And believe you me, you don't want to be anywhere near Tony when that kind of shit happens.

The biggest problem I had with Sabbath was the throne. The back of it was so high I couldn't hear the backline – the row of amps at the back of the stage, if you ain't familiar – so I had to rely on the monitor speakers. I'd never done a gig like that before. In a smaller place, on a different stage – or if I'd been sitting on a stool – I could have felt like I was part of the band. Instead, I felt like I was out there on my own. Meanwhile, I took out my hearing aids, 'cos I was worried the frequencies would get messed up and I'd end up singing flat, which had happened a few times when we did *The End Tour* in 2017.

But it couldn't have gone better. When the crowd chanted the tune of 'War Pigs' like they were cheering on England at the World Cup, it was just electrifying. Then we did 'N.I.B.', 'Iron Man' . . . and 'Paranoid'.

People ask me what I thought about Bill Ward taking off his shirt, and all I can say is, I'd have been worried if he hadn't. I mean, okay, he's not exactly Mr Universe – he's a seventy-seven-year-old bloke. But he's Bill, that's what he does. At every gig since 1968. So why the fuck would he stop now?

The only thing that was really frustrating for me was that I wanted to jump up and run around the stage. I tried a few times. You can see it on the tape. I wanted to get up from that throne *so badly*. But my legs are too weak now. And my balance has gone to shit. My trainer had told me, if you put your legs in a certain position, you can give it a go, see what happens. But nothing happened, and it pissed me off no end. But what can you do? Everything else about the gig was perfect. I mean, those fireworks after 'Paranoid' – they were the best I'd ever seen.

Geezer gave me a cake at the end, as you probably saw if you watched the video. But the problem is, none of us have changed since we were twenty years old. We're a bunch of jokesters. We never stop taking the piss. I was convinced Geezer was gonna smack it in my face or something. When he appeared out of nowhere holding what looked like a cream pie and went, 'All right, here you go,' all I could think was, what the fuck are you doing? I was convinced it was all some kind of wind-up. Then, when the show was over, I couldn't see what was going on over the back of my throne, so it felt like I was out there for a moment all on my own. That's why you could see me shouting 'TURN THE FUCKING STAGE!' to anyone who'd listen.

It was chaos, like it's always been.

But that's rock 'n' roll for you.

I wouldn't have it any other way.

Back to the Beginning was the best medicine I've had since all my medical shit started back in 2019. It was a magical night. It couldn't have been better.

Sharon worked so hard to make it happen. For two years, non-stop. She's like the new Bob Geldof. She did a phenomenal job. As did Tom and the army of other people involved. I had the easy part – all I had to do was perform. I had almost nothing to do with the planning. I had so many things go wrong with my health since that last big surgery in 2023, if felt like every day I'd just wake up, do what I was told, then go back to bed. My whole life was just getting wheeled in and out of rooms. I barely knew what time it was, never mind what day.

Back to the Beginning was the biggest metal show in history, or so I'm told. And although the early figures in the press of £140 million raised for the three charities were a bit misleading – I mean, Live Aid only raised £40 million on the day it was held – it must have been in the tens of millions. The show even ran *under* time. Nothing in the history of rock 'n' roll has run under time. It was like a military operation. All I can say is thank you and God bless to everyone who took part. None of the bands got paid, and they all came a very long way. As for which band Sharon kicked off the bill for demanding a fee, I don't want to know. I mean I think I *do* know . . . but I'd rather not focus on that.

I got such a kick out of watching it all back later.

When Sharon first told me Yungblud was gonna perform, I never realised he had such an incredible vocal range. But fuck me, the guy can sing. Everyone was just bowled over by his version of 'Changes'. It was phenomenal. He sang it so well, man. It's gonna be released as a single, apparently, with the proceeds going to charity.

I was also so happy to see Jake E. Lee up on stage, part of Tom's all-star supergroup. As I said earlier, he left my band in 1987 under unfortunate circumstances. After that, he was flying for a while. But the guy's had so much bad luck. He lost his wife, then the lead singer of his band, Badlands. Then of course he got shot in Las Vegas – which apparently happened 'cos he confronted two guys trying to steal a motorbike from one of his neighbours. He was much more badly injured than I thought. One of the bullets went through his lung.

Apparently, the gun they used was linked to a couple of murders, so the good news is that the guys who did it will probably be put away for a very long time. I hadn't spoken to Jake for thirty-eight years when I saw him at the show. There was a big crowd around me at the time, so we only managed to say a few words, but I texted him after, and told him that when I get it together, we should meet up. He said he'd love to.

The video messages during the show also meant the world to me. Thank you so much to everyone who took the time to record something. I was blown away by the kind words. Elton John, the guys in AC/DC, Billy Idol, Cyndi Lauper, Def Leppard, Jonathan Davis, Marilyn Manson, even Dolly Parton. I wish I had some great Dolly stories to tell you, but I'm just a fan, like everyone else. I did meet her in an elevator one time. I couldn't believe how tiny she was for someone with such a huge voice. Meanwhile, Ricky Gervais cracked me up by doing his message in the bath. I'll never forget the time we both went on *The Graham Norton Show*. I whispered in Sharon's ear that I needed to piss – 'cos I *always* need to piss – so Sharon asked Graham, then Ricky said he needed to go too. That clip's become a classic on YouTube.

The other fucking brilliant video was Jack Black doing 'Mr. Crowley'. He's such a talented guy, man. I went to the premiere of his movie *School of Rock*, back in the day. I absolutely loved it. And the kids who did 'Mr. Crowley' with him, they blew my mind. Tom Morello's son Roman was playing one of Randy Rhoads's guitars, and it was just fabulous.

I couldn't help but notice the crowd didn't like it when

Marilyn came on. But he's a good friend of mine, an all right guy. I just thought, give the guy a break.

The big surprise after the show was Sid proposing to Kelly. I had no idea he was gonna do that. But I'm glad he did, because they've got their little Sid together, and he's all right, Sid is, he's a nice guy. He's like a member of the family now. When he opened up with, 'Kelly, you know I love you more than anything else in the world,' I sussed out immediately what he was gonna do, so I went, 'Fuck off, you're not marrying my daughter!' I was just joking around. It was so nice he proposed to her. And he can't back out now, he's got six million fucking witnesses.

After more than thirty years of moving in the same circles, I also finally got to meet Axl Rose. It's incredible we'd never crossed paths before, given how much time I've spent with Slash and Duff McKagan.

It's funny, you build up a mental picture based on what you hear about someone, but Axl was nothing like that. Back in the day, when he first got famous, people would say he was awkward – just like they'd say, oh, Ozzy's crazy. But he was just a baby. And when you get fame at that age, it's a pretty toxic drug. As is money. And Guns N' Roses got more money than they probably knew how to handle. It's a total mind fuck, going from nothing to everything. I was lucky, I had bit of help with my money problems, 'cos I got married to my manager. Not everyone has that. Anyway, it was a great moment, meeting Axl, he's the nicest guy. I hope we get to hang out more in the future.

The final part of the show was the meet-and-greets

we did the following weekend at Comic Con Midlands at Birmingham's NEC. That was really special for me, 'cos like I said before, I love to meet the fans one on one.

The thing that really blows my mind is that so many young people are so into my music. They know as much about Sabbath and my solo albums as their parents and grandparents do. I mean, if my own dad had ever said to me, 'Oh, this guy Al Jolson, you've gotta listen to him, he's great' – just the fact that my dad liked him would have put me off. But I get these twenty-year-olds coming up to me with my face tattooed on every part of their body. Or they want me to sign my name so they can tattoo over it. And they come from all over the world. One family flew twenty hours from Malaysia. There were people from Saudi Arabia, Australia, South America, Canada, France, you name it.

Thank you to everyone who came, and God bless you. It meant the world to me.

So now I'm back at Welders, still on cloud nine after the show.

It's kind of fitting that Welders used to be a convalescent home. They'd send Second World War officers here to recover after they got limbs blown off in battle. Now there's a very different kind of patient here – me.

The funny thing is, the main reason Sharon wanted to buy this house was 'cos it was so far from the nearest pub. But now we've finally moved back in, there could be a pub halfway down the driveway and I'd need a fucking crane and a flatbed truck to get there.

But I'm comfortable here. I've got my red telephone box in the drive. Sid's bought this fabulous old Series I

Land Rover from 1948 that he parks right next to it. I've got my two four-legged friends, Wesley and Pickles, who came over from LA on a special airline just for dogs. They love nothing more than to shit on Sharon's favourite rugs. Best of all, I've got a custom gold-plated Zimmer frame with a bat on it wearing a crown, and two black tennis balls on the bottom to stop it scratching the floor. There's a matching wheelchair on the way.

Although I won't be performing again, I've already got an idea for a new album. Meanwhile, Sabbath's first manager – who's in his late eighties now – has just gone behind our backs and is planning to release a demo of ours from 1968 without our permission. He's also selling T-shirts and all other kinds of shit with our faces on it. It's unbelievable. There's not much we can do legally, thanks to the UK copyright laws, but it's funny how, fifty-seven years later, nothing ever changes. I mean, I get people need to make a living. But he couldn't have called us first?

I won't be going back to LA for a while. Maybe never, who knows. These days, it's a pain in the arse to fly. I need a week of tests just to get permission to get on a plane. Besides, LA's not exactly a place to retire to. I'm deafened by silence out here in the English countryside. There are no LAPD choppers circling overhead. No sirens blaring. No traffic at all hours. I like it. I've had a loud life. I'm ready for some quiet now.

Saying that, wherever Sharon goes, I'll go. But I'm okay if she wants to stay here. The food in England's better, as far as I'm concerned. The medical situation's better, 'cos you don't feel like you're getting shaken down. And England's so lush and green compared with dry and brown LA. It's funny – 'cos I always used to be on a world tour in the summer, it's been decades since I've spent time in England when the weather's nice. It's been a revelation just how beautiful it is when it's not pissing it down and blowing a gale. We've had Welders for well over thirty years now, and I'm just starting to fully appreciate it.

I got out into the garden yesterday in the sun. I've bought this off-road car thing – a Polaris, it's called – so our house manager can take me around the grounds.

We've got more than three hundred acres here, if you can believe it. One of the local farmers grazes his cattle out in the fields. When my legs get a bit stronger, I'm gonna go fishing in my lake. It's a man-made lake – Sharon had it dug out, then filled it with fish. Lake Ozzy, I'm calling it.

I've also got a big new home gym, full of apparatus. And I'm using it – twenty minutes of exercise, twice a day. I'm doing the exercise bike. Different weights. Legs one day. Arms the next. Meanwhile, Sharon says my blood pressure has calmed down now. Not that I'm out of the woods with my health, obviously. Parkinson's is a progressive disease. And that's just one of the many things wrong with me.

Every day I'm like, what's gonna happen next? It's never silly little things. It's always life-or-death. My latest problem is a dodgy heart valve, caused by the sepsis. The valve is 80 per cent blocked, apparently. The sepsis also gave me something called arrhythmia – when your heart can't keep time, like a drummer in a bad pub band – so cheers for that.

The docs would operate, but to do the operation I'd

have to stop taking my blood thinners, and that would be too dangerous. Meanwhile, the thinners mean if I ever fall over, I'd bleed out in about five seconds. I've honestly lost count of the ways in which getting old sucks.

On top of everything, I'm literally disintegrating. I'm taking shots to try to build up my bone density, but it's only a matter of time before another vertebra goes. I feel like a crumbling statue. My spine problems, my Parkinson's, my emphysema, my arrhythmia, my blood clots, my heart value ... it's all chipping away at the stone. I mean, if I was to go to bed tonight and not get up tomorrow, no one would be surprised. Death's been knocking at my door for the last six years, louder and louder. And at some point, I'm gonna have to let him in.

The funny thing is, I used to worry more about my mortality when I was younger. It's weird. You get closer to the end – the very thing you were scared of your whole life – and suddenly the weight's lifted off you. Not that I'm ready to go. But I've had a good run. I think I made a mark on the world. And I'm glad I didn't check out early, like so many others.

It's just crazy how quickly a lifetime goes. I say to my kids, get out there, travel, do your thing, 'cos when you start going downhill, it becomes a different fucking world, believe you me. Life's so short. People say you've still got your memories. But that goes both ways, of course. Because of the way I'm built, I tend to remember the bad things, like when Randy and Rachel were killed. That's forever etched in my heart.

When the end does come, I don't want to be cremated. It's like you were never here. You're just a bag of dust.

That's not for me. I wanna make the flowers grow. Not that my family ever want me to talk about death. Every time the subject comes up, they start waving their arms about, saying, 'No! No! Don't talk about that!' They don't even wanna *think* about it. The only conversation I've had with Sharon was when we decided we wanted to be buried together. I've also said to Sharon, don't you *dare* go before me. It's my biggest fear now, Sharon leaving this world before I do. If she does, I won't be too far behind. I live for the woman. When she went on her big diet a while ago, I was terrified of it going wrong. She lost so much weight, I thought she was gonna disappear. Meanwhile, there's been talk about us having some kind of suicide pact, but that's bullshit. We just don't want some drawn-out end on a breathing tube. I've said to Sharon, if that ever happens to me, *please* . . . turn me off. Or fly me to Switzerland, give me one final sip of the jolly juice and send me out like a Viking.

People ask me what I think's gonna happen in the afterlife. I say to 'em, I've no idea, but it won't be long now, so if you hang around a bit, maybe I can haunt you and give you the answer. As for what I want on my tombstone, that's one of the subjects my family definitely won't let me discuss.

Between you and me, though, I'm thinking something short and sweet.

'I told you I wasn't feeling well' should do the trick.

The one major blessing these days is that my addictions are finally under control. I've got so many doctors and nurses hovering over me at all times, there's not even the opportunity. Mind you, back in LA – in the months before we left for England – I did get hooked on apples for a while.

Not just any apples, mind you. They had to Pink Lady apples. None of that Granny Smith bullshit. And they had to be from Erewhon, the posh LA store. The thing with Pink Ladies is, they're not too sweet, but they're not too sour. They're in between. I got to the point where some nights l was eating twelve of 'em. I even hired a special guy to drive down to Erewhon and buy them. I didn't want to have 'em delivered in case I got brown ones, or ones with dents in.

Anyway, this guy was buying so many they started rationing him. It got to the point where I needed to join Pink Ladies Anonymous. It's a wonder I didn't wake up one day with an apple tree sprouting out of my arse.

But it's strange, the second I got to England I just stopped craving them. Maybe it was one of my medications that caused the addiction. Just the other day, they gave me a couple of slices of apple with my lunch, and I wasn't interested. So I guess I'm a recovered applea-holic now.

What I've realised is that the one place where I'm free of all my demons is on a stage. At Back to the Beginning, sitting on that throne, I felt at home, I felt at peace . . . I felt comfortable. I'm gonna miss doing it, going on stage. It's the only world I've known for fifty-seven years. There's *nothing* better than a good gig. The roar of a crowd, man, it's so contagious, so addictive. That's the magic, right there. It's funny, I spent my whole life trying to get high from every substance known to man. But looking back now, I realise I was just trying to get back the feeling of when I was up there on stage, doing my job.

The packed arena.

The thump of the bass drum you can feel in your stomach.

Forty or fifty thousand voices singing back your words.

All along, *that's* what I was chasing.

It was the best drug I ever took.

After I Am Ozzy, *never in a million years did I think I would ever write another memoir. As I've said repeatedly, my memory's not that sharp, especially when it comes to my health and my continuous doctors' visits. Thank you to everyone who helped me get all the details in the right order and made this book much more than just a medical journal . . . you know who you are. One thing's for sure: I won't be writing another one.*

God bless.

Love you all,

Ozzy

Thank you to the following . . .

My family: *Sharon, Aimee, Jack, Kelly, Louis, my sisters Jean and Gillian, my brother Paul, my nephew Terry. My grandchildren, Pearl, Andy, Minnie, Maple, Sidney, Maia and Elijah. Gina, Dean, Ollie and Amelia Maszlin.*

My healthcare team: *Dr Randy Schnittman, Dr Robert Bray, Dr Luke Macyszyn, David Wexler, Dr Dominique Fradin-Read, Dr Michele Tagliati, Dr Lawrence D. Piro, Natalia Rusadze and Gary Viles.*

My loyal team *(who have all been with me for far too long)*: *Lynn Seager, Michael Guarracino, John Fenton and Melinda Varga.*

My friends: *Zakk and Barbaranne Wylde, Billy Morrison, Slash, Jonathan Davis, Colin and Mette Newman, Adam Wakeman, Robert Trujillo, Tony Iommi, Geezer Butler, Bill Ward, Tommy Clueftos, Andrew Watt, Chad Smith, Steve Hewlett, Eddie Mendoza, Bill and Tani Austin, and everyone at Starkey Hearing and all my friends at Utah Airguns.*

Finally, to my fans: *You've been there for me, through the good, the bad and the ugly. You're always in my heart.*